Market Timing with No-Load Mutual Funds

Market Timing with No-Load Mutual Funds

Low-Risk High-Return Investing with No Commissions

**PAUL A. MERRIMAN
and MERLE E. DOWD**

An Owl Book
Henry Holt and Company | New York

First published in January 1987 by Henry Holt and Company, Inc.,
521 Fifth Avenue, New York, New York 10175.
Published in Canada by Fitzhenry & Whiteside Limited,
195 Allstate Parkway, Markham, Ontario L3R 4T8.

Library of Congress Cataloging-in-Publication Data
Merriman, Paul A., 1943-
Market timing with no-load mutual funds.
"An Owl book."
Bibliography: p.
Includes index.
1. Investment trusts. I. Dowd, Merle E. II. Title.
HG4530.M48   1986   332.63'27   86-9795
ISBN 0-8050-0121-2 (pbk.)

First Owl Book Edition—1987

Printed in the United States of America
10 9 8 7 6 5 4 3 2

ISBN 0-8050-0121-2

Contents

How This Book Will Help You

You can benefit from reading and using this book if—

• You are a busy, involved person with little time to pore over stock tables or evaluate alternative investments.

• You feel a need to increase your net worth or overall wealth—for whatever reason—to accumulate assets to supplement Social Security and a pension in retirement, to help children attend college, to start your own business, or simply to become financially independent.

• You wish to avoid risking your hard-earned cash.

• You are so involved at work or in outside activities that you sometimes forget about investing your money effectively, that is, with profit and prudence.

• You are disappointed with previous attempts to invest on your own or with the advice of brokers.

Some studies indicate that the average person, the unprofessional investor, gains very little from dabbling on a hit-or-miss basis in "the market." If this has been your experience, you will find the simple, easy program detailed in the following pages to be a logical and practical way to build your net worth with little of your time and with sleep-easy risks. Here's why:

You can control the two most important risks associated with any form of investing—security risk and market risk—with no-load mutual funds and market timing.

Security risk involves every kind of risk associated with picking individual stocks or attempting to forecast interest rates. Security risk affects every kind of investment: stocks, savings accounts, bonds, real estate, options, commodities, and others. Dabbling in any of these investments involves a security risk, popularly called "stock risk." The most effective way to reduce stock risk is through diversification. Mutual funds offer wide diversification with even the smallest investment. Thus, using no-load mutual funds reduces stock or security risk at no greater cost to you than to the biggest or richest investor.

Market risk is recognized in the axiom, "A rising tide lifts all boats." But the reverse also applies. A falling market drags most stocks and mutual funds down with it. So although mutual funds offer wide diversification to minimize stock risk, they offer little protection against market risk.

Market timing is a system for countering the up-and-down swings of the market. With market timing, you can be IN stocks during bull markets and IN money market mutual funds during bear markets. The combination offers a pragmatic plan to help you build your wealth successfully and with a minimum chance for loss. The following is a sample of the plans and ideas you can use:

• Expect to earn at least 20 percent per year on your investments in no-load mutual funds over a full market cycle with the aid of market timing.

• Wealth building within an IRA or a Keogh tax-deferred retirement plan can generate a net worth in these plans alone of $2 million or more over 30 years. Recognize that with a 20 percent annual return, your money doubles every 3.6 years. Tax-free compounding is incredibly effective in building assets.

• Appreciate the difference even a small variation of 1 percent per year makes in a long-term investment program. The difference is so striking that you will be motivated to start and continue a program of gaining a better return.

• Gaining $1 million in retirement assets doesn't require a big investment. A single IRA investment of $2,000 per year will do it in 25 years with 20 percent annual interest compounded monthly. Even $50 per month after an initial investment of $1,000 plus 30 years of compounding monthly at 20 percent per year will turn in over $1.5 million.

The benefit you gain from this book is the opportunity to accumulate at least $1 million over 25 years by investing $2,000 in an IRA or a Keogh. This investment program will take less than 30 minutes of your time *each year*.

You can learn how to generate your own switching signals. Or you can use market timing without having to perform any of the analyses—if you elect to use one of the many inexpensive or free timing services available. Another alternative is to turn over the responsibility of switching your investments to a market timer for a minimal cost.

Above all, this book will show you one of the only investments that can cut your risk in half along with the opportunities of doubling your return.

Preface

Synergism, according to one of Webster's dictionaries, is defined as "the simultaneous action of separate agencies which, together, have greater total effect than the sum of their individual parts." This book is the result of synergism.

Paul Merriman was attracted to the concept of market timing when he was the president of EMF Corporation, a firm that he took over only days before it was scheduled to enter bankruptcy. One of his responsibilities was to establish and manage the firm's profit-sharing trust. He surveyed numerous money managers for the job of investing the trust's assets for maximum gain with maximum safety. Of all the investment advisers he spoke with, the group whose program made the most sense, in his opinion, was the one that proposed investing in no-load mutual funds along with the application of market timing disciplines. He was surprised to discover that these firms charge as much as 3 percent of the assets under management and impose minimum account sizes as high as $500,000.

Because of the minimum-size account limitations and high fee schedules, market timing would be prohibitively expensive for the small investor. Yet, he reasoned, the small investor may have only an IRA as his or her only source of retirement funding and could use the tremendous benefits available with market timing. Following his rescue of the corporation from near bankruptcy and restoring it to financial health, Paul resolved to develop a system for managing no-load funds with market timing for every size of account anywhere in the country, including the first-time IRA investor with as little as $1,000.

Originally, all of his market timing work was done on a private management basis. He later found that many people had the necessary discipline to act on signals and would switch their funds themselves if they could avoid the technical analysis required to develop their own signals. *The Fund Exchange*, a telephone switch program, developed and literally expanded the potential for market timing no-load mutual funds to any size account in any location. He was convinced that the combination of no-load mutual funds and a low-cost market timing service represents the most liquid, low-risk, low-cost, and high-return investment available for the millions of persons looking for a way to make the most of their IRA investments. He wanted to find a way to share this information with every potential investor who would take the time to learn about this unique approach to investing.

Paul Merriman and Merle Dowd had crossed paths many times over the years. They first met as competitors working as stockbrokers with different firms. They met again when Merle was writing one of his 12 books, *How to Earn More Money from Your Crafts*. Paul and his wife, Joanne, own a company, TSI, Inc., a leading supplier of jewelry-making tools, equipment, and supplies. Joanne now runs the company. Merle devoted a part of his book to TSI's success.

They met again when Merle was researching an article for his nationally syndicated newspaper column, "Managing Your Money," dealing with market timing. Their conversation turned to investing, and Merle commented, "You know, Paul, I have a real problem with the mail I get from my column."

"How's that?"

"Well, many of the readers' letters ask for an absolutely safe investment that will return a maximum yield. You and I know that such an ideal investment vehicle does not exist. If I were to tell them to invest in government bonds because they are a direct obligation of the U.S. Treasury, they might not understand why the capital value of their investment goes up and down in response to changes in interest rates. I can tell them to buy bonds when interest rates are high and sell when interest rates are low, but few have the discipline to manage their investments in that manner. Or I could tell them to invest in various mutual funds, but many might respond to the advertising done by mutual fund companies without fully understanding the risks involved. Too little space is available to answer each letter with a full explanation—even if I had all the information, I would need to fully appraise their financial condition. So, I cop out. I tell them to study and develop their own expertise or at least learn enough to ask the right questions.

"It's frustrating to know that there is such a great need for information and direction and have only six hundred words each week to try to keep them informed. I guess it's better to light a small candle than to curse the darkness, but it gets to me. I wish I could do more."

"You know, you have just given me a great idea," Paul announced almost triumphantly. "We should write a book about market timing with no-load mutual funds." He explained the details.

Following this discussion, they agreed to collaborate on a book that would explain everything in layman's terms that a typical investor would need to know. Paul could use the book to explain the concept of market timing to potential clients. Merle could refer many of his readers to it for more information on the concept. Using the book, readers of his column would gain far more from their investments with a minimum commitment of time and understanding.

This is our book.

Market Timing with No-Load Mutual Funds

1

A Decision to Invest– Or Not

You have decided to invest. Or have you? It's an important decision, one that could change your life—for the better, if you make the right decisions.

Let's examine a decision path that could lead to investing to achieve some goal that is important to you financially. But first, look back on your life. You may remember several important forks in the road you have traveled. Each of those decisions to take one fork or the other has affected your life. If you examine those decisions thoughtfully, you will likely conclude that you could have changed your life. While you cannot go back and take another fork in the road, you can take the right road now. The decisions you make, which forks you take on the road, do make a difference.

Some of those decisions were indeed life determining. At some time you may have had to choose whether to attend college or go immediately into the work force or military service. If you selected college, you had to decide which college. At some time you may have considered whether to get married and to whom. Later, you may have consciously decided what kind of job to take, whether to have children or not, and where you preferred to live.

A small decision, possibly to buy this book, may also affect your financial security and life-style now and in retirement. Learning the power of market timing can literally change your life's financial direction. Your decision to continue using only

1

the banks could leave you with one-fifth to one-tenth the asset base at retirement you might have by following a different fork in the road. Electing to follow the guidelines you will find in this book could have a profound impact on your financial independence and wealth over the years.

INVESTING OBJECTIVES

Are you really concerned about retirement? Or do you only give it lip service? The record of persons who arrive at retirement with minimal resources is dismal. Social Security (SS) is, unfortunately, the backbone or base for many retirees even though it was never intended to provide a comfortable and secure retirement. Social Security aims only to provide a floor or base for minimal living to avoid abject poverty. Even more ominous is the realization that SS benefits are likely to be reduced or its levels changed to depend on your needs. The first step is already on the books for taxing up to half of SS benefits for those who make over $32,000 (couples filing jointly) or $25,000 for an individual. The political consensus is that those who do not need all of their SS benefits should not receive them even though they have contributed to the old-age security fund of Social Security all of their working years. Supplementing Social Security benefits in retirement calls for substantial investments built up over the years from savings and investment returns.

Okay, you're younger and not thinking about retirement. After all, there is plenty of time to worry about that. You have a bigger problem: kids who will want to attend college in a few years. But, you say, the kids can borrow from the government. Interest rates on student loans are cheap—under market rates—and the students can wait 10 months after graduation before beginning to repay the loans. If the kids are going to benefit from a college education, they can jolly well pay for it! No need for me to break my own bank. While you may not accept such thinking, the facts are that without some family help, the kids may not want to take on four or five years of college and mortgage their future in the bargain. Investing to build a fund to help your children through college could in-

Fig. 1-1. Decision path to financial security.

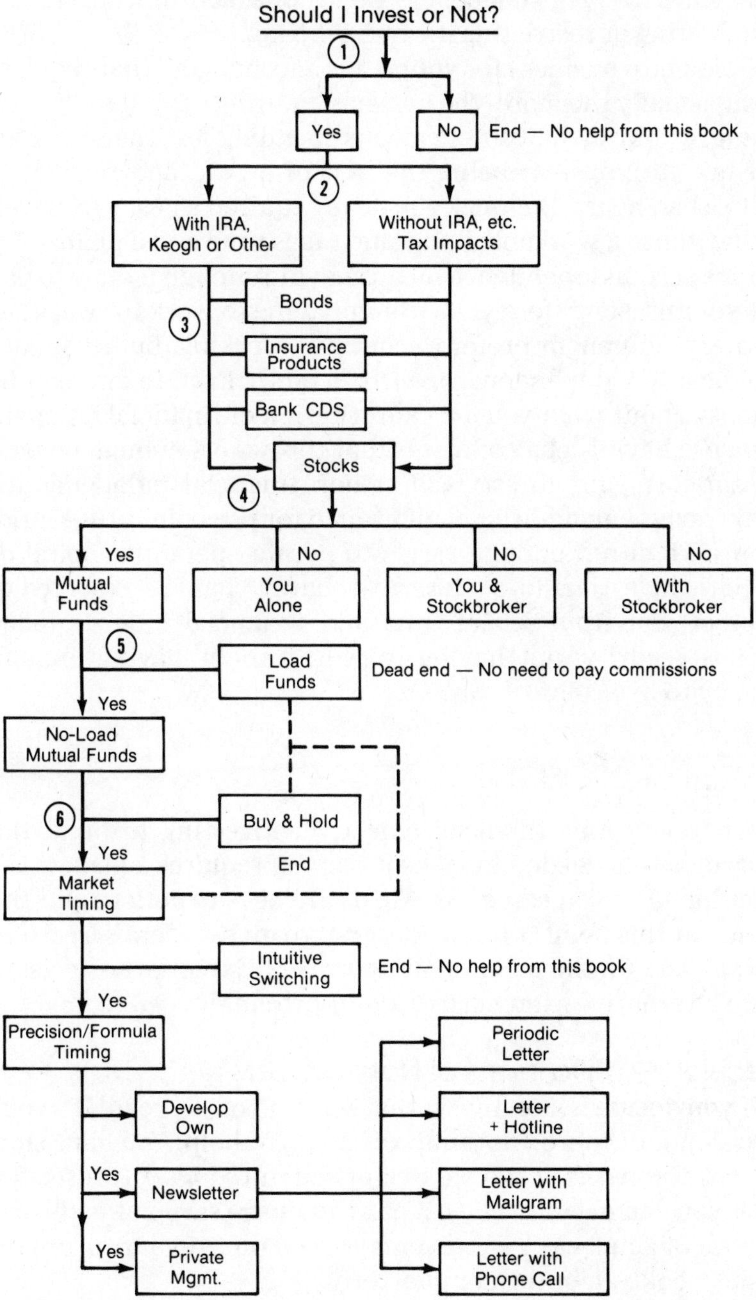

Should I Invest or Not?

① Yes / No — End — No help from this book

② With IRA, Keogh or Other / Without IRA, etc. Tax Impacts

③ Bonds / Insurance Products / Bank CDS

Stocks

④ Yes — Mutual Funds / No — You Alone / No — You & Stockbroker / No — With Stockbroker

⑤ Load Funds — Dead end — No need to pay commissions

Yes — No-Load Mutual Funds

⑥ Buy & Hold — End

Yes — Market Timing

Intuitive Switching — End — No help from this book

Yes — Precision/Formula Timing

Develop Own

Yes — Newsletter

Yes — Private Mgmt.

Periodic Letter

Letter + Hotline

Letter with Mailgram

Letter with Phone Call

clude profits or income that Uncle Sam would otherwise capture in taxes. This concept is being attacked in Congress by eliminating or restricting income splitting.

Going into business for yourself is another goal that requires cash, usually the more, the better. Acquiring capital for investment in your own business means spending less than your after-tax earnings—or being the heir of an old and rich uncle with a bad heart. But once you have acquired a nest egg, developing it into a workable lump sum takes time and a plan.

Financial independence means having enough money to pay for your present life-style without having to work for wages or a salary. You might prefer to continue working, but if you are financially independent, you don't really have to and can be choosy about what you do. One criterion of financial independence is having a bag of assets that throws off enough income to support your life-style. Further, financial independence may include an additional allowance for possible future inflation with either enough assets to permit spending capital or specific investments, such as gold shares, that are expected to protect you from severe inflation. Financial independence means security, not having to worry about having enough money to live comfortably.

INVESTING DECISIONS

Whatever your financial objective, investing to build the base of assets needed to make it happen requires a plan. It is a decision only you can make. Goals are keys to action, and the action at this point is to invest or not to invest. That's Decision Point No. 1 on the diagram in figure 1-1. Explore the decision path alternatives and make up your own mind.

Decision No. 1: To Invest or Not to Invest

If you decide not to invest, that's it. End of the road! It's your decision, but there's nothing we can do to help. You have shut us out. Cut us off at the pass. Short-circuited *your* future.

Or you can decide to invest cash you have saved already or a stream of small cash increments carved out of your future income weekly, monthly, or quarterly.

Decision No. 2: How to Invest

At the second fork in the road you have numerous choices, but let's follow a rational approach. Let's assume your goal is to build a retirement fund that will enable you to retire leisurely, travel, help your grandchildren, and not worry about outliving your resources. Depending on your age, a well-planned route to your retirement could land you there with $2 million.

You can choose to build your retirement plan without the tax advantages of an IRA, a Keogh or another arrangement. You can also go with an IRA and claim tax deferral advantages provided by the federal tax code. Most states go along, but be sure to check whether your state exempts the same $2,000 as the federal government. Look for more information about IRAs and Keoghs in chapter 6.

Let's assume for now that you plan to build retirement assets with annual savings of $2,000. You could invest each year's $2,000 contribution in an IRA or several IRAs, or you could invest the same $2,000 each year outside of an IRA. Figure 1-2 charts the difference in results you can expect assuming an average yearly return of 12 percent compounded annually. You can, of course, double those benefits if your spouse earns income that can be invested in his or her own IRA.

Since there appear to be major advantages to be gained from investing your retirement funds in an IRA compared to an investment program outside an IRA, at this fork in the road you decide to go with an IRA. Further, you decide to invest $2,000 each year.

Decision No. 3: Which Investment Vehicle?

As in any decision path, you are immediately faced with another multiple fork in the road. Investment choices for your IRA or Keogh (we will use only the IRA from this point on) include a bank, savings and loan, or credit union certificate of deposit (CD); one of the insurance company products, such as an annuity or one of the combination annuity-mutual fund tie-ups; stocks; bonds; mutual funds; limited partnerships, or some other vehicle. Each of these investments has its supporters, and most of these supporters are motivated by commissions. You would not pick a municipal bond; it is already tax advantaged and likely to pay a smaller dollar return than other possibilities. Before you decide, examine each of the primary candidates for its potential as a long-term retirement investment under the tax-sheltering umbrella of an IRA.

Bank, S&L, or credit union certificates of deposit are very low risk since they are insured up to $100,000 for each account. They offer a rate of return on a fixed capital base that varies from day to day or week to week. But once you buy a CD, the rate remains fixed until the CD matures. The returns on most CDs are compounded daily. If the CD you are considering does not offer daily compounding, look for one at a bank, S&L, or credit union that does. You can see the difference in table 1B. Over the long term, say 25 to 30 years, daily compounding could increase your retirement fund by as much as $74,698, or 15.5 percent. It is not, therefore, a detail to be ignored.

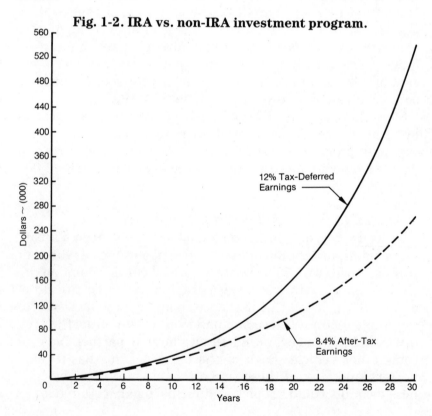

Fig. 1-2. IRA vs. non-IRA investment program.

One of the risks of investing in certificates of deposit that many security-conscious investors fail to consider is the roll-over risk. That is, you may be enjoying a high return in the 14 percent to 15 percent range over an 18-month maturity if you were lucky enough to lock in the high rate, but when it comes time to renew or roll over the CD, the rates may be down around the 7 percent to 9 percent range. Picking the time and the rate can incur substantial risks for the long term.

Table 1A. IRA vs. non-IRA growth assumes $2,000 is contributed to plan at beginning of each year and grows at 12 percent annually compounded. Non-IRA growth compounds at 8.4 percent after-tax rate on 12 percent gross yield assuming a 30 percent marginal tax rate.

	IRA			Non-IRA		
Year No.	Begin Year Total	Earnings at 12%	End Year Total	Begin Year Total	Earnings at 8.4%	End Year Total
1	$2,000	$240	$2,240	$2,000	$168	$2,168
2	$4,240	$509	$4,749	$4,168	$350	$4,518
3	$6,749	$810	$7,559	$6,518	$548	$7,066
4	$9,559	$1,147	$10,706	$9,066	$762	$9,827
5	$12,706	$1,525	$14,230	$11,827	$993	$12,821
6	$16,230	$1,948	$18,178	$14,821	$1,245	$16,066
7	$20,178	$2,421	$22,599	$18,066	$1,518	$19,583
8	$24,599	$2,952	$27,551	$21,583	$1,813	$23,396
9	$29,551	$3,546	$33,097	$25,396	$2,133	$27,529
10	$35,097	$4,212	$39,309	$29,529	$2,480	$32,010
11	$41,309	$4,957	$46,266	$34,010	$2,857	$36,867
12	$48,266	$5,792	$54,058	$38,867	$3,265	$42,131
13	$56,058	$6,727	$62,785	$44,131	$3,707	$47,838
14	$64,785	$7,774	$72,559	$49,838	$4,186	$54,025
15	$74,559	$8,947	$83,507	$56,025	$4,706	$60,731
16	$85,507	$10,261	$95,767	$62,731	$5,269	$68,000
17	$97,767	$11,732	$109,499	$70,000	$5,880	$75,880
18	$111,499	$13,380	$124,879	$77,880	$6,542	$84,422
19	$126,879	$15,226	$142,105	$86,422	$7,259	$93,682
20	$144,105	$17,293	$161,397	$95,682	$8,037	$103,719
21	$163,397	$19,608	$183,005	$105,719	$8,880	$114,599
22	$185,005	$22,201	$207,206	$116,599	$9,794	$126,394
23	$209,206	$25,105	$234,310	$128,394	$10,785	$139,179
24	$236,310	$28,357	$264,668	$141,179	$11,859	$153,038
25	$266,668	$32,000	$298,668	$155,038	$13,023	$168,061
26	$300,668	$36,080	$336,748	$170,061	$14,285	$184,346
27	$338,748	$40,650	$379,398	$186,346	$15,653	$201,999
28	$381,398	$45,768	$427,166	$203,999	$17,136	$221,135
29	$429,166	$51,500	$480,665	$223,135	$18,743	$241,879
30	$482,665	$57,920	$540,585	$243,879	$20,486	$264,364

IRAs offered by banks, S&Ls, and your credit union are easily accessible, inexpensive (low or nonexistent trust fees and annual management charges), and easy to understand. For these reasons, plus the insurance by FDIC, FSLIC, or National Credit Union Administration, 70 percent of IRA funds are invested in banklike products—CDs and money market deposit accounts. The $100,000 limit on insured coverage will one day be too little, however, now that the insuring organizations no longer cover accounts over $100,000 in a failed bank, S&L, or credit union. To avoid the $100,000 limit you will need to split

Table 1B. Importance of compounding rate. Note difference between accumulation assuming 12 percent nominal interest rate with daily compounding vs. annual compounding.

	Annual Compounding			Daily Compounding		
Year No.	Begin Year Total	Int. Rate	Yearly Int.	Begin Year Total	Interest Rate	Yearly Int.
1	100.00	12%	12.00	100.00	12.7475%	12.75
2	112.00	12%	13.44	112.75	12.7475%	14.37
3	125.44	12%	15.05	127.12	12.7475%	16.20
4	140.49	12%	16.86	143.32	12.7475%	18.27
5	157.35	12%	18.88	161.59	12.7475%	20.60
6	176.23	12%	21.15	182.19	12.7475%	23.23
7	197.38	12%	23.69	205.42	12.7475%	26.19
8	221.07	12%	26.53	231.61	12.7475%	29.52
9	247.60	12%	29.71	261.13	12.7475%	33.29
10	277.31	12%	33.28	294.42	12.7475%	37.53
11	310.58	12%	37.27	331.95	12.7475%	42.31
12	347.85	12%	41.74	374.26	12.7475%	47.71
13	389.60	12%	46.75	421.97	12.7475%	53.79
14	436.35	12%	52.36	475.76	12.7475%	60.65
15	488.71	12%	58.65	536.41	12.7475%	68.38
16	547.36	12%	65.68	604.79	12.7475%	77.10
17	613.04	12%	73.56	681.88	12.7475%	86.92
18	686.60	12%	82.39	768.81	12.7475%	98.00
19	769.00	12%	92.28	866.81	12.7475%	110.50
20	861.28	12%	103.35	977.31	12.7475%	124.58
21	964.63	12%	115.76	1,101.89	12.7475%	140.46
22	1,080.38	12%	129.65	1,242.35	12.7475%	158.37
23	1,210.03	12%	145.20	1,400.72	12.7475%	178.56
24	1,355.23	12%	162.63	1,579.28	12.7475%	201.32
25	1,517.86	12%	182.14	1,780.60	12.7475%	226.98
26	1,700.01	12%	204.00	2,007.58	12.7475%	255.92
27	1,904.01	12%	228.48	2,263.50	12.7475%	288.54
28	2,132.49	12%	255.90	2,552.04	12.7475%	325.32
29	2,388.39	12%	286.61	2,877.36	12.7475%	366.79
30	2,674.99	12%	321.00	3,244.15	12.7475%	413.55
31	2,995.99	12%	359.52	3,657.70	12.7475%	466.26

your IRAs into numerous pieces. Such splitting is permitted since you can have as many IRAs as you choose, but too many small IRAs may be impractical and difficult to monitor. If you have $500,000 or $1 million total in your IRAs, then many different IRAs would not be difficult or impractical to handle.

In our estimation, insurance products suffer three fatal flaws:

1. They are usually expensive, with significant sales charges and management fees being taken out of your IRA funds.

2. They generally offer lower yields than other equally accessible alternatives.

3. They often have heavy liquidation penalties if you decide to change your investment approach.

Common stocks are likely candidates. Studies by numerous authorities consistently prove that, over the long term and over a series of up-and-down cycles, stocks perform better than fixed-income securities. One study published by Murphy-Favre indicates that an unmanaged stock index outperformed debt instruments (CDs and bonds) by a three-to-one ratio from 1925 to 1981.

When you compare the benefits from investing in bank and S&L products (CDs, savings accounts, money market deposit accounts, and others), consider the underlying philosophy of the banks and other borrowers. Remember that when you deposit your cash in one kind of bank investment vehicle or another, you are really lending your money to the bank in exchange for rent, commonly known as interest. When you deposit cash in a checking account that pays no interest (rent), you are still lending the bank your cash in exchange for the convenience of writing checks. The bank's goal is to keep its cost of funds as low as possible; it does so by paying you as little interest as possible in order to borrow your money, whether that money is in the form of CDs or other products. The borrower (banks, S&Ls, and credit unions) will never pay you one penny more than they have to to convince you to lend them your money.

The market for interest-bearing instruments determines the rates, and the market is extremely competitive. The market for interest is truly an auction market, and one of the biggest influences of overall market rates is the weekly auction of treasury bills each Monday morning, orchestrated by the Federal Reserve System for the U.S. Treasury. Supply and demand fix the rates, and the interest paid on T-bills influences the rates paid by other borrowers. The underlying fact remains, however, that a borrower expects to pay as little as he needs to in order to get you to lend him your money. Frankly, we are not too interested in placing our money with people whose goal is to pay us as little as possible. We feel there may be a better path, and investing in stocks appears to be that better path for overall gain. On the basis of past performance, the litany of problems with fixed-income securities and an inner urge to avoid those borrowers who would pay us the least, we suggest and recommend investing your IRA funds in stocks. If you agree, we can move on to the next decision point.

Decision No. 4: Choosing an Investment Method

How will you invest your IRA funds in stocks? At this fork in the decision path, you are faced with four alternatives, as diagramed in figure 1-1.

One alternative is to follow the advice of a stockbroker. We, the authors, were licensed stockbrokers for years, but we are no longer active brokers for a variety of legitimate and personal reasons. We have seen the brokerage business from the inside. Many weaknesses are apparent from that view. This could be one of the mildest assertions you will read among these pages. Many dedicated stockbrokers continue to make money for their clients in the various markets. But many others offer little help and can dismantle your capital base with a surprising array of tools. The list of possible evils and pitfalls when working with a broker is long and ranges from the inept or fraudulent broker to the inherent costs of trading stocks. Further, your broker's motivation and compensation are in direct conflict with your goals as an investor. Despite the self-announced entreaties that a broker is unbiased, has the client's interests at heart, and works diligently to help the client make money in the market, the broker's job, when it comes down to the bottom line, is to generate commissions that support his personal and family life-style.

During bear markets, you benefit when you put funds in a money market fund or other cash equivalent, possibly T-bills. You would likely lose if you continued to trade stocks during bear markets. But a broker suffers a severe loss of personal income if he advises you to get out of stocks and put your money in a money market fund for two years. Very few brokers can afford to overcome this conflict of interest—the split between their need for income and your best interests as an investor.

Most brokers are trained to avoid future problems by keeping their risks to a minimum. For example, a broker will seldom put more than 10 percent to 15 percent of his clients into one stock. The reason for this limitation borders on the survival instinct. When a small percentage of his clients buys a specific stock, there is little chance that all of his clients will get mad at him at the same time should the stock turn sour and head south. While such a tactic may be good for the broker, it may not be good for you. If the broker has four hundred fairly active clients, only 40 to 60 may get a chance to buy shares from a hot initial offering. On the other hand, if the firm's research department unearths a really great stock, a broker will call no more than 50 to 75 of his clients. Will the broker call his smallest clients when his research department unearths a hot idea? Not likely. If he does get around to calling his small clients, several days might have passed, and the price of the stock might be several points higher. Brokers tend to deal with their IRA and other small clients only after they have serviced their more profitable clients. This is not the sort of relationship we want when our retirement security is at stake.

We dislike the odds of investing directly in stocks because you must invest a substantial sum if you are to have any sort of diversification. Also, the costs of getting into and out of stocks to avoid losses and to invest in up markets can be expensive. The actual costs will vary, of course, depending on whether you use a full-service or a discount broker. In our opinion, investing your IRA funds with the aid and advice of a stockbroker is out.

A second alternative calls for a team effort between you and your broker, but if using a broker leads to problems, certainly you compound those problems when *you* get into the act. The major problem to be faced is that neither of you has a definable discipline as to how and when to get into and out of the market. We believe that discipline, well defined and practiced, is essential for success in the market.

Most brokers will take the time to process your order if you initiate the contact. If you end up doing most of the work, however, you might as well work with a discount broker. We do not think you and a broker make a promising team for managing your retirement funds.

A third alternative calls for you to make your own decisions. If you are willing to spend one to three hours daily, you can probably make reasonable decisions. You might subscribe to a market letter that recommends stocks to buy and sell, and tells you when to trade. Before you depend on an advisory letter for market decisions, however, you should check it out. What is its track record? What system does it follow—a fundamental or a technical approach? How does it rate with one of the newsletter rating services, such as *The Hulbert Financial Digest*? If you are getting investment advice from a newsletter, you would likely use a discount broker for executions. A top-notch newsletter and a discount broker will probably cost less than trying to get advice and order execution from a full-service broker. You should be aware of one problem with using a popular newsletter (and if it isn't popular, it probably isn't all that good)—a newsletter's subscriber list may run into the thousands; some exceed 100,000. Advice to buy and/or sell in a large circulation newsletter is hardly unique. The advice to make a move in the market could and apparently does influence prices. When a buy signal is flashed to a newsletter's clientele, the many resulting orders may push up the price. So if you do not act immediately, you could pay too much for your shares.

Procrastination has foiled many a good investment program. If you avoid doing things when you receive the newsletter, you are not taking full advantage of your source. Generally, people don't have the discipline, the time, the motivation, or the interest to monitor their portfolio on a daily basis. You may fall into what has been a familiar trap to many investors: buying in active rising markets rather than in the valleys. The corollary is to sell into declining markets when you suddenly awake to the possibility of losing everything. Hope drives people into rising markets, and fear pushes them out during falling markets. With discipline you learn to do the contrary thing: buy when others are madly trying to unload their holdings and sell when buyers are clamoring for more shares. Thus, managing your own portfolio does not appear to be a good choice.

A fourth alternative calls for leaving the management of your retirement investments to a mutual fund. Mutual funds have been around for years but became viable investment vehicles when the Federal Investment Company Act of 1940 became law and was implemented to regulate their development. You should fully understand the concept of mutual funds and how you can use them effectively in your investment program. But first, here are a few basics on mutual funds:

Mutual funds are corporations. They sell shares to investors and invest the cash in shares of other companies, bonds, money market instruments, or other investment vehicles. There are two basic kinds of mutual funds. One is the closed-end fund that sells a set number of shares to investors at the time it is organized. Shares in closed-end mutual funds trade on exchanges or over the counter in the same manner as the shares of other corporations, with the price of the shares being determined by supply and demand. Closed-end mutual funds cannot be efficiently timed because of the expenses associated with switching. Since closed-end mutual fund shares are traded on an exchange or over the counter, a regular commission is charged when they are sold, and, in a separate transaction, the cash is transferred to a money fund. A similar commission is charged when money is moved back into the closed-end mutual fund. There is also no set price for closed-end fund shares, and if you need to liquidate in the wrong kind of market, you may have to sell your shares at a discount. If you have a substantial position (that is, a large number of shares), you may not get the same price as you would for a small number of shares. You may not get exactly the same price, either, as you would if you were liquidating a position in a no-load, open-end fund.

An open-end fund, the other kind of mutual fund, operates with a constantly changing number of shares. An open-end mutual fund stands ready on any business day to sell as many shares as an investor may choose to buy within the limits of the mutual fund's capital structure. The price of the shares is calculated at the end of each business day and is known as the net asset value (NAV). The NAV results from multiplying the price of each asset held in the fund's portfolio at the close of the day by the number of shares or increments of that asset owned by the fund, and then totaling all of the various assets to find the total worth of the fund's portfolio— including any cash. This total is divided by the number of shares held by investors in the fund to arrive at the net asset value per share. As an example, suppose a sample mutual fund held in its portfolio 1,000 shares of Stock A and 1,500 shares of Stock B. If Stock A closed at $10 per share, the total value of that asset would be $10,000. If Stock B closed at $5 per share, the total value of that asset would be $7,500. Combining the asset values yields a total of $17,500. If we assume that there are 10,000 shares in the mutual fund, dividing $17,500 by 10,000 yields a NAV of $1.75 per share. This is the number you will find reported in the mutual funds section of the *Wall Street Journal* and most other major metropolitan newspapers.

A significant advantage in using mutual funds is the low cost of their professional management and tremendous buying power. Because the fund advisors spread their commissions when buying stocks for the funds, mutual funds pay about one-ninth of what the public pays. Over millions of dollars of investments, the cost of managing mutual fund shares is almost infinitesimal compared to the costs of getting into and out of stocks or bonds on an individual basis. For example, if as an individual you were to approach the management company at Value Line, you would find that their minimum account size is $1 million and their fee at that level is 1 percent of the asset base. On the other hand, you could pick one of the public Value Line funds; the charge is $63/100$ of 1 percent per year, and the minimum account size is only $250.

You benefit from the opportunity of carefully examining the historical success or failure of a mutual fund's ability to make money for its shareholders in good times and bad. If you were to go to your broker, he or she would not likely open up the books for you to examine the record in bull and bear markets. A broker may perform fantastically well with aggressive accounts, but he may be lousy with conservative accounts. If yours is a conservative account, that broker would not likely perform well for you. But, you may never get an opportunity to review his past performance record with conservative accounts until one day you wake up and find your account balance has declined.

With mutual funds, you can pick the type of fund that interests you—aggressive, conservative, income, tax-free, or other. Then you can look at the fund's record in good times and bad. Few investors take full advantage of this tremendous benefit. Most investors tend to buy mutual funds based on their latest six months' performance, which is not very meaningful on a long-term basis.

Liquidity is another important benefit you gain from investing in mutual funds rather than individual stocks or bonds. Open-end funds will close out your position based on the NAV at the close of the business day that they receive your order.

Costs of getting in and out of mutual funds are also less than if you were to sell stocks or bonds. The difference between the bid and asked price, the spread, affects your investment costs this way: When you buy, you pay the asked price; when you sell, you receive the bid price. Depending on the stock and whether it is traded on an exchange or over the counter, the spread may be as much as $1 per share. As an example of the difference, consider the XYZ Corporation, one of the giants and high on the *Fortune* 500 list. XYZ Corporation's stock is traded on the New York Stock Exchange, and you typically see only the trading price in newspaper stock listings. On the specialist's book, however, the spread may be 1/8. If you follow a stock on the NASDAQ, you will find both the bid and asked prices. Little Company, Inc., is one of the small companies. In broker parlance it may trade at 15½ at 16½, meaning that if you are selling, the price is 15½, but if you are buying, the price is 16½. Thus, in addition to any commissions, you will lose the spread on a round-trip transaction. In a mutual fund, the value you receive is based on a formula that is described in the prospectus. In some cases the formula is based on the mean between the bid and asked prices or the last trade of the day, but it is a formula that does not change from day to day. Once a formula is established, it essentially means you can pay less when you buy and gain more when you sell than in the open market.

Because there are so many desirable features available to the retirement-oriented investor from using mutual funds, we recommend that you select open-end mutual funds as the investment vehicle for funding your retirement program. We immediately encounter the next fork in the path: Which kind of mutual fund—load or no-load?

Decision No. 5: Load or No-Load Mutual Fund

Open-end mutual funds are distributed in two ways: with a commission and without a commission. Those mutual funds that are typically sold by brokers are called "load" funds because they earn a commission on sales, typically 4 percent to 8½ percent of invested funds. Without quoting exactly from Webster's, load is generally defined as "a heavy burden." The commission certainly qualifies as a load under that definition. For example, if you were to invest $1,000 in a load fund with a broker who charges 8½ percent commission, the "load" or sales charge would be $85, leaving $915 of your original $1,000 to be invested in the mutual fund. Most or all of the commission charged for load funds stays with the broker and brokerage firm; little, if any, of the sales charge goes to the mutual fund.

No-load mutual funds do not charge a sales commission, as you might expect from the name. Investing in no-load funds is essentially a do-it-yourself operation, that is, you fill out the paperwork and deal directly with the fund by mail or telephone. These procedures are detailed later.

Whether to invest in a load or no-load fund is controversial. Since you will be making the decision at this fork in the road, you should understand the background thoroughly. The results of one study are reported in *The Handbook for No-Load Fund Investors*. The study compared two hypothetical funds, one a load fund and one a no-load fund. Both funds grow at an assumed average rate of 10 percent per year through bull and bear markets. To start, a lump sum of $10,000 is invested in each fund. All of the $10,000 invested in the no-load fund goes to work immediately. In the load fund $850, representing the load or sales charge at 8½ percent, is deducted up front from the amount being invested. Only $9,150 actually goes to work. The following is a quote from the handbook:

> At the end of year No. 1, the no-load investor's fund has grown 10 percent and now has a cash-in value of $11,000. The load fund has also grown 10 percent, but its cash-in value is only $10,065, or slightly more than the amount originally invested the year before. At the end of year No. 2, the no-load is worth $12,100 while the load fund is worth $11,072 or $1,028 less. The load fund investor lost the $850 and also loses forever the 10 percent per year growth on that portion of the investment. Over the years, the spread continues to widen. By the end of 10 years, still assuming equal growth rates, $10,000 in the no-load fund will have grown to $25,939 and the no-load investor will be $2,204 ahead. This is the real difference the load makes.

The chart in figure 1-3 illustrates this difference. You may also compare the load and no-load funds to a 100-yard race. If you are a load fund investor, you essentially give your opponent an 8½-yard head start.

Some brokers or load mutual fund salespersons attempt to make a case for the load funds by asserting that they can hire better people to assure better performance. Already noted is the fact that the load or sales charge is retained by the broker-dealer. Little or no part of the commission goes to the fund itself. Therefore, from the funds' perspective, both load and no-load funds operate as no-load funds.

Performance remains the key to long-term investment gains and should always be the key consideration when picking one or more mutual funds for investment. If no-loads do not perform as well as load funds, you would be penny wise and pound foolish to pick a no-load fund simply to save the commission. The records show, however, that no-load funds perform as well on average as load funds on the basis of the cash actually invested. Some load funds do better than the average no-load fund, and some no-load funds do better than the average load fund. As reported in the *The Handbook for No-Load Fund Investors*:

> As far back as 1962, a special study performed by the Wharton School of Finance for the Securities and Exchange Commission found "no evidence that higher sales charges go hand-in-hand with better investment performance. Indeed, the study showed that fund shareholders paying higher sales charges had a less favorable investment experience than those paying less."
>
> One of the best studies was an exhausting comparison of no-loads versus loads covering income, growth, and stability. It was conducted in 1971 by *Fundscope*, and concluded: "In the end, because so many no-load and so many load funds perform above average and so many below average, you must reach the conclusion there just is no relationship, no correlation, between load and results."
>
> In another 1971 study, the Hirsch Organization, publisher of *Smart Money*, evaluated all funds for a 20-year period and found that because no-loads didn't have a sales charge to penalize their shareholders, they had "a helluva head start."
>
> More recently, Computer Direction Advisors, Inc., a company specializing in computer-based financial evaluations, compared 82 no-load mutual funds with assets of $7.3 billion to 138 load mutual funds with assets of $22.0 billion. They found there was no significant difference in risk, diversification, rate of return or risk-adjusted performance over the one-, three- and five-year periods ending June 30, 1979.
>
> Similarly, Lipper Analytical Services, which tracks mutual fund performance, found the average no-load's gains for five-, 10- and 15-year periods ending in December 1983 were very close to the average for all funds.
>
> Look at it this way. If a load fund group drops the load, there is no reason for its performance to change. Its management has not changed. In the same vein, there are a few groups that manage both load and no-load funds. Dreyfus and Fidelity, for example. How can the load make a difference?

In sum, all of the facts show that a sales charge—or lack of one—is not a factor in achieving performance. The conclusion is inescapable; load or no-load, the basic product is the same. So, it's only logical to go no-load and save the commission expense.

Mutual funds make their money from management fees. These fees are based on the assets under management and vary from about .3 percent to 1½ percent of the asset base.

Fig. 1-3. No-load mutual fund starts with lead and grows faster than load fund with commission deducted at start. Both funds start with $10,000.

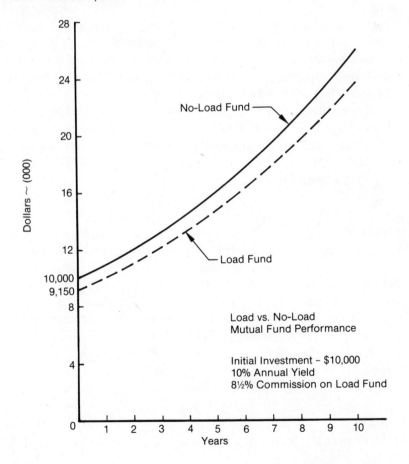

Load vs. No-Load
Mutual Fund Performance

Initial Investment – $10,000
10% Annual Yield
8½% Commission on Load Fund

Operating costs, such as printing, rent for office space, telephone, and similar expenses, are also charged against a mutual fund's income. Some funds will limit the combination of management fees and expenses to a defined ceiling, such as 1¼ percent of the asset base. If expenses exceed the expected limit, the difference will be charged to the managers rather than to the shareholders. All of the fees and expenses are fully disclosed in the prospectus that the investors in mutual funds receive prior to actual deposit of money. Thus, whether a mutual fund operates as a load or no-load fund makes little difference to the managers and investment advisors—only to the salesperson who sells you the load mutual fund shares.

There is literally a mutual fund for every taste and investment objective. You can invest in penny stock funds, gold funds, municipal bond funds, corporate bond funds, high-quality bond funds, junk bond funds, aggressive growth funds, income funds, funds that invest only in energy issues, and funds that emphasize social objectives. Some funds, called sector funds, are narrowly focused; others are broadly based. In any event, each fund discloses its record for any and all to see.

Numerous sources of specific and detailed information on no-load mutual funds are available. *Forbes* reports on more than six hundred funds, other than money market funds, in their issue that appears around the middle of August each year. The records of funds for the past 12 months and for the past 10 years are reviewed and rated according to their performance in up and down markets. *Money* magazine also reports periodically on mutual funds in special sections that review past performances. Summaries appear monthly in *Money*'s "Fund Watch" department. Several inexpensive newsletters provide more frequent information on no-load fund performance. The newsletters tend to concentrate on the no-loads because they offer a better deal for the investor. Since investing in no-load funds is a do-it-yourself project, newsletters aim their appeals directly at individual investors.

Picking a mutual fund from the hundreds available is analogous to picking a specific stock or bond. Although each of the funds is diversified, the objectives of specific funds will differentiate their performance in bull and bear markets. A no-load fund that invests in equities may do well in bull markets, while no-load bond funds may move little or not at all. A mutual fund, either load or no-load, that invests in penny stocks could fall precipitously in certain down markets. Money market funds maintain constant capital values and pay interest only to their shareholders. We expect to help you resolve some of this confusion in the succeeding pages.

Remember that many mutual funds claiming to be no-load funds charge various fees and penalties. Some other funds may charge a "low load" of 2 percent or 3 percent of the money invested. Other funds may charge a redemption fee if you redeem your investment within several months or several years. Others charge a minimal transaction fee for switching between funds.

As many as 250 presumably no-load mutual funds may also charge some of their marketing expenses to the fund's asset base rather than to incoming new deposits, under Section 12B.1 of the Federal Investment Company Act of 1940 as revised and approved by the Securities and Exchange Commission (SEC) in 1980. While these are not hidden charges (the SEC requires full disclosure of 12B.1 charges), they may not be as readily apparent as direct charges against new deposits.

For our purposes Decision No. 5 is relatively easy. Load funds are out because of their added cost. On average, no-load funds outperform load funds because they start with a lead of more cash in the account. Further, because no-loads offer greater flexibility, they provide important advantages for expanding your retirement investments. For all of these reasons, we recommend that you select no-load funds as your investment vehicle for building your retirement asset base.

Decision No. 6: Buy-and-Hold or Market Timing

When considering the management of your retirement investments, two risk factors are important: stock risk and market risk.

Stock risk—that is, picking a single issue of stock, bonds, options, or other securities—isolates the risk to one investment. For simplification, stock risk applies to the possibility of picking a stock or other security that declines or fails to perform.

Diversification within a mutual fund helps to minimize stock risk. The probability of loss from picking a bum stock is spread over a number of stocks, so diversification reduces risk.

Market risk—that is, the risk that the market as a whole will fall—affects mutual funds equally with individual stocks. This is where the axiom "A rising tide lifts all boats" comes from. Most serious stock analysts consider that only about 30 percent of the price of a stock results from a corporation's fundamentals. The remaining 70 percent of the stock's price at any specific time is determined mainly by the general market's condition. Since mutual funds invest in the common stocks of many corporations, a market that is declining will cause the net asset value (NAV) of equity funds to decline as well. Mutual fund managers and individuals all "fish from the same sea."

Will you simply buy and hold the funds? That is, will you put your $2,000 away each year in an IRA and let the fund managers invest it as they see fit? Since most funds tend to remain fully invested during bull and bear markets, the value of your shares will cycle up and down and likely vary around a trend line biased on the up side. Buying and holding no-load mutual fund shares, as with stocks, bonds, or other securities, thus involves market risk.

For over two hundred years the overall market has tended to move upward at about 5 percent per year. Over a long period you could expect this trend to develop a higher balance for your retirement fund. If the trend-generated increase does not keep up with inflation after taxes, you could be a net loser. Individual funds, like individual stocks, may do worse than the overall market. For example, a dollar invested in 1968 in Value Line Special Situations Fund declined to only 26 cents in 1974. There was nothing special about this performance, and such a decline was not an uncommon result for aggressive growth funds during that period. Remember, the fund was almost fully invested and highly diversified the whole time. Despite diversification, Value Line Special Situations Fund did not eliminate or even minimize market risk.

For a number of reasons it does not pay for most mutual funds to eliminate or even *try* to eliminate market risk. For one thing, if fund managers thought the markets were going to col-

lapse tomorrow, they would find it next to impossible to liquidate all of their holdings (at times they might own 50,000 to
100,000 shares of a particular stock). In falling markets it is not
uncommon for those kinds of stocks to go down 3, 4, 5, or 10
percent in one day. It does not make sense for funds to sell into
a panic.

Funds are generally evaluated by potential investors looking
at a fund's potential capabilities during a bull market. People
typically don't buy mutual funds in bear markets. Suppose you
read an article about one fund going down 25 percent and another fund declining 15 percent. The smaller loss would probably not be enough of an incentive to cause you to sit down and
write a check immediately and fire it off to the fund. People
just do not buy funds during bear markets, but they tend to be
large buyers and cannot get enough of the funds' shares during
bull markets. So, a mutual fund that may not have a great return in bear markets remains nearly 100 percent invested in
stocks that will, it is hoped, look good when the market turns
up again.

So-called defensive funds may attempt to break the fall of a
fund's shares during a bear market by switching out of equities
and buying T-bills or other short-term cash equivalents. But if
a fund remains in a defensive posture too long, it may give the
appearance that it does not know how to manage its assets
when the market is screaming upward. Funds have found that
it does not pay to liquidate their assets *en masse* during what
they might perceive to be a bear market. These funds also
present a growth face to investors, and growth is what shareholders are looking for—or they would not have selected that
fund. If they wanted to invest their money in a money fund,
they would go direct rather than invest their cash in a growth
fund that was temporarily in cash equivalents. Several no-load
mutual funds do switch funds internally at times. These internally timed funds may show a slower but consistent increase in
value over several cycles.

If you elect to invest your retirement cash in a growth fund
for a buy-and-hold posture, you can expect to watch the asset
value of the shares cycle up and down with a slight upward
bias. Obviously, some funds do better than others, and a few

report almost unbelievable and certainly unsustainable growth over short periods. Some expertise was involved, but a lot of the rise was probably due to luck—being in the right stocks at the right times. Picking one of these big winners can be difficult, but you might strike it lucky. We would prefer to take a more logical approach and insure lower but sustainable gains over the full period your retirement funds are invested for growth.

Market timing is the ultimate method of investing in mutual funds for long-term growth. It is simple to understand and simple to put into action. It is something any investor can do. We recommend that you avoid the buy-and-hold approach and embrace the concept of market timing, as explained in detail in chapter 2.

2

Market Timing—
What Is It?

Market timing is a technique for investing that will help you build wealth quicker, with less risk and with fewer demands on your time than any program or investment discipline we know. It's that simple.

Whatever your financial goal—an education fund for your children, retirement with or without an IRA or other deferred tax shelter, or simply becoming financially independent—you can reach your objective with greater assurance of success with market timing than with any other strategy. If you've heard this story for getting rich in the stock market before, recognize that market timing is neither entirely new nor risky. In fact, market timing is ultraconservative and appeals particularly to anyone who hates to lose. Why? Because market timing helps you avoid losses. Further, the benefits from using this proved technique are well documented by years of actual results.

If you have not heard about the substantial benefits to be derived from market timing, it is probably due to the large minimum account balances required—up to now. Instead of being limited to accounts of $100,000 or more—possibly much more—market timing is now available and particularly applicable to Individual Retirement Accounts (IRA) and Keogh plans.

GENERAL MARKET TIMING

As you know if you are a follower of the stock market, prices for shares move up and down. Market timing aims to ride stocks or mutual funds up but switch to money market mutual funds during market downswings. The trick is to recognize the beginnings and ends of cyclical trends. To recognize the turns, you need some sort of indicator, a signal that the market is likely to change direction. For example:

Suppose you decide to invest in a growth-oriented no-load stock fund. No-load mutual funds charge no fees for investing or for redemption of shares. Using one of the more volatile funds accelerates growth of share values during a market that is moving up. This type of fund may be a dog in a bear market. As share values move up smartly during the bull market cycle, your investment could increase by 50 percent or more within a 12-month span. But the market begins to cool, and your market indicator signals that it is time to get out. The share value may actually retrace part of its upward move before the indicator flashes a switch signal. Then, usually by telephone, you switch the cash value of your growth fund shares into a money market mutual fund. Money market funds exhibit one important quality: constant capital value, usually $1 per share. Switching to a money market fund is a defensive maneuver because it avoids the loss of capital. After the switch your capital is protected from any further decline in value and continues to earn interest while the market goes through its bear phase. Later, when the market finishes its downswing and begins to trend upward once again, the indicator signals another switch. You move the cash that has been earning interest in the money market fund back into the stock fund for another growth or bull market phase.

You have now completed one textbook cycle of market timing. Your cash increased in capital value during the bull market, earned interest while parked in a constant-capital money fund during the declining phase of the market, and moved back into the stock (equity) fund at the beginning of the next bull market phase. Instead of moving up and down with the same volatile stock mutual fund, however, you gained most of the up move, parked your cash in a money market fund while the market declined, and moved back into the equity fund with much more capital because you avoided the losses during the bear phase of the market.

The chart in figure 2-1 may help you visualize how your actions during a full market cycle increase your overall gain. Most market timers aim to be out of the market during most of the downswing. About 65 percent to 70 percent of the move is typical. On the upswing, market timers aim to participate in 65 percent to 70 percent of the change from the bottom to the top. No one can consistently pick the absolute tops and bottoms of a market cycle, and such efficiency is not needed to produce excellent and consistent results.

Fig. 2-1. Idealized comparison of market timing vs. buy-and-hold investing.

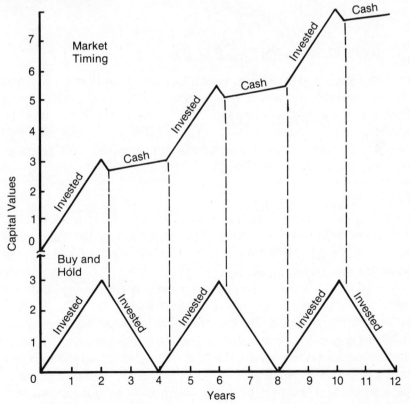

You can begin your market-timed investment program at any time. If the market should be in a down trend when you decide to invest, your cash would go directly into a money market fund rather than in an equity (stock) fund. When the indicators signal that a new up trend is under way, you simply switch cash from the money market fund into the equity fund for the ride up. Regular additions to your investment assets would be deposited first into the money fund and allowed to remain there until the check is cleared. This is usual fund policy but varies between funds. The additional money may then be switched into the equity fund depending on the market's condition. Depositing the additional cash directly into an equity fund could prevent its being switched to the money market fund for as many as 15 days, and that lack of mobility could result in a loss. Thus, regardless of the position of the equity fund versus the money market fund, new deposits will go directly to the money market fund.

MARKET TIMING–AN OLD DISCIPLINE

Numerous market timing techniques for avoiding losses have been around for years. Any action that helps to get out of positions to avoid or minimize losses or get in at desirable times to gain more can be called market timing. The technique is somewhat automatic or controlled by a formula or system to meet the general definition of market timing.

Stop-Loss Order

A stop-loss order, one form of limit order, continues to be a valuable tool for investors. The stop-loss order has been around on exchanges for years, but it was popularized by Nicholas Darvas in his book, *How I Made $2,000,000 in the Stock Market*. The technique was used so widely that some of its effects became known as the "Darvas Effects."

A stop-loss order works like this: You own Stock A, priced at $50 per share. The stock is relatively volatile; that is, the price moves up and down by as much as several points daily and not always in the same direction. You wish to avoid any big losses, so you place a limit order with your broker to sell the stock if the price should decline to $42 per share. The limit order is labeled "GTC," meaning Good Till Canceled. The broker files the order with the specialist at the exchange, possibly the New York Stock Exchange. The specialist enters the limit order on his book for possible action later. As long as Stock A trades above $42 per share, nothing happens. But if the price drops to $42 per share, the limit order automatically becomes a sell order. The specialist offers the shares of your Stock A to the next buyer at $42, and your stock is sold.

A stop-loss order avoids big losses, and that is one form of market timing. A rapid decline in the price of a stock can precipitate a larger-than-anticipated price swing by setting off stop-loss orders along the way. For example, when the price of Stock A drops to $42 per share and your shares trade, this may induce other holders to sell in the belief that the stock is headed down. If the stock should move to $40 where other stop-loss orders are filed, the decline continues and many shareholders are "stopped out." At some point canny traders will spot an oversold condition and buy shares of Stock A at bargain-basement prices. In a strong market, the price could easily move back to $45 or $50 per share. If such a rapid price reversal occurs within a few days, you could be out of the stock and the price still be around the price where you bought it. This is known as being "whipsawed." Thus, stop-loss orders do not offer a foolproof system for avoiding losses. In fact, no market timing technique can or will assure you against all losses. Stop-loss orders and other defensive techniques help give you an edge when used with understanding and experience. However, stop-loss orders cannot be used in buying or selling mutual funds of any kind.

Dollar-Cost Averaging

Dollar-cost averaging is another automatic system for timing buys but not sales of securities. Calling dollar-cost averaging a market timing strategy may be stretching the definition a bit, but dollar-cost averaging calls for automatic purchasing of shares on a predetermined schedule to take advantage of both the ups and downs in price. With dollar-cost averaging you buy a specific dollar amount of a stock or mutual fund at regular intervals regardless of the share prices. Under this system you end up with a lower average price for the shares you hold than if you had bought them at irregular intervals or bought a specific number of shares each time instead of a fixed dollar amount.

Dollar-cost averaging is less likely to produce results equivalent to in-and-out market timing using mutual funds because the system includes no sell discipline. We know of cases where astute investors followed a rigid program of acquiring stocks or mutual funds over periods of 15 or 20 years with excellent results. A major bear market near the end, however, wiped out as much as 75 percent of their portfolios' value because they did not cut their losses in a bear market. Half of the investment program can be excellent in some markets, but without a definite and planned program for avoiding losses, the dollar-cost averaging advantages of acquiring stocks or mutual fund shares can be negated.

Market Timing Indicators

As you will have already perceived, one of the key elements in any successful market timing program is an indicator or group of indicators that will help you determine when to move cash from an equity or growth investment into a money market fund or from a money market fund back into the equity or growth fund. Unfortunately, the perfect indicator does not exist and never will.

A perfect indicator would signal a change in the trend of the market the day before the reversal actually occurs, and the indicator would signal such changes accurately and predictably. Technical analysts are constantly searching for one or several signals that when interpreted separately or together would provide a forecast of market and individual stock direction. The technicians use a variety of statistical analyses, usually with the help of a computer, to search past market actions for some clue to what happened before the market actually moved.

Two types of indicators are usually involved. The first type is the forecasting indicator. Analysts would like to discover an indicator that would flash a signal early as a notice that the market is due to advance or decline. The second general type of indicator is the trend indicator. Most market timers use the trend indicators to key their actions, and they are known generally as trend followers. The basic indicator for trend following is the moving average. An indicator based on moving averages that you can construct and maintain yourself is detailed in chapter 5.

Market Timing Discipline

Probably the most important characteristic of market timing is discipline—particularly a sell discipline. Many investors, often keyed by their brokers, buy regularly, possibly using some system, information supplied by an analyst, or a hunch or hot tip heard at a cocktail party. Most of the action happens on the buy side.

When you adopt market timing, you embrace both a buy and sell discipline that follows a prescribed formula. Whether you do your own switching or turn over the tasks to a market timer, both the buy and sell sides get equal attention because they are equally important. Buy and sell signals are automatic in a market timing program. When the indicator flashes a signal to move from a growth mutual fund into a money market fund, you "sell." When the indicator says to move your cash parked in a money fund into equities, you "buy." It's that simple. The important benefit for you is that you have sold before encountering a huge loss.

When you move cash out of a money market fund into a stock or equity fund, there is no capital gain, either short or long term. You will have earned interest income that is taxable at ordinary income rates. But when you move your cash out of an equity (growth) fund and into a money market fund, that action constitutes a sale for tax purposes.

If you had kept your cash in the stock or equity fund for at least six months and your account shows a capital gain, the difference will be taxed as a long-term capital gain for a favorable tax treatment. Should there be a loss, highly unlikely in a well-managed market timing program, it would be a long-term loss for tax purposes if your cash had remained in the equity fund for at least six months. Formerly, the holding period for long-term capital gain or loss treatment was one year. The Deficit Reduction Act of 1984 shortened the holding period to six months for transactions that were entered into after June 22, 1984. Any gains or losses incurred when the holding period is less than six months are short term and taxed at ordinary income rates.

No-Load Mutual Funds

At last count there were more than seven hundred no-load mutual funds grouped into families that include money market funds. Appendix A lists many of the no-load mutual funds according to their family affiliation. It is important to select funds within the same family to facilitate switching with a minimum loss of time and/or minimum expense. Mutual funds are organized to provide a specific type of investment and are known by such general labels as equity, bond, income, tax-free, or money market funds.

An *equity* fund aims for capital growth by investing in the common stocks of other corporations. With hundreds of equity funds around, specialization among funds is common.

Aggressive equity funds invest in the common stocks of emerging growth companies, probably in some new and exotic high-technology field. The objective is to buy the stocks of these companies while they are small and unknown, and share prices are low. After holding these shares for months or years, the share prices will have escalated, it is hoped, and the NAV of the fund will have risen to yield a capital gain when sold or switched to a money market fund. Many equity funds are known to be highly volatile, with wide and often rapid price swings; hence the name, aggressive equity funds.

Growth equity funds invest in large capitalization corporations with a history of steady, if not sensational, growth.

Income funds aim to provide income from bonds, real estate, stocks known to pay high proportions of earnings as dividends, and certificates of deposit or Treasury bills.

Municipal bond funds pass tax-free interest through to fund shareholders. Tax-free dividends may also escape state income taxes when the portfolio is structured to hold only the bonds of one state where the tax on municipal bond interest is also exempted. These are generally referred to as "double tax-frees."

Money market mutual funds invest only in short-term market instruments, such as certificates of deposit, T-bills, bankers' acceptances, and commercial paper. The main characteristic of market instruments is their short maturity, sometimes figured in days. With a short maturity, changes in the interest environment have little effect on the capital value of the securities. Thus, money market funds can maintain a constant capital value or NAV of $1 per share. Interest income is passed through to shareholders, but there can be no capital gain or loss, and that is the primary benefit of being in a money market fund during declining markets.

Since market timing requires switching from equity or growth situations into stable or fixed capital investments and vice versa, no-load mutual funds offer the ideal combination.

HAZARDS OF MARKET TIMING

Despite the advantages and benefits to be derived from the use of market timing by individual investors, not everyone is pleased by the prospect of significant moves into or out of the market at specific points or times. Analysts and market observers express some concern that normal market actions could be affected, possibly even manipulated, if huge blocks of stocks are sold in response to signals from market timers. Much like the "Darvas effect," market timing might influence the prices of securities in the market under certain conditions. While these concerns continue to be expressed, little evidence is available to support them on a long-term basis.

When mutual funds are used as the vehicle for market timing, the managers of the funds may find that some of their actions are limited. If a large block of a mutual fund's shares should be switched from an equity fund into a money market mutual fund, the managers might have to sell stocks being held by the fund at what they consider an inopportune time. Ordinarily, small redemptions of shares or switches of shares into a family money market fund cause few problems. The cash for redemption may come either from investments by new or existing shareholders or from a small pool of cash kept in a bank or its own money market fund for the day-to-day liquidation of shares. The fund may also tap into a prearranged line of credit from a bank to provide cash needed for a larger-than-expected influx of redemption orders. But a massive switch could strain the resources of a fund and force it to sell securities into a down market at a loss. In these cases the fund managers believe their freedom of action is being taken away by outside managers. In one instance, a sizable mutual fund was suddenly faced with a need for $15 million as a result of a switching signal. While the managers disagreed with the market timer's decision, they had little choice but to comply. Instead of selling securities to raise the cash, however, the fund managers borrowed the cash for switching into the money market fund and held the securities. As it turned out, the market timers were right, and the value of the securities that were retained in the portfolio declined.

The potential problems associated with massive and sudden switches of equity assets into a money fund or vice versa worry some fund managers so much that they have erected barriers to frequent switching. Imposing a redemption fee is the most common deterrent. When switching out of an equity fund into a money market fund costs 1 percent to as much as 5 percent, the value of the switch must be looked at more closely, or so goes the thinking among fund managers opposed to switching. The imposition of low-load sales charges to invest in certain "hot" funds may also deter the investor who is looking to switch out of the equity fund when the trend changes from up to down. Generally, the best defense against load and redemption charges is to avoid those fund families that impose charges or otherwise discourage switching.

Despite the expressed concerns about market timing, Charles Schwab has announced a program whereby no-load funds may be switched among different funds, including money market funds, on an almost unlimited basis. (More on this program later in chapter 5.) Such a far-reaching program could not have been developed without the complete cooperation of the no-load mutual funds involved—and isn't that a stamp of approval for switching by the no-load mutual fund industry? Charles Schwab's strong endorsement of switching no-load mutual funds can be interpreted as a very strong statement that market timing with no-load mutual funds is not only here to stay but is likely to increase among mutual fund investors who are interested in building their asset base with minimum risk.

TIMING IN UP AND DOWN MARKETS

Time can be an important factor in any market timing program. What the market in general is doing obviously impacts the results from your investment program. To gain insight into what can happen over a period of 15 years, consider the following three programs:

1. A diversified aggressive growth mutual fund offers the potential of outstanding gains—as much as 50 percent to 100 percent per year. Assume that this fund is managed by some of the best equity managers in the business and has earned numerous favorable reports in the financial press. You are told that losses may occur from time to time, but the large gains should more than make up for the losses.

2. The same diversified aggressive growth mutual fund as in No. 1 offers the same performance but with the discipline the Merriman Growth Equity Model supplies for market timing. Expectations are for sizable gains in up markets with smaller losses, possibly minimal gains, in bear markets.

3. U.S. Treasury bills are bought and rolled over to provide a loss-free investment program. Inflation may be a factor in determining after-inflation gains or losses of actual purchasing power.

Each December 31 you review the performance of these three portfolios with the following results:

1970: The aggressive fund without timing declined 34.4 percent. The mutual fund with timing was up 10.5 percent. T-bills were up 6.5 percent. Even though timing won, you might be uneasy about being in a fund that lost more than one-third of its value in one year. Although timing wins by a small advantage over T-bills, you may not think timing was worth the risk.

1971: The fund was up 17.6 percent, but with timing, the increase was 35.9 percent. T-bills gained 4.3 percent. You are likely to believe solidly in market timing discipline; however, it will be another five years before you feel that confident again.

1972: The fund suffers a setback of 11 percent. With timing there is still a 4.5 percent loss. The winner is T-bills, up 4.1 percent—with no risk.

1973: It happens again! The fund is down 45.5 percent, but with timing the loss is cut to 1.6 percent—but still a loss. T-bills show a gain—again.

1974: This is the year that most investors threw in the towel and decided the stock market was not for them, even with the diversification afforded by a professionally managed mutual fund. The fund loses another 30 percent. The timed fund and T-bills both turn in a gain of 7.1 percent.

1975: This is the first year you would win with a buy-and-hold position in the fund—up 47 percent. With timing your investment is up 34 percent. T-bills gain 5.8 percent. The 47 percent gain during 1975 just makes up for the 30 percent loss in 1974. Remember, it takes a 100 percent gain to make up for a 50 percent loss.

1976: The fund on buy-and-hold was up 52.7 percent, the market-timed fund was up 57.8 percent, and T-bills were up 5 percent.

1977: In this mixed year the fund was up 12.3 percent, market timing was up 3.5 percent, and T-bills were up 5.3 percent.

1978: The fund was up 21.1 percent, timing was up 17 percent, and T-bills were up 7.2 percent.

1979: The fund on buy-and-hold topped three portfolios with a solid gain of 43.6 percent, the timed fund was up 26 percent, and T-bills were up 10 percent.

1980: The buy-and-hold fund gained 54.4 percent, with the timed fund turning in a 78.4 percent gain. T-bills were up 11.5 percent.

1981: The fund without timing lost 2.2 percent. The timed fund was at 8.5 percent. T-bills won with a 14.1 percent gain. At the end of 12 years, each of the three approaches has won four times.

1982: The buy-and-hold fund was up 23.1 percent, and the timed fund gained 30.7 percent. T-bills were up 10.7 percent.

1983: The fund alone with a 19.4 percent gain barely topped the fund with timing with a 21.4 percent gain. T-bills were a distant third at 8.6 percent.

1984: Another reversal, with the buy-and-hold fund dropping 25.5 percent, the timed fund dropping 5.7 percent, and T-bills gaining 9.6 percent.

1985: The buy-and-hold fund was up 21.1 percent, the timed fund up 21.1 percent, and T-bills up 7.6 percent.

For a year-by-year summary of results with an aggressive growth fund on buy-and-hold and market timed programs versus T-bills, see table 2A. Similar results using a conservative growth-income fund versus T-bills are detailed in table 2B.

From this mixed bag of results, as summarized in table 2A, you can learn the following about investing in growth funds with and without market timing versus Treasury bills:

1. The only way to guarantee a gain at year-end is to invest in short-term, risk-free debt instruments, specifically T-bills.

2. In all three of the assumed portfolios, there were up to five years between winning years. You should be patient no matter which approach you use.

3. Although the number of winning years may be approximately the same, long-term results were not. If you had in-

Table 2A. Aggressive growth fund vs. U.S. Treasury bills.

Year	Fund Buy & Hold	Fund Timed	U.S. Treasury Bills	Average All Three	Average T-Bills & Timing
1970	-34.4%	+10.5%	+ 6.5%	- 5.8%	+ 8.5%
1971	+17.6%	+35.9%	+ 4.3%	+19.3%	+20.1%
1972	-11.0%	- 4.5%	+ 4.1%	- 3.8%	- .2%
1973	-45.5%	- 1.6%	+ 7.0%	-13.3%	+ 2.7%
1974	-30.0%	+ 7.1%	+ 7.1%	- 5.3%	+ 7.1%
1975	+47.0%	+34.0%	+ 5.8%	+28.9%	+19.9%
1976	+52.7%	+57.8%	+ 5.0%	+38.5%	+31.4%
1977	+12.3%	+ 3.5%	+ 5.3%	+ 7.0%	+ 4.4%
1978	+21.2%	+17.0%	+ 7.2%	+15.1%	+12.2%
1979	+43.6%	+26.0%	+10.0%	+26.5%	+18.0%
1980	+54,4%	+78.4%	+11.5%	+48.1%	+45/0%
1981	- 2.2%	+ 8.5%	+14.1%	+ 6.8%	+11.3%
1982	+21.1%	+30.7%	+10.7%	+21.5%	+20.7%
1983	+19.4%	+21.4%	+ 8.6%	+16.5%	+15.0%
1984	-25.5%	- 5.7%	+ 9.6%	- 7.2%	+ 2.0%
1985 (11-29)	+13.8%	+12.1%	+ 7.0%	+10.7%	+ 9.6%
Average	+ 9.8%	+20.7%	+ 7.7%	+12.7%	+14.2%

vested $10,000 in each approach in 1970, the results as of December 31, 1985, were as follows:

Buy-and-hold	$23,176
Market timing	$171,023
T-bills	$ 32,969

Table 2B. Conservative growth-income vs. U.S. Treasury bills.

Year	Fund Buy & Hold	Fund Timed	U.S. Treasury Bills	Average All Three	Average T-bills & Timing
1970	+ 6.7%	+19.3%	+ 6.5%	+10.8%	+12.9%
1971	+13.5%	+19.4%	+ 4.3%	+12.4%	+11.9%
1972	+ 9.1%	+ 2.0%	+ 4.1%	+ 5.1%	+ 3.1%
1973	-15.9%	+ 8.8%	+ 7.0%	- .3%	+ 7.9%
1974	-16.1%	+ 7.1%	+ 7.1%	- .6%	+ 7.1%
1975	+41.7%	+22.3%	+ 5.8%	+23.3%	+14.1%
1976	+34.5%	+29.2%	+ 5.0%	+22.9%	+17.1%
1977	+ 1.8%	+ 4.2%	+ 5.3%	+ 3.8%	+ 4.8%
1978	+11.8%	+16.5%	+ 7.2%	+11.6%	+11.9%
1979	+27.6%	+15.5%	+10.0%	+17.7%	+12.8%
1980	+27.8%	+35.0%	+11.5%	+24.8%	+23.3%
1981	+16.4%	+ 6.2%	+14.1%	+12.2%	+10.1%
1982	+29.7%	+20.6%	+10.7%	+20.3%	+15.7%
1983	+ 6.5%	+ 8.4%	+ 8.6%	+ 7.8%	+ 8.5%
1984	+ 2.7%	+14.1%	+ 9.6%	+ 8.8%	+11.9%
1985 (11-29)	+19.0%	+15.8%	+ 7.0%	+13.9%	+11.4%
Average	+13.5%	+15.3%	+ 7.7%	+12.2%	+11.5%

3

Market Timing Performance

E very good theory requires definitive proof of its validity before it can be used with confidence. So it is with market timing. Market timing as a concept has long been used in stock market strategy. The use of market timing specifically with no-load mutual funds is newer, but 14 years of actual experience have proved its usefulness. Market timing became a viable strategy at about the time money market mutual funds came into being, around 1972. With a money market fund available for switching into during downtrends of the market, little- or no-cost switching by telephone became a practical maneuver. Parking capital in a money market fund minimized periodic losses inherent in buy-and-hold positions. Prior to 1972, market timing was practiced by switching out of mutual funds into Treasury bills during bear markets. While this procedure was a bit unwieldy, it worked to preserve large capital positions.

Over the past 14 years, the concept has been refined and expanded to encompass billions of dollars of investments. Annual increases in the total value of investments averaged more than 20 percent per year for numerous market timers using no-load funds.

Before getting into the specifics of market timing performance, recognize what an average 20 percent gain will do for your investment goals. Using the familiar "Rule of 72," dividing the 20 percent annual gain into 72 yields 3.6, meaning that a lump sum invested at a 20 percent annual return would double in 3.6 years. If you were to invest $2,000 in an IRA, for example, *and not add to it*, after 40 years your balance would grow to $2,939,543 (the start of year 41 equals the end of year 40), as shown in table 3A. Such is the incredible power of compound interest. After 20 years an initial deposit in an IRA of $2,000 compounding at 20 percent each year on average would grow to $30,814. Since both of these examples are within an IRA, no tax would be levied on the income each year. Taxes levied at ordinary income rates would be payable on IRA cash for the year it is withdrawn.

Table 3A details the year-by-year increase in value for a single deposit of $2,000 over the total 40-year span at interest rates of 5, 10, 15, and 20 percent. Table 3B looks at the growth of a retirement fund within an IRA with annual additions of $2,000 at annual yields of 10, 15, and 20 percent. After 25 years the total has reached $1,134,755 (the start of year 26 equals the end of year 25). Contributions at $2,000 per year total only $50,000. For comparison, table 3B shows the growth of capital within an IRA where the average yearly rate of only 10 percent is assumed for the same 25 years and reaches a total of $218,364 (the start of year 26 equals the end of year 25). You will see from the comparison of figures in table 3B that the difference in yearly rate is enormous—$914,391 for these two examples over a 25-year period. Also consider that the 10 percent yearly rate is about what you can expect from bank-type IRA programs.

One other point here. Over 25 years you will have invested $50,000 at the rate of $2,000 per year. However, only part of that $50,000 is actually out of pocket for the year deposited because each $2,000 is a before-tax contribution. If you are in a 40 percent marginal tax bracket, your actual out-of-pocket cash contribution drops to $1,200. The other $800 is your tax saving for the year. In effect, Uncle Sam invests the other $800 for your benefit.

Look at the power of compounding your investment within an IRA another way. From the figures in table 3C note the difference that a 1 percent change in average annual growth can make over the period a retirement plan is in force.

Suppose that annual growth averages only 19 percent instead of 20 percent. After 40 years an initial deposit of $2,000 would grow to $2,939,543 (the start of year 41 equals the end of year 40) at 20 percent annual return. With an annual return of 19 percent, the comparable total is $2,103,335, for a difference of $836,208—for only a 1 percent higher rate. The build-

Table 3A. Growth of $2,000 with no additional deposits over years at 5, 10, 15, and 20 percent annual yields.

Year No.	5% Start	Addition	10% Start	Addition	15% Start	Addition	20% Start	Addition
1	$2,000	$100	$2,000	$200	$2,000	$300	$2,000	$400
2	$2,100	$105	$2,200	$220	$2,300	$345	$2,400	$480
3	$2,205	$110	$2,420	$242	$2,645	$397	$2,880	$576
4	$2,315	$116	$2,662	$266	$3,042	$456	$3,456	$691
5	$2,431	$122	$2,928	$293	$3,498	$525	$4,147	$829
6	$2,553	$128	$3,221	$322	$4,023	$603	$4,977	$995
7	$2,680	$134	$3,543	$354	$4,626	$694	$5,972	$1,194
8	$2,814	$141	$3,897	$390	$5,320	$798	$7,166	$1,433
9	$2,955	$148	$4,287	$429	$6,118	$918	$8,600	$1,720
10	$3,103	$155	$4,716	$472	$7,036	$1,055	$10,320	$2,064
11	$3,258	$163	$5,187	$519	$8,091	$1,214	$12,383	$2,477
12	$3,421	$171	$5,706	$571	$9,305	$1,396	$14,860	$2,972
13	$3,592	$180	$6,277	$628	$10,701	$1,605	$17,832	$3,566
14	$3,771	$189	$6,905	$690	$12,306	$1,846	$21,399	$4,280
15	$3,960	$198	$7,595	$759	$14,151	$2,123	$25,678	$5,136
16	$4,158	$208	$8,354	$835	$16,274	$2,441	$30,814	$6,163
17	$4,366	$218	$9,190	$919	$18,715	$2,807	$36,977	$7,395
18	$4,584	$229	$10,109	$1,011	$21,523	$3,228	$44,372	$8,874
19	$4,813	$241	$11,120	$1,112	$24,751	$3,713	$53,247	$10,649
20	$5,054	$253	$12,232	$1,223	$28,464	$4,270	$63,896	$12,779
21	$5,307	$265	$13,455	$1,345	$32,733	$4,910	$76,675	$15,335
22	$5,572	$279	$14,800	$1,480	$37,643	$5,646	$92,010	$18,402
23	$5,851	$293	$16,281	$1,628	$43,289	$6,493	$110,412	$22,082
24	$6,143	$307	$17,909	$1,791	$49,783	$7,467	$132,495	$26,499
25	$6,450	$323	$19,699	$1,970	$57,250	$8,588	$158,994	$31,799
26	$6,773	$339	$21,669	$2,167	$65,838	$9,876	$190,792	$38,158
27	$7,111	$356	$23,836	$2,384	$75,714	$11,357	$228,951	$45,790
28	$7,467	$373	$26,220	$2,622	$87,071	$13,061	$274,741	$54,948
29	$7,840	$392	$28,842	$2,884	$100,131	$15,020	$329,689	$65,938
30	$8,232	$412	$31,726	$3,173	$115,151	$17,273	$395,627	$79,125
31	$8,644	$432	$34,899	$3,490	$132,424	$19,864	$474,753	$94,951
32	$9,076	$454	$38,389	$3,839	$152,287	$22,843	$569,703	$113,941
33	$9,530	$476	$42,228	$4,223	$175,130	$26,270	$683,644	$136,729
34	$10,006	$500	$46,450	$4,645	$201,400	$30,210	$820,373	$164,075
35	$10,507	$525	$51,095	$5,110	$231,610	$34,741	$984,447	$196,889
36	$11,032	$552	$56,205	$5,620	$266,351	$39,953	$1,181,336	$236,267
37	$11,584	$579	$61,825	$6,183	$306,304	$45,946	$1,417,604	$283,521
38	$12,163	$608	$68,008	$6,801	$352,249	$52,837	$1,701,124	$340,225
39	$12,771	$639	$74,809	$7,481	$405,087	$60,763	$2,041,349	$408,270
40	$13,410	$670	$82,290	$8,229	$465,850	$69,877	$2,449,619	$489,924
41	$14,080	$704	$90,519	$9,052	$535,727	$80,359	$2,939,543	$587,909

ups of capital for shorter periods with yields of 19, 20, and 21 percent are detailed in table 3C.

Boxcar numbers are captivating to consider. But recognize from these analyses how much more you gain after a number of years from only 1 percent more in annual return. The buildup from compounding is particularly important for re-

Table 3B. Growth of $2,000 plus additions of $2,000 annually at 10, 15, and 20 percent annual yields.

Year No.	19% Start	Addition	20% Start	Addition	21% Start	Addition
1	$2,000	$380	$2,000	$400	$2,000	$420
2	$2,380	$452	$2,400	$480	$2,420	$508
3	$2,832	$538	$2,880	$576	$2,928	$615
4	$3,370	$640	$3,456	$691	$3,543	$744
5	$4,011	$762	$4,147	$829	$4,287	$900
6	$4,773	$907	$4,977	$995	$5,187	$1,089
7	$5,680	$1,079	$5,972	$1,194	$6,277	$1,318
8	$6,759	$1,284	$7,166	$1,433	$7,595	$1,595
9	$8,043	$1,528	$8,600	$1,720	$9,190	$1,930
10	$9,571	$1,818	$10,320	$2,064	$11,120	$2,335
11	$11,389	$2,164	$12,383	$2,477	$13,455	$2,826
12	$13,553	$2,575	$14,860	$2,972	$16,281	$3,419
13	$16,128	$3,064	$17,832	$3,566	$19,699	$4,137
14	$19,193	$3,647	$21,399	$4,280	$23,836	$5,006
15	$22,840	$4,340	$25,678	$5,136	$28,842	$6,057
16	$27,179	$5,164	$30,814	$6,163	$34,899	$7,329
17	$32,343	$6,145	$36,977	$7,395	$42,228	$8,868
18	$38,488	$7,313	$44,372	$8,874	$51,095	$10,730
19	$45,801	$8,702	$53,247	$10,649	$61,825	$12,983
20	$54,503	$10,356	$63,896	$12,779	$74,809	$15,710
21	$64,859	$12,323	$76,675	$15,335	$90,519	$19,009
22	$77,182	$14,665	$92,010	$18,402	$109,527	$23,001
23	$91,847	$17,451	$110,412	$22,082	$132,528	$27,831
24	$109,297	$20,767	$132,495	$26,499	$160,359	$33,675
25	$130,064	$24,712	$158,994	$31,799	$194,034	$40,747
26	$154,776	$29,407	$190,792	$38,158	$234,782	$49,304
27	$184,184	$34,995	$228,951	$45,790	$284,086	$59,658
28	$219,179	$41,644	$274,741	$54,948	$343,744	$72,186
29	$260,822	$49,556	$329,689	$65,938	$415,930	$87,345
30	$310,379	$58,972	$395,627	$79,125	$503,275	$105,688
31	$369,351	$70,177	$474,753	$94,951	$608,963	$127,882
32	$439,527	$83,510	$569,703	$113,941	$736,846	$154,738
33	$523,037	$99,377	$683,644	$136,729	$891,583	$187,232
34	$622,415	$118,259	$820,373	$164,075	$1,078,816	$226,551
35	$740,673	$140,728	$984,447	$196,889	$1,305,367	$274,127
36	$881,401	$167,466	$1,181,336	$236,267	$1,579,494	$331,694
37	$1,048,867	$199,285	$1,417,604	$283,521	$1,911,188	$401,349
38	$1,248,152	$237,149	$1,701,124	$340,225	$2,312,537	$485,633
39	$1,485,301	$282,207	$2,041,349	$408,270	$2,798,170	$587,616
40	$1,767,508	$335,827	$2,449,619	$489,924	$3,385,785	$711,015
41	$2,103,335	$399,634	$2,939,543	$587,909	$4,096,800	$860,328

tirement plans using either an IRA or a Keogh.

Market timing has proved its value by regularly delivering an average annual rate of 18 percent to 22 percent—or more. Market timing is effective because it avoids losses during periodic downturns. Investment funds parked in a money market mu-

Table 3C. Effect of 1 percent difference in yield over 40-year retirement investment.

Year No.	10% Start Total	Annual Earnings	15% Start Total	Annual Earnings	20% Start Total	Annual Earnings
1	$2,000	$200	$2,000	$300	$2,000	$400
2	$4,200	$420	$4,300	$645	$4,400	$880
3	$6,620	$662	$6,945	$1,042	$7,280	$1,456
4	$9,282	$928	$9,987	$1,498	$10,736	$2,147
5	$12,210	$1,221	$13,485	$2,023	$14,883	$2,977
6	$15,431	$1,543	$17,507	$2,626	$19,860	$3,972
7	$18,974	$1,897	$22,134	$3,320	$25,832	$5,166
8	$22,872	$2,287	$27,454	$4,118	$32,998	$6,600
9	$27,159	$2,716	$33,572	$5,036	$41,598	$8,320
10	$31,875	$3,187	$40,607	$6,091	$51,917	$10,383
11	$37,062	$3,706	$48,699	$7,305	$64,301	$12,860
12	$42,769	$4,277	$58,003	$8,701	$79,161	$15,832
13	$49,045	$4,905	$68,704	$10,306	$96,993	$19,399
14	$55,950	$5,595	$81,009	$12,151	$118,392	$23,678
15	$63,545	$6,354	$95,161	$14,274	$144,070	$28,814
16	$71,899	$7,190	$111,435	$16,715	$174,884	$34,977
17	$81,089	$8,109	$130,150	$19,523	$211,861	$42,372
18	$91,198	$9,120	$151,673	$22,751	$256,233	$51,247
19	$102,318	$10,232	$176,424	$26,464	$309,480	$61,896
20	$114,550	$11,455	$204,887	$30,733	$373,376	$74,675
21	$128,005	$12,800	$237,620	$35,643	$450,051	$90,010
22	$142,805	$14,281	$275,263	$41,289	$542,061	$108,412
23	$159,086	$15,909	$318,553	$47,783	$652,474	$130,495
24	$176,995	$17,699	$368,336	$55,250	$784,968	$156,994
25	$196,694	$19,669	$425,586	$63,838	$943,962	$188,792
26	$218,364	$21,836	$491,424	$73,714	$1,134,755	$226,951
27	$242,200	$24,220	$567,138	$85,071	$1,363,706	$272,741
28	$268,420	$26,842	$654,208	$98,131	$1,638,447	$327,689
29	$297,262	$29,726	$754,339	$113,151	$1,968,136	$393,627
30	$328,988	$32,899	$869,490	$130,424	$2,363,763	$472,753
31	$363,887	$36,389	$1,001,914	$150,287	$2,838,516	$567,703
32	$402,276	$40,228	$1,154,201	$173,130	$3,408,219	$681,644
33	$444,503	$44,450	$1,329,331	$199,400	$4,091,863	$818,373
34	$490,953	$49,095	$1,530,731	$229,610	$4,912,235	$982,447
35	$542,049	$54,205	$1,762,340	$264,351	$5,896,682	$1,179,336
36	$598,254	$59,825	$2,028,691	$304,304	$7,078,019	$1,415,604
37	$660,079	$66,008	$2,334,995	$350,249	$8,495,622	$1,699,124
38	$728,087	$72,809	$2,687,244	$403,087	$10,196,747	$2,039,349
39	$802,896	$80,290	$3,092,331	$463,850	$12,238,096	$2,447,619
40	$885,185	$88,519	$3,558,181	$533,727	$14,687,716	$2,937,543
41	$975,704	$97,570	$4,093,908	$614,086	$17,627,259	$3,525,452

tual fund during bear markets continue to grow from compounding interest income while other parts of the market may be declining.

Let's look at some examples.

Greenwich Monitrend

Greenwich Monitrend is an investment adviser currently managing more than $100 million in individual and institutional accounts. Monitrend's first trade took place on August 12, 1971. Since that date each of the trades has been audited by Reitman & Reitman, Certified Public Accountants (New York). The total results of Monitrend's action are reproduced, with permission, in table 3D. Results over the period from 1971 through 1985 show a compounded annual growth rate of 22 percent based on the Lipper Growth Fund Index. A buy-and-hold program over the same period produced a compounded

Table 3D. Comparison of results between a buy-and-hold investment of $1.00 in the Lipper Growth Fund Index vs. an investment of $1.00 in a market timing program with the same index but utilizing Greenwich Monitrend's actual equity market buy/sell decision.

Date	Value of Original $1.00 Invested		Percent Change for Period	
	Timed Program	Buy/ Hold	Timed Program	Buy/ Hold
8/12/71	$1.00	$1.00	- -	- -
12/31/71	$1.19	$1.09	+ 19.1	+ 9.99
12/31/72	$1.46	$1.26	+ 22.88	+ 14.72
12/31/73	$1.77	$0.92	+ 21.25	- 27.01
12/31/74	$2.14	$0.64	+ 20.95	- 30.06
12/31/75	$3.11	$0.84	+ 45.32	+ 32.02
12/31/76	$4.00	$0.99	+ 28.54	+ 16.68
12/31/77	$4.28	$1.02	+ 6.75	+ 3.75
12/31/78	$5.75	$1.14	+ 34.53	+ 11.10
12/31/79	$7.03	$1.45	+ 22.24	+ 27.35
12/31/80	$9.95	$1.99	+ 41.39	+ 37.25
12/31/81	$12.56	$1.82	+ 27.31	- 8.4
12/31/82	$16.28	$2.18	+ 28.59	+ 20.24
12/31/83	$16.93	$2.66	+ 4.01	+ 21.94
12/31/84	$15.78	$2.59	- 6.80	- 2.79

annual growth rate of 8.5 percent. A sizable portion of the difference resulted from the funds' following the market down during the declines of 1972, 1973, and 1974. During most of that period Monitrend's assets were safely protected and continued to earn interest in money market mutual funds. The chart reproduced as figure 3-1 clearly shows the steady rise of Monitrend's market-timed portfolio compared to a buy-and-

Fig. 3-1. Greenwich Monitrend market timing performance. (See table 3D for numbers and details.)

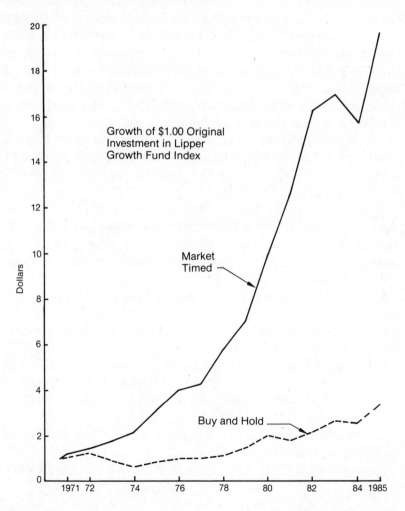

hold program. About four years of limited growth in the buy-and-hold mode were required to recover from the losses experienced during the down years of 1972 to 1974.

Donoghue's SLYC System

William E. Donoghue, founder and head of The Donoghue Organization, is generally recognized as the guru of money market mutual funds. The Donoghue Organization publishes *Money Fund Report* and *Moneyletter*. Donoghue and Thomas Tilling have written two editions of the *No-Load Mutual Fund Guide*, the latest edition being a paperback published by Bantam Books in early 1984. More recent books are *Guide to Finding Money to Invest* by William E. Donoghue and *Donoghue's Investment Tips for Retirement Savings*. The Donoghue Organization also publishes the *Mutual Fund Almanac*, a yearly updated performance report on many load and no-load mutual funds other than the money market funds. Histories of funds are reproduced for the past 10 years. It is a treasure trove of historical data but, like all market information, it represents the past. What happened in the past may or may not be relevant to future performance.

As part of their book, *No-Load Mutual Fund Guide*, Donoghue and Tilling introduced what they call their SLYC system, basically a market timing device based on average money fund rates. The acronym SLYC stands for four elements of their investment plan:

S for safety heads the list, to help you avoid unnecessary risk.

L stands for liquidity—"so you don't tie up your money and lose profitable opportunities."

Y brings in the ever-present need for yield, or a return on your investment. In their system, Donoghue and Tilling attempt to reach the highest overall yield consistent with acceptable risk.

C was added to the previous acronym, SLY, for catastrophe proofing, so you "can sleep nights."

Donoghue's SLYC system came from a long-term analysis of

stock market activity. One study disclosed a 30-year return for stocks at around 10 percent. The book also mentions the "dart board" approach and its surprisingly good results. Even so, as other market analysts quickly discovered, the return would have been substantially higher if the losses during bear markets had been eliminated or reduced. Donoghue and Tilling looked for some indicator to help them avoid the downturns. They recognized that stock prices had reacted negatively to interest rates over the past several cycles.

Because interest rates are so pervasive in current markets for stocks, bonds, real estate, and other investments, Donoghue based his SLYC system on changing interest rates. He thereby reasoned that investments should be in stocks whenever yields exceed 10 percent and should be out of stocks when yields fall below 10 percent. From this general caveat, he devised the "12 percent solution" as detailed in table 3E. The average rate of interest paid by the money market funds is the key indicator here. Donoghue's research indicates that stocks experience difficulties in staging much of a rally when interest rates are relatively high. He defines 13 percent as a relatively high barrier. Behind that thinking is the realization that corporations borrow scads of money to finance their operations. When the cost of money is high, profits will likely suffer, plans

Table 3E. SLYC switch points.

Donoghue's (30-day) Money Market Fund Average	Investment in Stocks (Mutual Funds)	Investment in Money Market Fund
Rising Interest Rates		
Below 10%	100%	0%
10%-11%	75%	25%
11%-12%	50%	50%
12%-13%	25%	75%
Above 13%	0%	100%
Falling Interest Rates		
13%-12%	25%	75%
12%-11%	50%	50%
11%-10%	75%	25%
Below 10%	100%	0%

for expansion will be curtailed, and then the prices of the corporations' stocks will probably drop. Experience indicates that higher interest rates tend to stifle stock prices, and the expectations of lower interest rates tend to boost prices. Thus, tying the SLYC system to interest rates involves considerable logic. However, using interest rates as an indicator results in using secondary information rather than specific price changes.

How has the SLYC system performed? According to the research department at The Donoghue Organization, the performance of the SLYC system has been traced in detail from May 1, 1979. If you had invested $10,000 on that date and switched back and forth according to the indicators, it would have grown to $26,939 through May 30, 1984, for an annual compounded growth rate of 21.92 percent. These figures include the reinvestment of all dividends and capital gains, if any. This is a relatively short time period as stock market cycles go. Use it with caution. Obviously, if the overall annual compounded rate is 21.92 percent, significant yields occurred during the time the money was invested in one or more no-load equity funds, since the interest payable on funds in a money market fund would average substantially less. A different time period would likely show a different annual compounded rate. Further, since market timing calls for your capital to be in a money market fund about half the time, the yields from money market funds during those periods will have a substantial effect on the overall performance.

Money Performance Summary

Performance results from 12 respected market timing organizations were summarized as part of an article, "Services That Time Your Trades," that appeared in *Money* magazine's May 1984 issue. The top timing organization among the 12 was Greenwich Monitrend Corp. with an overall compounded annual return of 21.6 percent during a five-year period beginning March 15, 1979. The lowest of the 12 timing services recorded an annual compounded return of 11.6 percent.

Analysis of 12 different services called for a consistent basis for the results to be comparable. Actual switch dates used by each of the services were used in the analysis, but for the period that money was invested in equity funds, a consistent rate of return equal to the return compiled by the Lipper Growth Fund Index was used rather than the actual earnings recorded for each service. The Lipper Growth Fund Index is a composite of returns on 30 growth stock funds. During the periods when the timing services switched out of equity funds, the rate paid on 90-day Treasury bills was credited to funds for the period.

The range of performance turned in by the 12 timing services representing the five-year compounded rate of return varied by almost 100 percent (from 11.6 percent to 21.6 percent). Thus, merely timing your investments offers no assurance of superior results—you also need a superior timer. Further, timing services exact a fee for their services, and they may limit minimum investments if they manage the funds directly. Of the services surveyed in the *Money* article, fees ranged from 2 percent to 3 percent of funds under management. Minimum amounts accepted ranged from zero to $150,000. Some of the timing services surveyed by *Money* also charged a substantial one-time account-opening fee. A market timer may charge a 2 percent fee for an account of $100,000 and a 1 percent fee for an account of $1 million or more.

The average number of switches per year varied from a low of 1.6 to as many as 8.8. The trader who traded most frequently turned in a performance near but not at the bottom of the range. For more information, you might want to study the complete article in the May 1984 issue of *Money*.

The Paul A. Merriman & Associates equity switching model was submitted to Moniresearch, the same analysts who developed the data for the *Money* article. Moniresearch used timing signals from the Merriman models and the same Lipper Growth Fund Index for performance results when the money was in the equity fund. According to this study the Merriman model turned in a performance of 21.9 percent growth rate compounded annually. The Merriman model called for an average of four switches per year compared to the average of 3.3 switches per year for the 12 market timers in the *Money* article. After considering the fees charged, PM&A rated No. 1, ahead of the 12 other timers.

Wall Street Week Technical Market Index

Probably the most widely watched timing indicator is the *Wall Street Week* Technical Market Index (TMI), shown weekly on many Public Broadcasting System stations. The TMI consists of 10 individual indicators that are generally unrelated. These 10 indicators show as plus, minus, or neutral, and the consensus is the sum of the 10 indicators. If all happened to be in neutral, the TMI would be zero for the week. If seven of the indicators are in plus territory and three in minus territory, the TMI for the week is shown as plus 4—a bullish sign meaning that the TMI was confirming a positive tone to the market. A net plus 5 or higher reading means investors should buy shares in the market. If the net reading should be a minus 5, however, meaning that at least five more indicators were in minus territory than in plus ground, the TMI would be bearish, that is, investors should sell. The full range of consensus indications is detailed in chapter 4.

Louis Rukeyser, host of *Wall Street Week*, refers to the indicators as "elves" and to their originator, Robert J. Nurock, as "Chief Elf." Mr. Nurock is the originator of the Technical Market Index and publishes a newsletter, *The Astute Investor* (Investor's Analysis, Inc., P.O. Box 988, Paoli, PA 19301). The Technical Market Index is updated and presented each week on the broadcast. See your local newspapers for time and station.

How have the "elves" scored with their predictions? According to Chief Elf Nurock, over the nine-and-a-half-year period from October 18, 1974, through April 13, 1984, the TMI correctly forecast the Dow Jones Industrial Average (the Dow) 74 percent of the time 26 weeks in advance and 94 percent of the time 52 weeks in advance. Over the recent five-year period, the TMI has been correct 70 percent of the time in forecasting the Dow five weeks in advance, 75 percent of the time 26 weeks in advance, and 100 percent of the time 52 weeks in advance. While these correct forecasts of the Dow represent highly significant statistical readings, you would have to invest in one of the index mutual funds to participate in the market. Thus, any specific percentage gain in a portfolio or for a specific sum of original cash is not possible since you "can't buy the Dow."

NoLoad Fund X

NoLoad Fund X is a monthly newsletter published by DAL Investment Co. (235 Montgomery Street, San Francisco, CA 94104) that reports on the performance of about 350 no-load mutual funds. The format of the report divides the funds into six categories, with three categories devoted to equity growth funds. Class 1 funds are rated "Most Speculative," Class 2 funds are rated "Speculative," and a more conservative group of growth funds in Class 3 are rated "High Quality." The various classifications reflect aggressiveness of the funds' objectives and the volatility of their performances.

Another feature of the newsletter is a listing of the five no-load equity funds in each group that showed the best performance over the preceding month. In this section, called "Following the Stars," each of the top five funds carries a double asterisk, calling your attention to those funds that turned in the best overall performance for their shareholders.

NoLoad Fund X carries this concept one step further. Editor Burt Berry recommends a market timing system that calls for you to invest in the top-rated fund noted in "Following the Stars." As long as your fund remains in the Star Box—that is, remains among the five best performing funds for each classification—you stick with that fund, but if your fund drops out of the top five, you withdraw your entire investment from that fund and immediately reinvest the proceeds with the new top-rated fund. Keeping your money invested in a fund that is doing better than the others will keep your equity growing rapidly. Berry's model differs from the usual market timing plan where funds are shifted out of an equity fund into a money market fund during market declines.

How did the *NoLoad Fund X* model perform? Over the period from August 31, 1976, through December 31, 1985 (nine years and four months), the model for Class 3 funds grew at an annually compounded rate of 28.1 percent. In other words, $10,000 invested in the top Class 3 fund on August 31, 1976, and switched as noted above, grew to $101,470 by December 31, 1985. This increase includes the reinvestment of all dividends and capital gains paid. Results do not take any taxes on income into effect. An allowance for the time lost in switching was included in the program. When the model called for a change, the fund to be dropped was sold on the second Friday of the month, and the money was reinvested a week later. In most cases an investment was closed out from one fund and

Table 3F. Rankings of top five no-load mutual funds in three growth fund categories for December 1985— *NoLoad Fund X.*

Months Starred			CLASS 1		
Con-secu-tive	In Past Year	F*X Score	MOST SPECULATIVE GROWTH FUNDS	Total Assets ($ Mil)	% in Cash & Equiv.
2	4	35.00	Pac Horiz Agg Gth	$102	8%
1	1	32.23	Fin Str Leisure	7	13
1	4	31.28	Fin Str Pacific	5	8
4	4	31.08	Fin Str Health	6	6
1	1	27.90	Berger 100	12	4

Months Starred			CLASS 2		
Con-secu-tive	In Past Year	F*X Score	SPECULATIVE GROWTH FUNDS	Total Assets ($ Mil)	% in Cash & Equiv.
3	5	36.43	GT Glbl Pacific	$ 49	6%
4	7	29.25	PRO Med Tech	98	7
2	2	27.33	North Star Regional	89	13
1	4	22.40	Gradison Emerg Gth	17	19
4	4	22.38	Meridian	18	7

Months Starred			CLASS 3 #		
Con-secu-tive	In Past Year	F*X Score	HIGHER QUALITY GROWTH FUNDS	Total Assets ($ Mil)	% in Cash & Equiv.
11	11	35.73	Transatlantic	$ 85	7%
11	11	34.75	Price Int'l	625	3
3	3	29.60	NoEast Inv Gth	16	14
11	11	28.88	Scudder Int'l	640	3
1	8	26.10	Vang Tr Int'l	652	3

[r] = Sales are (temporarily) restricted. Check with fund.

the funds reinvested in a different fund family. Telephone switching directly was not possible. Telephone switching could be effected through the Schwab Marketplace, with a fee being paid (see chapter 10).

For comparison, the Vanguard Index Trust showed a compounded growth rate of 12.8 percent for the same period. An initial investment of $10,000 on August 31, 1976, grew to $30,932 by December 31, 1985, under the same conditions. The Vanguard Index Trust is designed as a proxy for the overall market and tends to reflect the Standard & Poor's 500 average fairly closely. For another comparison, consider the performance of the Reserve Fund, the original money market mutual fund. An initial $10,000 invested on the same date, August 31, 1976, grew to $24,514 by December 31, 1985, for a compounded growth rate of 10.1 percent.

Perhaps not so surprising is the performance of the conservative or "High Quality" classification of funds: The Class 3 funds outperformed both the "Most Speculative" and "Speculative" classifications. Recognize, however, that the nine-plus years covered in the performance report were generally bullish periods for the market. The *NoLoad Fund X* model has not been tested in a long-term bear market.

Hulbert Financial Digest Performance Ratings

The *Hulbert Financial Digest* (HFD) is a monthly newsletter that reviews, rates, and compares many advisory services, including a wide selection of market timers. Each monthly issue reports on the performance of the stock picks and timing moves recommended by the most prominent newsletters. HFD's method is to follow the picks and advice of the newsletter writers. The performance ratings include increases or decreases in portfolio value for the preceding month and for several preceding years. HFD's tables also report risk ratings, the number of stocks in a portfolio and a rating on the clarity and completeness of the newsletter. A portion of the Performance Ratings for December 1985 is reproduced in table 3G. For more detailed information on how the ratings are compiled, write to *Hulbert Financial Digest* (643 South Carolina Avenue, S.E.,

Table 3G. Performance ratings (May 30, 1986, *Hulbert Financial Digest*).

NEWSLETTER (Composition of Portfolio)	5/86 Gain	1986 Gain	1985 Gain	1984 Gain	1983 Gain	1982 Gain	1981 Gain	7/1 to 12/31/80 Gain	Risk Rating Note 1
Addison Report (Portfolios fully invested in "monitored" lists)									
a. Conservative stocks (Fully invested)	+5.0%	+19.8%	+15.3%	+4.4%	+28.9%	n/a	n/a	n/a	4.09
b. Speculative Stocks (Fully invested)	+5.2%	+20.8%	+17.6%	-13.6%	+89.6%	n/a	n/a	n/a	5.92
BI Research (Portfolio fully invested in stocks rated "Buy")	+1.5%	+5.9%	+65.9%	+14.3%	n/a	n/a	n/a	n/a	9.88
Cabot Market Letter (Model Portfolio: Stocks and, at times, T-Bills)	+6.5%	+16.5%	+37.4%	-22.7%	+7.3%	+32.8%	+2.5%	n/a	6.63
(Cabot Market Letter–Timing Only)	+4.7%	+16.8%	+26.3%	+0.7%	+16.4%	+13.9%	-3.7%	n/a	n/a
Calif. Technology Stock Letter (Model Portfolio: Stocks & T-Bills)	-3.5%	+8.9%	-5.9%	-47.9%	+1.7%	n/a	n/a	n/a	8.36
(Calif. Technology Stock Letter–Timing Only)	+3.0%	+11.9%	+25.5%	+1.2%	+15.4%	n/a	n/a	n/a	n/a
Canadian Business Service Investment Report									
a. Very Conservative Stocks (Fully invested)	+1.0%	+6.3%	+20.7%	-4.9%	n/a	n/a	n/a	n/a	3.85
b. Conservative stocks (fully invested)	+3.2%	+20.4%	+17.2%	+.3%	n/a	n/a	n/a	n/a	4.05
c. Average risk stocks (fully invested)	-4.9%	+37.6%	+39.7%	-6.4%	n/a	n/a	n/a	n/a	5.54
d. Higher risk stocks (fully invested)	+0.2%	+13.7%	+21.4%	-10.7%	n/a	n/a	n/a	n/a	5.11
e. Speculative stocks (fully invested)	-3.2%	+26.2%	+13.8%	-10.8%	n/a	n/a	n/a	n/a	7.09
The Chartist									
a. Actual Cash Account (Stocks and, at times, T-Bills)	+4.4%	+17.9%	+23.3%	+1.0%	+25.1%	+32.7%	-9.7%	+23.4%	3.73
(Actual Cash Account–Timing Only)	+2.3%	+9.3%	+20.6%	+5.0%	+16.2%	+12.1%	n/a	n/a	n/a
b. Traders' Stocks (fully invested)	+7.6%	+35.9%	+52.2%	+6.4%	+30.5%	n/a	n/a	n/a	5.74
Dessauer's Journal (International Portfolio: Stocks,Bonds,Currencies)	+2.5%	+23.1%	+41.8%	-0.0%	+21.0%	+20.1%	n/a	n/a	3.15
Dow Theory Forecasts (Portfolios fully invested in each list's stocks)									
a. Income Stocks (Invested in those "especially recommended")	+4.6%	+22.3%	+35.1%	+12.9%	+20.5%	+20.2%	-8.2%	+14.9%	3.01
b. Investment Stocks (Invested in those "especially recommended")	+6.6%	+25.9%	+35.3%	+2.3%	+15.6%	+28.4%	-4.2%	+21.8%	3.64
c. Growth Stocks (Invested in those "especially recommended")	+2.4%	+18.3%	+28.8%	-6.8%	+11.7%	+14.9%	+5.2%	+22.5%	4.65
d. Speculative Stocks (Invested in those "especially recommended")	+5.3%	+16.8%	+35.3%	-4.7%	+11.7%	+13.4%	-5.9%	+27.5%	4.43
e. Low-Priced Stocks (Invested in those "especially recommended")	+1.6%	+12.7%	n/a	n/a	n/a	n/a	n/a	n/a	n/a
f. Special Situations Stocks (Fully invested)	+4.3%	+13.8%	n/a	n/a	n/a	n/a	n/a	n/a	n/a
Dow Theory Letters (Recommendations in "Investment Position" Box)	+4.0%	+5.6%	-5.9%	+1.8%	-6.8%	+19.2%	+10.2%	n/a	2.87
Emerging & Special Situations (Fully invested in stocks rated "buy")	-2.4%	+9.0%	+44.2%	-4.6%	+6.6%	n/a	n/a	n/a	7.41
Fund Exchange Report (Mutual Funds)									
a. Balanced Model Portfolio	+3.8%	+16.2%	+20.2%	n/a	n/a	n/a	n/a	n/a	3.30
b. Conservative Growth Model Portfolio	+3.1%	+16.5%	+28.6%	n/a	n/a	n/a	n/a	n/a	3.29
c. Conservative Growth Margined Portfolio	+7.9%	+35.4%	+45.5%	n/a	n/a	n/a	n/a	n/a	5.40
d. Aggressive Growth Model Portfolio	+5.7%	+21.9%	+29.7%	n/a	n/a	n/a	n/a	n/a	4.21
e. Aggressive Growth Margined Portfolio	+8.3%	+40.4%	+40.1%	n/a	n/a	n/a	n/a	n/a	6.86
f. Taxable Bond Model Portfolio	-0.0%	+7.1%	+18.9%	n/a	n/a	n/a	n/a	n/a	1.67
g. Gold Model Portfolio	+0.5%	+1.9%	-9.9%	n/a	n/a	n/a	n/a	n/a	4.46

Fundline ("Fund-A-Month Accumulation Portfolio"—Mutual Funds)	-0.9%	+10.4%	n/a	n/a	n/a	n/a	n/a	n/a	n/a
(Fundline—Timing Only)	+2.5%	+13.8%	n/a	n/a	n/a	n/a	n/a	n/a	n/a
Garside Forecast (Fully invested in recommended stocks)	-4.3%	+6.0%	+17.8%	+1.6%	n/a	n/a	n/a	n/a	3.56
Granville Market Letter (*Not* including phone service)									
a. Open Stock Positions (was "Aggressive Traders' Portfolio)	+1.6%	-7.9%	-22.7%	+2.9%	-25.2%	-29.7%	-3.3%	+10.6%	3.85
b. Option Portfolio (Fully invested when in options))	+7.9%	-64.3%	-97.8%	n/a	n/a	n/a	n/a	n/a	33.77
Growth Fund Guide									
a. Aggressive Growth Funds (Fully invested in funds most highly rated)	+6.6%	+29.2%	+33.8%	-18.3%	+22.4%	n/a	n/a	n/a	4.78
b. Growth Funds (Fully invested in funds most highly rated)	+4.9%	+23.5%	+31.2%	+0.8%	+24.2%	n/a	n/a	n/a	3.78
c. Quality Growth Funds (Fully invested in funds most highly rated)	+1.1%	+13.6%	+26.4%	+5.5%	+22.4%	n/a	n/a	n/a	2.48
d. Special Situations Funds (Fully invested in funds most highly rated)	+1.8%	+27.8%	+20.9%	-3.6%	+30.3%	n/a	n/a	n/a	4.35
Growth Stock Outlook (Supervised Portfolio: Stocks, T-Bills)	+2.4%	+10.1%	+24.7%	+3.5%	+33.1%	+24.0%	+11.8%	+34.0%	3.05
(Growth Stock Outlook—Timing Only)	+2.5%	+9.3%	+19.5%	+5.4%	+17.6%	+18.5%	-0.6%	+14.9%	n/a
Harry Browne's Special Reports (Variable [Speculative] Portfolio)	+2.1%	+12.6%	+14.8%	+4.1%	+8.1%	+17.2%	-6.9%	n/a	1.95
Heim Investment Letter (Usually stocks and/or T-Bills)	+0.5%	+2.9%	+4.8%	+1.6%	+2.6%	-8.4%	+10.5%	+2.6%	0.80
High Technology Growth Stocks									
a. Model Portfolio: Stocks, T-Bills	+0.9%	+16.9%	-4.8%	-36.3%	n/a	n/a	n/a	n/a	8.96
(High Technology Growth Stocks Model Portfolio—Timing Only)	+4.6%	+16.5%	+25.5%	+1.5%	n/a	n/a	n/a	n/a	n/a
b. Timeliness Portfolio (Stocks, T-Bills)	+2.0%	+29.1%	n/a	n/a	n/a	n/a	n/a	n/a	n/a
High Technology Investments									
a. Long-Term Portfolio I (Stocks and, at times, T-Bills)	-3.6%	-1.6%	+50.0%	-23.3%	+3.5%	n/a	n/a	n/a	9.47
b. Long-Term Portfolio II (Stocks and, at times, T-Bills)	-1.3%	-0.3%	+103.3%	-2.6%	-19.2%	n/a	n/a	n/a	10.54
(Long-Term Portfolio II—Timing Only)	-0.1%	+0.2%	+15.8%	+8.6%	+12.0%	n/a	n/a	n/a	n/a
Howard Ruff's Financial Success Report									
a. "Phantom Investor" (Stocks, commodities, coins, T-Bills)	n/a	n/a	+2.3%	-13.2%	-14.9%	+43.8%	-2.4%	-6.8%	n/a
b. "Optimum Switch Hitter" (Mutual Funds)	n/a	n/a	+12.6%	n/a	n/a	n/a	n/a	n/a	n/a
Holt Investment Advisory									
a. Aggressive Portfolio (At times, stocks, bonds, options, T-Bills)	-3.8%	-7.8%	-17.4%	-0.4%	-8.2%	-11.8%	+7.9%	-6.1%	3.90
(Holt Investment Advisory Aggressive Portfolio—Timing Only)	-1.3%	-3.7%	-5.4%	-1.2%	-6.6%	+4.0%	+11.4%	-6.7%	n/a
b. Investors' Portfolio	+0.4%	+4.3%	n/a	n/a	n/a	n/a	n/a	n/a	n/a
Indicator Digest									
a. Growth Portfolio: Stocks, T-Bills	+2.2%	+13.4%	+6.9%	-10.3%	+11.8%	n/a	n/a	n/a	3.50
(Indicator Digest Growth Portfolio—Timing Only)	+3.2%	+11.8%	+18.7%	+1.1%	+17.0%	n/a	n/a	n/a	n/a
b. Total Return Portfolio (Stocks, Funds, T-Bills)	+0.2%	+13.2%	n/a	n/a	n/a	n/a	n/a	n/a	n/a
Insider Indicator (Portfolio fully invested in past year's 'buys')	+3.3%	+16.4%	+25.6%	n/a	n/a	n/a	n/a	n/a	4.05
Insiders (Insiders Portfolio)	+4.8%	+15.9%	+20.2%	n/a	n/a	n/a	n/a	n/a	4.10
International Harry Schultz Letter									
a. US Stocks in the "List" (formerly "Investment Table")	+3.6%	+13.2%	+8.7%	+7.4%	+2.1%	-5.5%	-17.5%	+41.2%	2.86
b. Non-US Stocks in the "List" (Fully invested)	-5.1%	+25.7%	n/a	n/a	n/a	n/a	n/a	n/a	n/a
c. Portfolio constructed out of gold/silver trading advice (non-margined)	-4.3%	-2.9%	-2.8%	+20.3%	n/a	n/a	n/a	n/a	2.38

Table 3H. Timing scoreboard.

The following tables compare the records of various newsletters in timing the stock, gold and bond markets. Chosen for the comparison have been the intermediate trading systems maintained by these newsletters. Within each category, each system earns the same rate of return when in the market and the same rate of return when in cash. The tables were designed to aid, in particular, the mutual fund switcher. Thus, in the event a newsletter recommends actually going short the market on a sell signal, we calculate two portfolios for it—one which does go short and the other which goes into cash as would a mutual fund investor. In addition, the transactions reflected below all were made at the closing price on the day subscribers would have been able to act on the advice. No commissions were debited. In addition we show the number of switches generated by each trading system. (The figure is in the parenthesis following that period's gain or loss.) A switch into or out of the market is counted as one switch, so a roundtrip in and out of the market counts as two switches.

NEWSLETTER (Portfolio to compare to)	5/86 Gain	1986 Gain	1985 Gain	1984 Gain	1983 Gain	1982 Gain	1981 Gain	7/1 to 12/31/80
STOCK MARKET TIMING—Records Trading the NYSE Composite								
Astute Investor (Technical Market Index, a.k.a. Wall Street Week Index)								
a. 100% cash on sell signals	+4.7%(0)	+16.8%(0)	+26.2%(0)	+8.5%(1)	+26.9%(1)	n/a	n/a	n/a
b. 100% short on sell signals	+4.7%(0)	+16.8%(0)	+26.2%(0)	+8.5%(1)	+24.3%(1)	n/a	n/a	n/a
Bob Brinker's Marketimer (Stock market timing model)								
a. 100% short on sell signals	-4.4%(1)	+12.4%(2)	n/a	n/a	n/a	n/a	n/a	n/a
b. 100% cash on sell signals	+0.5%(1)	+15.3%(2)	n/a	n/a	n/a	n/a	n/a	n/a
Dines Letter								
a. Short-Term Trading Signals: 100% short on sells	+4.7%(0)	+16.8%(0)	+11.1%(4)	-9.3%(7)	+6.9%(2)	-6.3%(3)	+19.4%(1)	-7.3%(1)
b. Short-Term Trading Signals: 100% cash on sells	+4.7%(0)	+16.8%(0)	+21.2%(4)	-1.3%(7)	+12.6%(2)	+13.2%(3)	+17.2%(1)	+11.3%(1)
Dow Theory Letters (Primary Trend Index: 100% cash on sells)	+4.7%(0)	+16.8%(0)	+14.8%(5)	-2.1%(3)	+17.5%(0)	+12.3%(1)	+1.6%(1)	+19.2%(0)
Elliott Wave Theorist								
a. Traders	+4.7%(0)	+16.8%(0)	+26.2%(0)	n/a	n/a	n/a	n/a	n/a
b. Investors	+4.7%(0)	+16.8%(0)	+26.2%(0)	+9.8%(3)	+24.4%(1)	+10.2%(8)	-8.7%(0)	+15.7%(1)
Fund Exchange Report (Equity Trading Model)	+4.7%(0)	+16.8%(0)	+24.3%(2)	+7.6%(3)	n/a	n/a	n/a	n/a
Investor's Intelligence (Mutual Fund Switching Advice)	-0.5%(0)	+2.8%(0)	+7.7%(¼)	n/a	n/a	n/a	n/a	n/a
Investech Market Letter (Mutual Fund Switching Advice)	+3.7%(0.35)	+13.6%(1.6)	+16.0%(1.2)	n/a	n/a	n/a	n/a	n/a
Lynn Elgert Report (Advice For Mutual Fund Investors)	+5.0%(1)	+15.5%(3)	+25.7%(2)	n/a	n/a	n/a	n/a	n/a
Market Logic (Mutual Fund Switching Advice)	+4.7%(0)	+16.8%(0)	+26.2(0)	+1.3%(0)	+17.5%(0)	+17.9%(½)	+2.2%(¼)	+12.5%(0)
Mutual Fund Strategist								
a. Compuvest Timing Model	+4.7%(0)	+16.8%(0)	+28.1%(2)	n/a	n/a	n/a	n/a	n/a
b. Cycle/Reversal Discriminator	+2.7%(1)	+12.5%(7)	+28.6%(8)	n/a	n/a	n/a	n/a	n/a
Nicholson Report (Market Mood Indicator: 100% cash on sells)	+2.7%(1)	+11.4%(9)	+14.3%(15)	-3.2%(26)	-4.0%(24)	n/a	n/a	n/a
Professional Tape Reader (Group Intensity: 100% Cash on Sells)	+0.7%(.25)	+3.5%(1.15)	+16.7%(2.3)	+1.3%(4½)	+16.3%(4½)	+9.5%(7½)	-2.7%(8)	+12.9%(1)

Professional Timing Service

a. Supply/Demand Formula Re: DJIA (100% short on sells)	-4.4%(0)	+13.6%(1)	+11.2%(1)	+2.5%(3)	+17.5%(2)	-24.5%(2)	+20.0%(3)	-3.2%(2)
b. Supply/Demand Formula Re: DJIA (100% cash on sells)	+0.5%(0)	+16.1%(1)	+20.6%(1)	+11.4%(3)	+25.7%(2)	+1.2%(2)	+13.3%(3)	+14.2%(2)
c. Supply/Demand Formula Re: S&P 500 (100% Short on sells)	-4.4%(0)	+13.6%(1)	+8.2%(2)	n/a	n/a	n/a	n/a	n/a
d. Supply/Demand Formula Re: S&P 500 (100% Cash on sells)	+0.5%(0)	+16.1%(1)	+19.7%(1)	n/a	n/a	n/a	n/a	n/a
Stockmarket Cycles (Mutual Fund Switching Advice)	+3.2%(1)%	+15.2%(2)	+27.1%(4)	n/a	n/a	n/a	n/a	n/a
Switch Fund Advisory (Inactive Investors Switch Signals: no shorting)	+4.7%(0)	+16.8%(0)	+26.2%(0)	+1.3%(0)	+17.5%(0)	+32.4%(1)	+14.7%(1)	+19.2%(0)
Systems & Forecasts								
a. Time Trend: No Shorting	+1.4%(2)	+9.3%(4)	+22.5%(10)	+8.6%(15)	+18.7%(7)	n/a	n/a	n/a
b. Mutual Fund Trading Advice	+1.8%(0.9)	+11.7%(4.9)	+20.1%(10.2)	n/a	n/a	n/a	n/a	n/a
Telephone Switch Newsletter (Equity/Cash Switching Advice)	+4.7%(0)	+16.8%(0)	+23.6%(1)	+4.7%(3)	+17.5%(0)	+30.3%(1)	+0.7%(1)	+19.2%(0)
Value Line Investment Survey (Market timing advice: no shorting).	+4.7%(0)	+16.8%(0)	+26.2%(0)	+1.3(0)%	+10.7%(1)	+10.9%(0)	+6.79,(1)	+19.2%(0)
Weber's Fund Advisor (No Shorting)	+4.7%(0)	+16.8%(0)	+26.2%(0)	n/a	n/a	n/a	n/a	n/a
Zweig Forecast–Short Term Trading Index (No shorting)	+2.7%(1)	+13.1%(4)	+24.6%(14)	n/a	n/a	n/a	n/a	n/a
NYSE Composite	+4.7%	+16.8%	+26.2%	+1.3%	+17.5%	+14.0%	-8.7%	+19.2%

GOLD MARKET TIMING—Records Trading Gold's London P.M. Fixing Price

Elliott Wave Theorist								
a. Traders (Shorting allowed)	+0.7%(0)	-4.6%(2)	-11.1%(7)	n/a	n/a	n/a	n/a	n/a
b. Investors (No shorting)	+0.5%(0)	+2.8%(0)	+7.6%(0)	n/a	n/a	n/a	n/a	n/a
Fund Exchange Report (Gold Switching Model) (No shorting)	+0.5%(0)	+1.0%(2)	-3.6%(6)	-1.3%(6)	n/a	n/a	n/a	n/a
Garside Forecast (Gold Bell Ringer)								
a. 100% short on sells	-0.7%(0)	+5.0%(0)	+4.1%(1)	n/a	n/a	n/a	n/a	n/a
b. 100% cash on sells	-0.7%(0)	+5.0%(0)	+8.0%(1)	n/a	n/a	n/a	n/a	n/a
Market Logic (Gold Model)(No shorting)	+0.5%(0)	+6.3%(1)	+11.6%(3)	-4.0%(3)	n/a	n/a	n/a	n/a
Telephone Switch Newsletter (Gold/Cash Switch Advice)	+0.5%(0)	-4.3%(2)	+2.0%(2)	n/a	n/a	n/a	n/a	n/a
Zweig Forecast (Gold Model)(No shorting)	+0.5%(0)	+2.3%(2)	+3.3%(4)	n/a	n/a	n/a	n/a	n/a
Gold Bullion	-0.7%	+5.0%	+6.1%	-19.2%	n/a	n/a	n/a	n/a

BOND TIMING RECORDS—Records Trading the Dow Jones 20 Bond Average

Elliott Wave Theorist								
a. Traders	+1.3%(0)	+3.8%(5)	+1.4%(4.5)	n/a	n/a	n/a	n/a	n/a
b. Investors	+0.5%(0)	+6.9%(3)	+10.8%(1½)	n/a	n/a	n/a	n/a	n/a
Fund Exchange Report (Bond Switch Advice: All Cash on Sells)	-1.0%(1)	+8.3%(1)	+16.3%(6)	+11.7%(5)	n/a	n/a	n/a	n/a
Garside Forecast (Bond Bell Ringer)								
a. 100% short on sells	+1.8%(0)	-7.7%(0)	-15.6%(0)	n/a	n/a	n/a	n/a	n/a
b. 100% cash on sells	+0.5%(0)	+2.8%(0)	+7.6%(0)	n/a	n/a	n/a	n/a	n/a
Lynn Elgert Report (Monetary Model/Bond Switching Advice)	+0.5%(0)	+3.2%(1)	+8.5%(2½)	n/a	n/a	n/a	n/a	n/a
Systems & Forecasts (Monetary Model)	-1.0%(1)	+8.3%(1)	+15.1%(8)	n/a	n/a	n/a	n/a	n/a
Dow Jones 20 Bond Average	-1.5%	+7.7%	+15.6%	+4.3%	n/a	n/a	n/a	n/a

Washington, DC 20003) and request a copy of "An Introduction to the *Hulbert Financial Digest.*"

A Timing Scoreboard is another feature of each monthly issue of HFD. Market timing organizations are rated according to the effectiveness of their switching signals. The Timing Scoreboard from the June 1986 issue is reproduced in table 3H. Note that the reports are divided into equity, gold, and bond sections. Timing signals are reported for stock portfolios and for services that concentrate only on the switching of mutual funds. Note that many of the equity (stock) mutual fund gains for 1985 exceed the 20 percent floor commonly referred to in other sections of this book. You should not be surprised because the New York Stock Exchange (NYSE) average (table 3H) gained 26.2 percent during the 1985 year. During 1984 the NYSE gained a measly 1.3 percent, while many of the market timers turned in performances several times better. These reported gains confirm that market timing does not necessarily improve fund performances during bull markets, but market

Table 3I. Growth of an IRA in Value Line Special Situations Fund assuming a $2,000 contribution at the start of each calendar year. Note the increasing value of the fund's balance with market timing vs. buy-and-hold using the Merriman Equity Switch Model. All dividends and capital gains are considered to be reinvested.

Year	Annual Invest- ment	Total Invest- ment	Buy/Hold % Change	Buy/Hold Value	Switching % Change	Switching Value
1970	$2,000	$2,000	- 34.4%	$1,312	+ 10.5%	$2,210
1971	$2,000	$4,000	+ 17.6	$3,895	+ 35.9	$5,721
1972	$2,000	$6,000	- 11.0	$5,246	- 4.5	$7,374
1973	$2,000	$8,000	- 45.5	$3,949	- 1.6	$9,224
1974	$2,000	$10,000	- 29.5	$4,194	+ 7.1	$12,021
1975	$2,000	$12,000	+ 47.0	$9,105	+ 34.0	$18,788
1976	$2,000	$14,000	+ 52.7	$16,957	+ 57.8	$32,803
1977	$2,000	$16,000	+ 12.3	$21,289	+ 3.5	$36,022
1978	$2,000	$18,000	+ 21.2	$28,226	+ 17.0	$44,485
1979	$2,000	$20,000	+ 43.6	$43,403	+ 26.0	$58,571
1980	$2,000	$22,000	+ 54.4	$69,906	+ 78.4	$108,050
1981	$2,000	$24,000	- 2.2	$70,102	+ 8.5	$119,414
1982	$2,000	$26,000	+ 23.1	$89,031	+ 30.7	$158,689
1983	$2,000	$28,000	+ 19.4	$108,691	+ 21.4	$195,076
1984	$2,000	$30,000	- 25.5	$82,465	- 5.7	$185,843
1985	$2,000	$32,000	+ 21.1	$102,287	+ 21.1	$227,478

timing substantially improves performance in bear markets when compared to a buy-and-hold program.

Paul A. Merriman & Associates

Paul A. Merriman, co-author of this book, aims his market timing service principally at the long-term management of retirement accounts—IRA, Keogh and others. Retirement accounts avoid tax complications. If switch timing is constrained by income tax considerations, the overall performance may be affected.

Paul A. Merriman & Associates offers three models: an equity fund switching model, a bond fund switching model, and a gold fund switching model. They have developed a proprietary equity switching system that has been backtested for periods beginning with 1970. Actual figures represent a two-and-a-half-year time period that began July 31, 1983. Backtesting a model involves tracing the history of market moves and switching funds from an equity fund into a money market

Table 3J. Growth of an IRA in Value Line Special Situations Fund assuming a $2,000 contribution at the start of each calendar year run in reverse order using the Merriman Equity Switch Model. All dividends and capital gains are considered to be reinvested.

Year	Annual Invest- ment	Total Invest- ment	Buy/Hold % Change	Value	Switching % Change	Value
1985	$2,000	$2,000	+ 21.1%	$2,422	+ 21.1%	$2,422
1984	$2,000	$4,000	- 25.5	$3,294	- 5.7	$4,170
1983	$2,000	$6,000	+ 19.4	$6,322	+ 21.4	$7,490
1982	$2,000	$8,000	+ 23.1	$10,244	+ 30.7	$12,404
1981	$2,000	$10,000	- 2.2	$11,974	+ 8.5	$15,628
1980	$2,000	$12,000	+ 54.4	$21,576	+ 78.4	$31,449
1979	$2,000	$14,000	+ 43.6	$33,855	+ 26.0	$42,145
1978	$2,000	$16,000	+ 21.2	$43,456	+ 17.0	$51,650
1977	$2,000	$18,000	+ 12.3	$51,048	+ 3.5	$55,528
1976	$2,000	$20,000	+ 52.7	$81,004	+ 57.8	$90,779
1975	$2,000	$22,000	+ 47.0	$122,015	+ 34.0	$124,324
1974	$2,000	$24,000	- 29.5	$87,431	+ 7.1	$135,293
1973	$2,000	$26,000	- 45.5	$48,740	- 1.6	$135,096
1972	$2,000	$28,000	- 11.0	$45,158	- 4.5	$130,927
1971	$2,000	$30,000	+ 17.6	$55,458	+ 35.9	$180,647
1970	$2,000	$32,000	- 34.4	$37,693	+ 10.5	$201,825

Fig. 3-2. Comparison of buy-and-hold vs. market timing performance for IRA using the Merriman Equity Switch Model with Value Line Special Situations Fund. (See table 3I for numbers and details.)

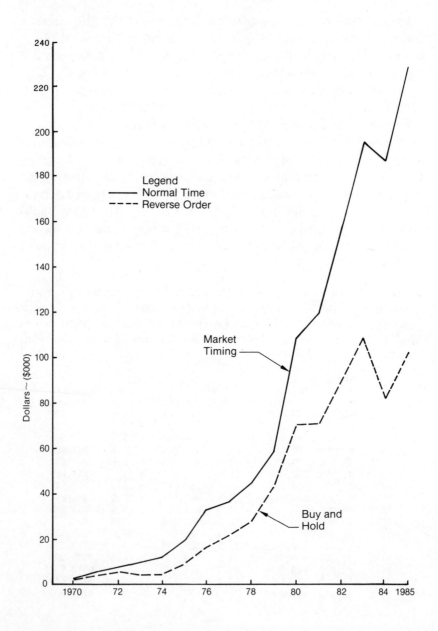

Fig. 3-3. The Value Line Special Situations Fund.

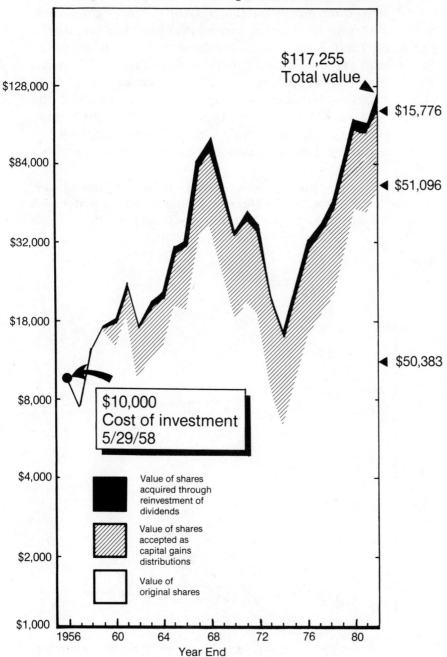

fund or 90-day U.S. Treasury bills according to model indicators. When equity advances triggered the reverse signal, funds
were withdrawn from the money market fund and invested in
the equity fund. Annual results of these transactions are noted
in tables 3I and 10A, using the Value Line Special Situations
Fund, generally considered an aggressive growth fund. Note
the comparison between the buy-and-hold results and the
switching results over the 16-year period in Value Line Special
Situations Fund. Figure 3-2 shows these results graphically.

The sequence of price movements over the years can affect

**Fig. 3-4. Comparison of buy-and-hold vs. market timing per-
formance for IRA using the Merriman Equity Switch Model with
Value Line Fund. (See table 3K for numbers and details.)**

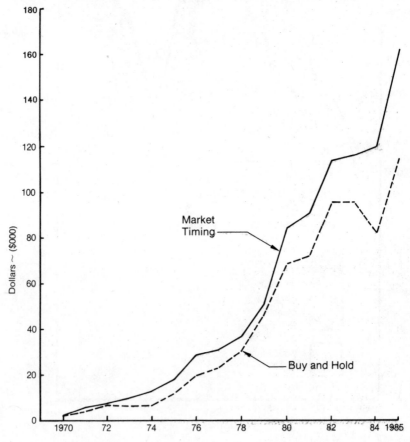

any market timing system's performance. Paul examined the effect of reversing the order of switching signals and looking at the market in reverse order. Table 3J records how his equity

Table 3K. Value Line Fund.

Year	Annual Invest- ment	Total Invest- ment	Buy/Hold % Change	Value	Switching % Change	Value
1970	$2,000	$2,000	- 25.1%	$1,498	+ 9.8%	$2,196
1971	$2,000	$4,000	+ 16.8	$4,086	+ 27.3	$5,342
1972	$2,000	$6,000	+ 10.5	$6,725	+ 4.9	$7,702
1973	$2,000	$8,000	- 29.7	$6,134	+ 2.5	$9,945
1974	$2,000	$10,000	- 22.4	$6,312	+ 7.1	$12,793
1975	$2,000	$12,000	+ 39.0	$11,534	+ 20.2	$17,781
1076	$2,000	$14,000	+ 43.0	$19,382	+ 45.1	$28,702
1977	$2,000	$16,000	+ 9.5	$23,413	+ 1.1	$31,040
1978	$2,000	$18,000	+ 19.3	$30,318	+ 12.3	$37,104
1979	$2,000	$20,000	+ 44.1	$46,570	+ 32.1	$51,656
1980	$2,000	$22,000	+ 41.6	$68,775	+ 57.4	$84,455
1981	$2,000	$24,000	+ 2.4	$72,474	+ 5.2	$90,951
1982	$2,000	$26,000	+ 28.1	$95,401	+ 23.5	$114,794
1983	$2,000	$28,000	- 1.7	$95,745	- .6	$116,093
1984	$2,000	$30,000	- 15.2	$82,888	+ 1.6	$119,982
1985	$2,000	$32,000	+ 34.6	$114,259	+ 33.0	$162,236

switching model performed beginning with 1985 and moving back to 1970. On a buy-and-hold basis, the performance changed radically from an average of 13 percent compounded annually to only 1 percent in reverse order. But the switching

Table 3L. Value Line Fund (reverse order).

Year	Annual Invest- ment	Total Invest- ment	Buy/Hold % Change	Value	Switching % Change	Value
1985	$2,000	$2,000	+ 34.6%	$2,692	+ 33.0	$2,660
1984	$2,000	$4,000	- 15.2	$3,979	+ 1.6	$4,735
1983	$2,000	$6,000	- 1.7	$5,877	- .6	$6,695
1982	$2,000	$8,000	+ 28.1	$10,090	+ 23.5	$10,738
1981	$2,000	$10,000	+ 2.4	$12,380	+ 5.2	$13,400
1980	$2,000	$12,000	+ 41.6	$20,362	+ 57.4	$24,240
1979	$2,000	$14,000	+ 44.1	$32,224	+ 32.1	$34,663
1978	$2,000	$16,000	+ 19.3	$40,829	+ 12.3	$41,173
1977	$2,000	$18,000	+ 9.5	$46,898	+ 1.1	$43,648
1976	$2,000	$20,000	+ 43.0	$69,924	+ 45.1	$66,235
1975	$2,000	$22,000	+ 39.0	$99,974	+ 20.2	$82,018
1974	$2,000	$24,000	- 22.4	$79,132	+ 7.1	$89,983
1973	$2,000	$26,000	- 29.7	$57,036	+ 2.5	$94,283
1972	$2,000	$28,000	+ 10.5	$65,235	+ 4.9	$101,001
1971	$2,000	$30,000	+ 16.8	$78,530	+ 27.3	$131,120
1970	$2,000	$32,000	-25.1	$60,317	+ 9.8	$146,166

model yielded a respectable 20 percent—lower than the 23 percent noted for the forward model but not significantly different, as in the case of the buy-and-hold program.

The Value Line Special Situations Fund reports in its prospectus an increase of 1,172.6 percent in the value of an investment in the fund's shares from May 29, 1956, through December 31, 1982, as shown in figure 3-3. An investment of $10,000 in Special Situations Fund on May 29, 1956, would have grown to $117,255 by the close of business on December 31, 1982; this includes $15,776 of dividends reinvested throughout the years as paid and $51,096 in capital gains distributions also invested in additional shares of the fund. The value of the

Fig. 3-5. Comparison of buy-and-hold vs. market timing performance for IRA using the Merriman Equity Switch Model with Value Line Income Fund. (See table 3M for numbers and details.)

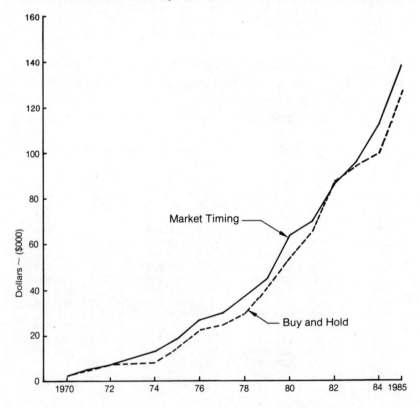

original shares grew to $50,383 during the period. The value of the shares dropped significantly from an interim high in 1968 to a low of less than $16,000 during the downturn of 1974, before rising again to $117,255 at the end of 1982. Reducing these losses during downturns by switching improves overall performance and proves the benefits of market timing.

The Value Line Special Situations Fund adopts an aggressive investment approach and tends to be more volatile in its up-and-down cycling than the more conservative Value Line Fund. Again, using PM&A's proprietary model for the period from 1970 through 1985, a buy-and-hold program delivered 5.4 percent per year with the Value Line Fund while the switching program delivered 19.4 percent per year com-

Fig. 3-6. Comparison of buy-and-hold vs. market timing performance with an initial investment of $10,000 using the Merriman Gold Switch Model with United Services Gold Shares. (See table 3N for numbers and details.)

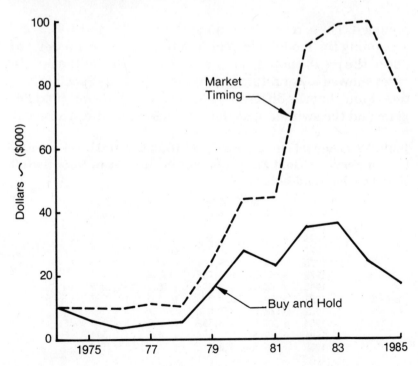

Table 3M. Growth of an IRA in Value Line Income Fund assuming a $2,000 IRA contribution at the start of each calendar year. Note the increasing value of the fund's balance with market timing vs. buy-and-hold using the Merriman Equity Switch Model. All dividends and capital gains are considered to be reinvested.

	Annual Invest-	Total Invest-	Buy/Hold		Switching	
Year	ment	ment	% Change	Value	% Change	Value
1970	$2,000	$2,000	+ 6.7%	$2,134	+ 19.3%	$2,386
1971	$2,000	$4,000	+ 13.5	$4,692	+ 19.4	$5,237
1972	$2,000	$6,000	+ 9.1	$7,301	+ 2.0	$7,382
1973	$2,000	$8,000	- 15.9	$7,822	+ 8.8	$10,207
1974	$2,000	$10,000	- 16.1	$8,241	+ 7.1	$13,074
1975	$2,000	$12,000	+ 41.7	$14,511	+ 22.3	$18,435
1076	$2,000	$14,000	+ 34.5	$22,208	+ 29.2	$26,403
1977	$2,000	$16,000	+ 1.8	$64,643	+ 4.2	$29,595
1978	$2,000	$18,000	+ 11.1	$29,601	+ 16.5	$36,809
1979	$2,000	$20,000	+ 27.6	$40,323	+ 15.5	$44,825
1980	$2,000	$22,000	+ 26.8	$53,665	+ 35.0	$63,213
1981	$2,000	$24,000	+ 16.4	$64,794	+ 6.2	$69,257
1982	$2,000	$26,000	+ 29.7	$86,632	+ 20.6	$85,935
1983	$2,000	$28,000	+ 6.5	$94,393	+ 8.4	$95,322
1984	$2,000	$30,000	+ 2.7	$98,996	+ 14.1	$111,044
1985	$2,000	$32,000	+ 23.9	$125,133	+ 20.6	$136,331

pounded. These results are shown in tables 3K and 10B.

Running the model one year at a time in reverse order produced the results noted in table 3L. The results for the reverse order showed lower returns, as in the case of the Special Situations Fund, but the differences between the buy-and-hold program and the switching model were less dramatic. These var-

Table 3N. Comparison of growth of $10,000 initial investment in United Services Gold Shares using the Merriman Gold Switch Model vs. buy-and-hold.

	Buy/Hold		Switching	
Year	% Change	Value	% Change	Value
1975	- 38.9%	$6,110	- 5.3%	$9,470
1976	- 41.1	$3,599	+ 5.0	$9,944
1977	+ 39.9	$5,035	+ 11.8	$11,117
1978	+ 9.0	$5,488	- 8.4	$10,183
1979	+187.2	$15,762	+142.6	$24,704
1980	+ 78.9	$28,198	+ 78.4	$44,072
1981	- 28.0	$20,303	+ 1.1	$44,557
1982	+ 72.4	$35,002	+107.6	$92,500
1983	+ 1.0	$35,352	+ 6.3	$98,328
1984	- 29.6	$24,888	+ 1.0	$99,311
1985	- 26.8	$18,218	- 21.7	$77,760

ied looks at fund performance can give you an idea of what happens when either a buy-and-hold mutual fund investment program or one coupled with market timing is initiated in a bear market and moves into a bull market, or vice versa. The trend of the overall market obviously affects the results from any investment program. The big benefit from market timing comes from the elimination of most of the losses during bear markets, as confirmed by running programs in reverse order.

Many investors may perceive market timing to be most effective in combination with volatile equity funds, but investments in these funds, with or without market timing, will not be suitable for everyone. Market timing is also applicable to conservative equity funds, gold funds, and various taxable and tax-free bond funds.

Fig. 3-7. Comparison of buy-and-hold vs. market timing performance with an initial investment of $10,000 using the Merriman Bond Switch Model with Dreyfus Tax-Exempt Bond Fund and Dreyfus A-Bond Plus Fund. (See table 3K for numbers and details.)

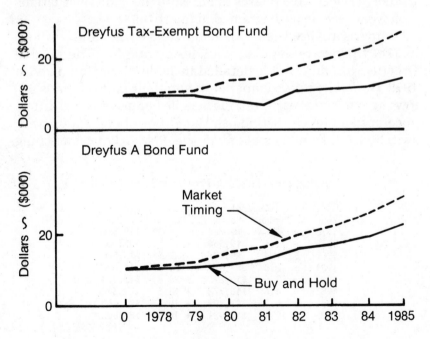

An income fund is sometimes referred to as a "widows and orphans fund" because it is less risky than most equity funds. Performance of the Value Line Income Fund is detailed in table 3M. The average annual return under a buy-and-hold program is 12.6 percent compared to the market timed average of 15.3 percent. The chart in figure 3-5 compares differences visually.

Table 3P. Dreyfus A-Bond Plus.

Year	Buy/Hold % Change	Buy/Hold Value	Switching % Change	Switching Value
1978	+ 1.3%	$10,130	+ 8.3%	$10,830
1979	+ 5.3	$10,667	+ 8.4	$11,740
1980	+ 5.3	$11,232	+ 25.4	$14,722
1981	+ 9.2	$12,266	+ 10.6	$16,282
1982	+ 26.2	$15,491	+ 18.6	$19,311
1983	+ 7.7	$16,684	+ 12.7	$21,764
1984	+ 12.5	$18,770	+ 17.7	$25,616
1985	+ 21.4	$22,787	+ 17.2	$30,021

Volatile gold funds benefit hugely from market timing. Table 3N details the difference between results with the PM&A gold switching model and a buy-and-hold program based on the United Services Gold Shares Fund. Note the wide fluctuations from year to year, as diagramed in figure 3-6.

Comparisons between two bond funds with and without market timing are detailed in tables 3P and 3Q. The taxable Dreyfus A Bond Fund is detailed in Table 3P beginning with 1978. Generally tax-exempt bonds and their mutual funds follow the same market pattern as taxable bonds; only the difference in yield levels distinguish them. Both bond funds were switched following signals from the PM&A bond switching

Table 3Q. Dreyfus Tax-Exempt Bond Fund.

Year	Buy/Hold % Change	Buy/Hold Value	Switching % Change	Switching Value
1978	- 3.0%	$9,700	+ 3.5%	$10,350
1979	- 1.4	$9,564	+ 6.3	$11,002
1980	- 14.3	$8,197	+ 22.9	$13,522
1981	- 10.0	$7,377	+ 6.6	$14,414
1982	+ 39.6	$10,298	+ 24.4	$17,931
1983	+ 4.6	$10,772	+ 13.6	$20,370
1984	+ 8.7	$11,709	+ 10.3	$22,468
1985	+ 19.4	$13,981	+ 10.5	$26,625

model. Results are diagramed in figure 3-7.

The choice of a mutual fund and the selection of a market timer compatible with your investment objectives must be carefully considered since the combination can produce highly profitable results, while an incompatible combination may lead to disappointing investment results.

4

Technical Indicators for Market Timing

Most market timers depend almost exclusively on technical analysis rather than fundamental analysis. This emphasis represents a major difference in their approach to the market compared to the fundamentalists. Technical analysis also depends on a disciplined approach to the market, and it is discipline, or lack of it, that accounts for the success or failure of most investors.

Definitions first.

Fundamentalists are those stock market analysts, followers, or investors who base their decisions to buy or sell specific stocks or other securities on inside and outside influences.

Outside influences might be an analysis of the economic conditions prevalent at a specific time, such as the actual or expected rate of inflation, money market conditions (including short- and long-term interest rates), and various indicators of the world's economic condition.

Inside influences are those that affect a specific corporation. Balance sheet data (such as debt/equity ratio, capitalization structure, current ratio between short-term assets and liabilities, and numerous other bits of data that experience has shown to reflect the solidity or weakness of a corporation) form the basis for fundamentalists' decisions. Earnings or income information in the form of sales/inventory ratio, competition, profits as a percent of sales and as a return on investment, sales/share ratio, the history of sales growth, and the stability of operations may affect the fundamentals of a company. The projected sales growth and the profits to be realized from those sales affect the worth placed on a corporation by investors. One of the key investment criteria is the price/earnings ratio (P/E), which is the price of a stock relative to its earnings either for the current year or projected for the next one or several years. For investors interested in income, the dividend payout ratio or the percentage of profits paid out in the form of dividends to stockholders can be an important factor in deciding whether to buy or sell the stock. Unfortunately, all of these criteria can be positive about one or many stocks and the market could still go down. One estimate has it that about 30 percent of a stock's price may be determined by the stock's fundamentals as perceived by market analysts. The other 70 percent of a stock's value may result from overall market conditions.

Technicians use mathematics and the theory of probabilities to help them make decisions. Most data can be displayed graphically in the form of charts, usually based on the calendar since much of the data is related to time. The sorts of data they analyze might include the New York Stock Exchange Index and similar indexes reflecting the prices of the markets, such as the advance/decline ratio, put/call ratio, odd-lot short/overall short ratios, on-balance volume, insider buying and selling, and indications of advisor sentiment. The technician recognizes that price movements, along with volume and other indicators, represent the sum of many individuals' thinking, and he considers his charts the consensus or "indicator of central tendency."

Technicians are constantly looking for the "perfect indicator," the one that will always flash a signal of the market's or a stock's position one day to several weeks in advance. The indicator is expected to be right every time. Can you imagine the worth of such an indicator? It would be so valuable that technicians continue to study and search with the zeal and dedication of those who looked for the Holy Grail or the Fountain of Youth. So far, the perfect indicator has eluded searchers.

Fundamental analysis seldom provides a precise timing date for getting into or out of the market. It may yield general information to buy on weakness, hold for a long term, or sell on rallies rather than a point in time when you should stop being a bear and start being a bull—or vice versa. The technician generally believes that all of the information available to fundamentalists is also available to many, many people, and the current price reflects the sum of all of those bits of information and opinions. The technical analyst attempts to determine what the marketplace is thinking on balance. He or she is really looking for the trend and the probability that the trend will continue in a specific direction. Fundamentalists generally look long-term, and technicians tend to be relatively short-term oriented.

Wall Street Week TMI

In chapter 3, the performance of the Technical Market Index (TMI), a widely watched index shown weekly on the Public Broadcasting System (PBS) network show *Wall Street Week (WSW)*, was shown to be a reliable indicator of the direction of the Dow Jones Industrial Index and, presumably, the market for stocks as a whole. The TMI is actually a collection of 10 individual indicators originated by Robert J. Nurock, editor and publisher of *The Astute Investor* and a frequent guest panelist on the *WSW* show. Examining the makeup of the index will give you an idea of how the indicators contribute to the overall TMI. The following information is used with the express permission of Robert J. Nurock (Investor's Analysis, Inc., P.O. Box 988, Paoli, PA 19301).

The Technical Market Index consists of 10 indicators that may be in plus, minus, or neutral territory. When the 10 indicators are totaled, the net or algebraic sum represents the position of the TMI. For example, suppose seven of the indicators are in plus territory, two are minus, and one is neutral; the net or algebraic sum is a plus 5. Under the formula for using the TMI, a plus 5 would be a buy signal, indicating that the stock market as represented by the Dow Jones Industrial Index was down and about to reverse direction or start an upward trend. A plus 5 signal means to buy for the long term. Similarly, a minus 5 signal strongly suggests that holders of stocks sell, as the consensus of the 10 indicators is forecasting a switch in direction to a downward trend. Such signals have been quite accurate, although the signals sometimes appear early; a plus 5 buy signal appeared on the *WSW* show on the third Friday of May 1984, but the overall market did not take off on a big upswing until August 1, 1984.

Table 4A. Technical Market Index Readings.

+5 or higher	Extremely bullish—buy now
+4	Strongly bullish—get ready to buy
+3	Bullish
+2	Mildly bullish
+1	Neutral
0	Neutral
-1	Neutral
-2	Mildly bearish
-3	Bearish
-4	Strongly bearish—get ready to sell
-5	Extremely bearish—sell now

A typical weekly reading may be:

4 indicators positive	+4
5 indicators neutral	0
1 indicator negative	-1
Index reading	+3
Interpretation	Bullish

The 10 technical indicators are constructed from data generally available through such sources as the *Wall Street Journal* and the various exchanges. The 10 indicators are as follows:

1. Dow Jones Momentum Ratio is a typical moving average that measures the point differential between the DJIA and its 30-day moving average.

2. New York Stock Exchange (NYSE) Hi-Lo Index compares the average number of stock issues making new highs and new lows on a daily basis over the past two weeks.

3. Market Breadth Indicator is a 10-day moving average of advances minus declines.

4. Arms (Trading) Index is another 10-day moving average; this indicator uses the ratio of the volume going into advancing stocks versus the volume going into declining stocks on the NYSE.

5. Prices of NYSE Stocks Versus Their Moving Averages are two moving averages: the percentage of NYSE stocks above their 10-week and 30-week moving averages.

6. Premium Ratio on Options compares the average premium on all listed put options to the average premium on all listed call options on a weekly basis according to data from the Options Clearing Corp., 141 W. Jackson Boulevard, Chicago, IL 60604.

7. Advisory Service Sentiment rates the forecasts of leading advisory services. The ratio is the percentage of the services' bearishness.

8. Low-Price Activity Ratio is a measure of the activity in speculative stocks relative to more seasoned issues. This ratio is published weekly in *Barron's* on the Market Laboratory page.

9. Insider Activity Ratio relates the insiders who sell to those who buy on a weekly basis.

10. Fed Policy is a guide to Federal Reserve Board policy as that policy is reflected in the level of the federal funds rate relative to the discount rate on a daily basis. A high federal funds rate relative to the discount rate signifies that money is "tight" and borrowing is discouraged. The opposite indicates "easy" money, and the expansion of business is encouraged.

Many of the 10 indicators used in the Technical Market Index are complex, difficult to compute, and not all that easy to understand. However, the final result is easy to understand and to use. The final Index is a simple number with a plus or minus in front with specific meanings, as we have seen in table 4A.

Moving averages play an important role in market timing. Understanding how moving averages are computed and why they are significant will help you to appreciate their effectiveness in calling market turns. Chapter 5 will advance your knowledge of market timing in two ways:

1. You will learn how to construct a front-loaded moving average and how to apply it to market timing.

2. You can use your own moving average to call market turns. The moving average you will learn to construct has been back-tested to prove its effectiveness. Thus, when you construct your own average and keep it current on a daily or weekly basis, you are as up to date as any market timer.

5

Constructing Your Own Timing Indicator

You can construct your own market timing indicator and keep it current by spending as little as five minutes every week. This indicator, designed specifically for this book, provides timely signals for switching from growth stock funds to money market funds and from money market funds back to growth funds. We have dubbed this market timing indicator the "3-A Signal System." It may help you gain from 18 percent to 22 percent per year on average—or more. Nothing projected into the future can be guaranteed, of course, but on the basis of historical performance, you may be able to double your investable assets about every three-and-a-half to four years—before taxes.

Backtested with the aid of a simulated computer program, the 3-A Signal System turned in a performance about 40 percent greater than the Lipper Growth Fund Index. Using the Lipper Growth Fund Index of 30 growth mutual funds as a proxy for a growth mutual fund during periods of market uptrends and switching to U.S. Treasury bills during periods of market downtrends, the 3-A Signal System turned in an average annual growth rate of 12.9 percent over 15 years, from September 1970 through September 1985. A buy-and-hold strategy using the same Lipper Growth Fund Index turned in a performance average of 9.1 percent per year over the 15-year period. If you combine the 40 percent improvement in average yearly performance with aggressive mutual fund picking, the achievement of 18 percent to 22 percent or more on average yearly is clearly attainable.

The Merriman Growth Equity Model was tested against the Lipper Growth Fund Index; it turned in an average performance of about 14.7 percent per year, and over the past 15 years simulated performance has shown 21 percent to 23 percent per year using specific growth mutual funds. Thus, the attainment of 18 percent to 22 percent annual gains, or more, appears to be a reasonable expectation. But, there are no guarantees.

Comparing timing signals against the Lipper Growth Fund Index provides a common base for comparison. Stephen Shellans, president of Moniresearch Corporation (P.O. Box 19146, Portland, OR 97219), analyzed the performances of the 12 market timers that were reported in *Money* magazine in May 1984, using the same index as a base. If you should develop your own indicator and would like to test it against the common denominator of the Lipper Growth Fund Index, Steve Shellans at Moniresearch will run the simulation for you for a reasonable fee. One of the best references on developing timing indicators is *Stock Market Trading Systems* by Gerald Appel and Fred Hitschler (Dow Jones-Irwin, 1818 Ridge Road, Homewood, IL 60430).

3-A SIGNAL SYSTEM

Like most of the market timing indicators, the 3-A Signal System uses a moving average. In fact, it makes use of three moving averages, hence the name. In this case the base is a 33-week moving average of the three Dow Jones averages—the DJIA (Dow Jones Industrial Average), DJTA (Dow Jones Transportation Average), and the DJUA (Dow Jones Utility Average). All of these averages are widely reported in daily newspapers. The closing figures each Friday are the numbers used in computing the index. First, however, a bit of background on moving averages and how they are computed.

A moving average is a statistical tool for smoothing data; that is, a moving average removes the ragged and jagged peaks and valleys of daily or weekly data and presents the result in an average format. The smoothed line helps analysts to see the underlying movements, directions, and rates of change. Technically, a moving average eliminates the "noise" in an array of data.

As you might expect from the name, a moving average is, first of all, an average. Statisticians make use of a variety of tools loosely called averages or "indications of central tendency." You may be familiar with the mean or common mathematical average. Computing the mean is simple. You add all the numbers together and divide by the number of entries. In the example shown in table 5A, a series of daily closings of the New York Stock Exchange Composite from early January 1986 are averaged using three different mathematical manipulations.

1. The first series, one you are probably familiar with, is a simple mean. The total for 10 days is 1,204.58; when divided by the 10 entries, it yields a mean of 120.46. For a moving average, you drop the top number and add the most recent number to include 10 numbers one period later. Again referring to table 5A, note that for Day No. 11, the total is 1204.18 from adding the 10 entries beginning with 121.50 for Day No. 2 (dropping the number for Day No. 1) and ending with 120.34 for Day No. 11. Again dividing by 10 yields a new average for 10 days of 120.42. The moving average proceeds one day at a time by repeating the process. This common mean is frequently used as the basis for indicator systems, and a 39-week moving average may be found as the key factor in several indicators.

2. The second series is a weighted average. In this example, weights are applied by multiplying the number of each succeeding day by the NYSE Composite Average for each day of the series. This method of weighting gives increasing weight to more recent numbers. To compute this example of a front-loaded average, multiply the first number, 120.74, by 1; the second number, 121.50, by 2; and so on until the tenth number, 120.62, is multiplied by 10. The total of weighting numbers is 55. Divide the total of 6,607.20 by 55 for the weighted average of 120.13—slightly less than the previously computed mean. The weighted average is less than the mean because the trend of the market averages was down for the 10 days considered and the weighted average emphasized the more recent num-

bers. Computing a weighted moving average involves considerable computation—even with a computer or programmable calculator; therefore, this form of moving average is seldom used.

3. The exponential average is another method for attributing more weight to recent numbers. It is simple to compute although the formulas may appear complex at first glance. Computing an exponential average avoids the need for regularly processing a long string of numbers, as in the mean or weighted average. Two computations are involved in setting up an exponential moving average. You first compute the Smoothing Constant (SC) using the following formula:

$$\text{Smoothing Constant} = \frac{2}{(N + 1)}$$

N = the number of days, weeks, or other periods to be averaged. Referring to table 5A and the 10-day moving average of N = 10, the formula is:

$$\text{Smoothing Constant} = \frac{2}{(10 + 1)} = 2 \text{ divided by 11, or } 0.18$$

Thus, for a moving exponential average of 10 numbers, the SC equals 0.18. Use this Smoothing Constant in computing the exponential average (EA) as follows:

$$\text{New EA} = [(A - B) \times SC] + B$$

where A is equal to the current number and B is equal to the previous exponential average.

Refer to table 5A for the following example:

120.74 = current NYSE average (first on list) or A
120.74 = previous exponential average or B*
First EA = [(120.74 – 120.74) × .18] + 120.74
         = (0 × .18) + 120.74
         = 0 + 120.74 = 120.74—the EA for Day No. 1

Because there is no previous day's exponential average (*),

the calculation assumes the EA equals the current day's number. To begin a new series, you must calculate exponential averages for at least the number of periods averaged before the exponential average is stabilized. In computing the example exponential average in table 5A, the EA for Day No. 2 thus equals the NYSE Composite figure for Day No. 1. The second day's EA computes as follows:

$$\begin{aligned} \text{Second EA} &= [(121.50 - 120.74) \times .18] + 120.74 \\ &= [.76 \times .18] + 120.74 \\ &= .1368 + 120.74 \\ &= 120.8768 \text{ or } 120.88 \end{aligned}$$

Table 5A. Computations for three moving averages.

Week No.	NYSE Comp.	Mean 10-Day Total	10-Day Average	Weight Factor	Weighted Average Weighted Index	10-Day Total	Weighted Average
1	120.74			1	120.74		
2	121.50			2	243.00		
3	121.38			3	364.14		
4	123.14			4	492.56		
5	120.20			5	601.00		
6	118.87			6	713.22		
7	118.82			7	831.74		
8	119.19			8	953.52		
9	120.12			9	1,081.08		
10	120.62	1204.58	120.46	10	1,206.20	6607.2	120.13
11	120.34	1204.18	120.42	55			
12	119.86	1202.54	120.25				
13	118.95	1200.11	120.01				
14	117.75	1194.72	119.47				
15	118.14	1192.66	119.27				

Exponential Average			
Daily NYSE Comp.	Exp. Ave.	+ 1.5%	- 1.5%
120.74	120.74	122.55	118.93
121.50	120.88	122.69	119.06
121.38	120.97	122.78	119.15
123.14	121.36	123.18	119.54
120.20	121.15	122.97	119.33
118.87	120.74	122.55	118.93
118.82	120.39	122.20	118.59
119.19	120.18	121.98	118.37
120.12	120.17	121.97	118.36
120.62	120.25	122.05	118.44
120.34	120.26	122.07	118.46
119.86	120.19	121.99	118.39
118.95	119.97	121.77	118.17
117.75	119.57	121.36	117.78
118.14	119.31	121.10	117.52

In the example in table 5A, all EAs from Day No. 10 on are meaningful and may be used statistically.

Using an exponential average avoids the need to keep and manipulate a long string of numbers; for example, to compute the EA for Day No. 11 from table 5A, all you need is the NYSE Composite Average for Day No. 11 (120.34) and the previous EA for Day No. 10 (120.22). Using these numbers and the formula above, you compute the new EA of 120.24 for Day No. 11. You wouldn't need to know any of the prior figures.

The moving average for Day No. 10 is 120.22, close to the weighted 10-day average of 120.13—and far easier to compute once you have the smoothing constant and an ongoing exponential average. Further, the exponential average is easy to set up on a computer using a spreadsheet program.

The 3-A Signal System uses a 33-week exponential moving average of the three Dow Jones averages. The smoothing constant is .05882 (2 divided by 33 + 1). The exponential averages for the years 1983, 1984, and 1985 are displayed in table 5B along with two other series for each Dow Jones average that will be explained later. A chart of the three averages is shown in figure 5-1. Notice how the moving averages smooth the jagged weekly closing figures.

REFINING THE 3-A SIGNAL SYSTEM

Moving average systems generally work by calling for action on penetrations—when the index line penetrates or crosses the moving average in one direction or another. For example, if the 33-week moving average appears above the line for weekly closing figures and the difference grows smaller until the weekly index line intersects or penetrates the moving average line, you might consider this a signal to "buy." In your market timing system, a penetration up through the moving average line to a position higher would be a signal to switch out of your money market fund into your growth equity fund because the market appears to be trending up. That is, prices represented by the Dow Jones averages of stock prices have been moving up for some period.

When the index line is above its moving average, moves

down, and penetrates the moving average to a position below it, the market appears to be trending down. Such a downward penetration would be a signal to sell stocks or to switch out of your growth equity fund into your money market fund. You would wait out the bear phase with your capital safely protected in a money market fund.

While single moving averages provide more direction than a simple plot of prices or indexes, you can encounter whipsaws or short-term reversals that would get you into and out of the market within days or weeks. Long-term moving averages— say for 52 or 65 weeks—would surely eliminate most whipsaws, but they tend to be unresponsive to market changes. You can lose more of an uptrend and suffer more losses during downtrends with an indicator that is unresponsive to long-term market trends. Moving averages tend to perform best during long-term market trends, either up or down. They perform less well when the market is moving up and down in cycles of a few weeks to a few months.

The 3-A Signal System incorporates two refinements of single moving averages to avoid most whipsaws without losing large chunks of trends in either direction.

Filter Zones

A filter zone is the first refinement. Simply stated, it is a zone or band around the moving average that enlarges the depth of the moving average. For a penetration to occur, the actual index line moving up through the moving average must first cross the moving average line and then the upper edge of the band before you would act. Figure 5-2 charts a small section of the 3-A Signal System around two penetration points on the Dow Jones Industrial Average. Note the upper and lower band limits that are defined as plus 1½ percent and minus 1½ percent for a total band width of 3 percent of the moving average value at each weekly point. Note, too, the values for the filter band limits in the portion of the moving average computation in table 5B. These band limits and the band width resulted from a series of trial-and-error widths to determine the optimum responsiveness without encountering an unreasonable number of whipsaws.

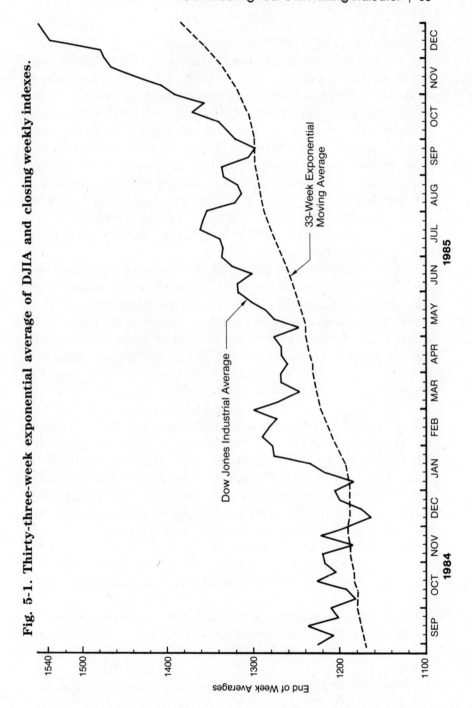

Fig. 5-1. Thirty-three-week exponential average of DJIA and closing weekly indexes.

Multiple Moving Averages

Rather than a single moving average and signals generated when a crossover occurs, with or without a filter zone, two or more moving averages improve the reliability of indicator systems. Various combinations of multiple moving averages can and do generate different buy-and-sell signals—or switch signals in a market timing program. The multiple moving averages may be of different time periods for the same variable or different variables based on identical moving average periods. In a multiple moving average indicator system, nothing happens when a single crossover occurs, but when a second or third crossover confirms the market's direction, the system generates a switching signal.

The 3-A Signal System maintains three moving averages, one for each of the Dow Jones averages—industrial, transportation, and utility. Each is a 33-week exponential average of the prices at the close of a week's trading, usually at the end of Friday's. If a holiday interrupts the market on Friday, the week's closing price is Thursday's. Each of the moving averages includes a filter band with a width of 3 percent from edge to edge, 1½ percent on either side of the moving averages. Buy-and-sell signals occur according to the movements of the three index lines and their moving averages. A "buy" signal means to move out of a money market fund and buy shares of your selected growth mutual fund. A "sell" signal means to sell your shares in the growth mutual fund and move the cash balance into your money market fund. If you have set up accounts in both mutual funds according to instructions given later in this book, you can make these switches by telephone. Buy and sell according to the following rules:

—Buy when at least two of the weekly index lines are above the upper band limits of their respective exponential moving averages.

—Sell when any one of the index lines is below the lower band limit of its moving average and the other two are in neutral territory; that is, within the filter zone of their moving averages.

These buy-and-sell points do not occur often. Over the 15-

year simulation period, only 31 switches took place, or just over two per year. A switch is a round trip involving one sell and one buy transaction. Note the two penetrations that occurred during the week of February 3, 1985, calling for "sell" in figures 5-2 and 5-3. A "buy" signal occurs during the week of August 3, 1985. In both cases only the industrial and transportation indexes collaborate to generate the sell and buy signals.

Fig. 5-2. Dow Jones Industrial Averages, 1984.

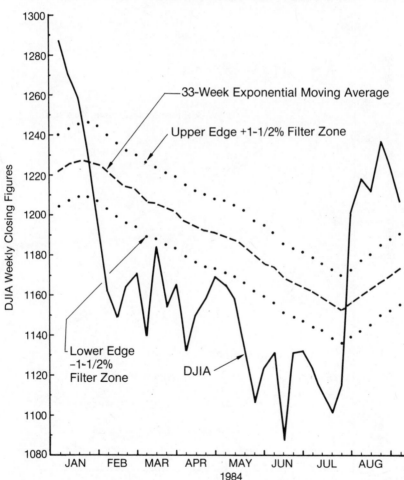

Visually picking off the penetration points from charts similar to those in figures 5-2 and 5-3 is easier than picking reversals only from tabular data. Unless you are adept at plotting the figures or have access to a computer that can chart the data, such as Microsoft's Chart software, diagramming the data can be time-consuming. You can pick up the reversals by noting the data in an array of prices and moving averages similar to those in table 5B.

Fig. 5-3. Dow Jones Transportation and Utility Averages, 1984.

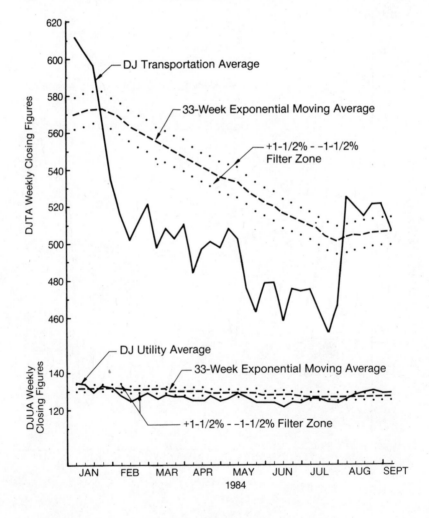

Table 5B. Index data.

Date 1984	DJIA	Exp. Ave.	+1.5%	-1.5%	Transport	Exp. Ave.	+1.5%	-1.5%	Utility	Exp. Ave.	+1.5%	-1.5%
Jan 1	875	850.00	864.24	838.70	380.30	340.00	347.51	337.23	109.02	105.00	106.82	103.66
8	866.53	851.47	865.14	839.57	368.67	342.37	349.08	338.76	107.68	105.24	106.96	103.80
15	847.6	852.36	864.86	839.30	352.63	343.92	349.60	339.26	104.18	105.38	106.89	103.73
22	845.03	852.08	864.44	838.89	342.03	344.43	349.45	339.12	104.06	105.31	106.81	103.66
29	871.1	851.66	865.60	840.01	356.14	344.29	350.16	339.81	107.51	105.24	106.95	103.79
Feb 5	851.03	852.81	865.49	839.91	357.17	344.99	350.89	340.52	106.95	105.37	107.04	103.88
12	833.81	852.70	864.33	838.82	347.54	345.70	351.00	340.62	105.2	105.46	107.03	103.87
19	824.3	851.59	862.73	837.23	343.13	345.81	350.84	340.47	104.91	105.45	107.00	103.83
26	824.39	849.98	861.21	835.75	336.38	345.65	350.28	339.93	107.23	105.42	107.11	103.94
Mar 5	807.36	848.48	858.75	833.37	322.82	345.11	348.95	338.64	107.68	105.52	107.23	104.06
12	797.37	846.06	855.84	830.55	320.00	343.80	347.53	337.26	106.01	105.65	107.26	104.09
19	805.65	843.20	853.60	828.37	329.16	342.40	346.74	336.49	106.58	105.67	107.31	104.14
26	817.92	840.99	852.23	827.04	332.32	341.62	346.19	335.96	108.57	105.72	107.48	104.30
Apr 2	838.57	839.63	852.16	826.98	339.34	341.07	346.08	335.85	110.2	105.89	107.74	104.55
9	842.94	839.57	852.36	827.17	348.84	340.97	346.86	336.31	110.52	106.14	108.00	104.81
16	843.42	839.77	852.58	827.38	346.57	341.73	347.09	336.61	112.27	106.40	108.35	105.15
23	862.16	839.98	853.91	828.67	345.61	341.96	347.53	336.83	114.59	106.75	108.82	105.60
30	865.68	841.29	855.36	830.08	349.26	342.39	348.16	337.26	115.77	107.21	109.33	106.10
May 7	869.2	842.72	856.94	831.61	352.90	343.01	348.62	337.86	116.95	107.71	109.88	106.63
14	857.78	844.28	857.75	832.40	350.84	343.47	347.98	338.32	115.57	108.26	110.32	107.06
21	835.9	845.07	857.20	831.87	333.56	342.89	346.67	337.74	113.78	108.69	110.62	107.35
28	819.54	844.53	855.71	830.42	320.14	341.55	345.21	336.43	119.09	108.99	111.22	107.94
Jun 4	804.98	843.06	853.44	828.41	317.07	340.11	343.92	335.01	111.52	109.58	111.34	108.05
11	809.74	840.82	851.58	826.41	318.50	338.84	341.90	333.76	109.96	109.69	111.36	108.06
18	788.62	838.99	848.57	823.49	305.01	336.85	340.62	331.80	106.7	109.71	111.18	107.89
25	803.08	836.03	846.60	821.58	315.35	335.58	339.37	330.55	106.57	109.53	111.00	107.72
Jul 2	796.99	834.09	844.39	819.43	314.60	334.35	338.54	329.33	106.17	109.36	110.81	107.53
9	814.12	831.91	843.33	818.40	320.59	333.54	337.90	328.54	106.82	109.17	110.67	107.40
16	828.67	830.86	843.20	818.27	322.69	332.90	337.03	327.91	107.37	109.03	110.57	107.30
23	830.57	830.74	843.19	818.26	318.35	332.05	335.64	327.07	106.45	108.93	110.42	107.16
30	808.6	830.73	841.87	816.98	308.75	330.68	333.63	325.72	103.22	108.79	110.09	106.83
Aug 6	784.34	829.42	839.17	814.37	297.06	328.70	331.65	323.77	104.51	108.46	109.85	106.61
13	788.05	826.77	836.86	812.13	295.49	326.75	331.25	321.84	106.31	108.23	109.74	106.49
20	869.29	824.49	839.54	814.72	320.04	326.35	332.65	321.46	115.36	108.12	110.17	106.91
27	883.47	827.13	842.90	817.99	349.82	327.73	332.82	322.82	114.25	108.54	110.51	107.24

Table 5B *(cont'd)*

Date 1984	DJIA	Exp. Ave. 850.00	+1.5%	-1.5%	Transport	Exp. Ave. 340.00	+1.5%	-1.5%	Utility	Exp. Ave. 105.00	+1.5%	-1.5%
Sep 3	925.13	836.01	848.55	823.47	369.68	330.20	335.15	325.25	117.29	109.37	111.01	107.73
10	906.82	840.18	852.78	827.58	369.60	332.52	337.50	327.53	114.48	109.67	111.32	108.03
17	916.94	844.69	857.36	832.02	362.26	334.27	339.28	329.25	115.63	110.02	111.67	108.37
24	919.52	849.09	861.83	836.36	369.60	336.34	341.39	331.30	117.06	110.44	112.09	108.78
Oct 1	907.74	852.54	865.33	839.76	365.03	338.03	343.10	332.96	115.91-	110.76	112.42	109.10
8	986.85	860.44	873.35	847.54	385.79	340.84	345.95	335.73	120.25	111.32	112.99	109.65
15	993.1	868.25	881.27	855.22	401.98	344.44	349.60	339.27	121.26	111.90	113.58	110.22
22	1031.46	877.85	891.01	864.68	439.37	350.02	355.27	344.77	121.54	112.47	114.16	110.78
29	991.72	884.54	897.81	871.28	420.19	354.15	359.46	348.84	119.19	112.86	114.56	111.17
Nov 5	1051.78	894.38	907.80	880.97	452.19	359.92	365.31	354.52	122.55	113.43	115.14	111.73
12	1039.92	902.94	916.49	889.40	444.84	364.91	370.38	359.44	119.42	113.79	115.49	112.08
19	1021.25	909.90	923.55	896.25	433.15	368.92	374.46	363.39	119.37	114.11	115.83	112.40
26	1007.36	915.63	929.37	901.90	424.91	372.22	377.80	366.63	116.14	114.23	115.95	112.52
Dec 3	1031.36	922.44	936.28	908.60	445.37	376.52	382.17	370.87	116.74	114.38	116.10	112.67
10	1018.76	928.11	942.03	914.18	438.92	380.19	385.89	374.49	118.17	114.60	116.32	112.88
17	1011.5	933.01	947.01	919.02	444.32	383.96	389.72	378.20	117.29	114.76	116.48	113.04
24	1045.07	939.60	953.70	925.51	447.17	387.68	393.50	381.87	118.03	114.95	116.68	113.23
31	1045.54	945.89	960.08	931.70	448.38	391.25	397.12	385.38	119.46	115.22	116.95	113.49
Jan 7 83	1076.07	953.55	967.85	939.25	460.37	395.32	401.25	389.39	124.49	115.76	117.50	114.03
14	1080.53	961.02	975.43	946.60	467.68	399.57	405.57	393.58	124.63	116.29	118.03	114.54
21	1052.98	966.43	980.92	951.93	448.79	402.47	408.50	396.43	125.05	116.80	118.55	115.05
28	1064.75	972.21	986.79	957.63	460.37	405.87	411.96	399.79	123.62	117.20	118.96	115.44
Feb 4	1077.91	978.43	993.10	963.75	485.07	410.53	416.69	404.37	125.05	117.66	119.43	115.90
11	1086.52	984.79	999.56	970.01	479.91	414.61	420.83	408.39	123.66	118.02	119.79	116.25
18	1092.82	991.14	1,006.01	976.27	480.70	418.50	424.78	412.22	124.12	118.38	120.15	116.60
25	1120.94	998.78	1,013.76	983.79	492.30	422.84	429.18	416.50	124.82	118.75	120.54	116.97
Mar 4	1140.96	1,007.14	1,022.25	992.03	511.12	428.03	434.45	421.61	129.29	119.37	121.17	117.58
11	1117.74	1,013.64	1,028.85	998.44	503.34	432.46	438.95	425.98	126.98	119.82	121.62	118.02
18	1117.74	1,019.77	1,035.06	1,004.47	506.27	436.80	443.36	430.25	126.25	120.20	122.00	118.40
25	1140.09	1,026.84	1,042.25	1,011.44	515.57	441.44	448.06	434.82	126.34	120.56	122.37	118.75
Apr 1	1130.03	1,032.91	1,048.41	1,017.42	507.39	445.32	452.00	438.64	124.54	120.80	122.61	118.98
8	1124.71	1,038.31	1,053.89	1,022.74	509.37	449.08	455.82	442.35	124.31	121.00	122.82	119.19
15	1171.34	1,046.14	1,061.83	1,030.45	529.94	453.84	460.65	447.03	126.06	121.30	123.12	119.48
22	1196.3	1,054.97	1,070.80	1,039.15	527.24	458.16	465.03	451.29	127.17	121.64	123.47	119.82

Date 1984	DJIA	Exp. Ave. 850.00	+1.5%	-1.5%	Transport	Exp. Ave. 340.00	+1.5%	-1.5%	Utility	Exp. Ave. 105.00	+1.5%	-1.5%
29	1226.2	1,065.04	1,081.02	1,049.07	524.94	462.09	469.02	455.15	128.41	122.04	123.87	120.21
May 6	1232.59	1,074.90	1,091.02	1,058.77	552.10	467.38	474.39	460.37	129.11	122.46	124.30	120.62
13	1218.75	1,083.36	1,099.61	1,067.11	547.87	472.11	479.20	465.03	129.61	122.88	124.72	121.04
20	1190.02	1,089.63	1,105.98	1,073.29	539.62	476.09	483.23	468.94	128.88	123.23	125.08	121.38
27	1216.14	1,097.07	1,113.53	1,080.62	545.10	480.14	487.35	472.94	130.12	123.99	125.49	121.78
Jun 3	1213.04	1,103.90	1,120.45	1,087.34	551.06	484.32	491.58	477.05	129.61	124.15	125.85	122.13
10	1196.11	1,109.32	1,125.96	1,092.68	572.94	489.53	496.87	482.19	126.8	124.44	126.02	122.29
17	1241.69	1,117.13	1,133.89	1,100.38	581.12	494.92	502.34	487.49	129.06	124.68	126.31	122.58
24	1225.26	1,124.46	1,141.33	1,107.59	589.29	500.47	507.97	492.96	128.41	124.93	126.55	122.81
Jul 1	1207.23	1,130.39	1,147.35	1,113.43	586.61	505.53	513.12	497.95	128.92	125.18	126.80	123.05
8	1192.31	1,134.91	1,151.93	1,117.89	575.28	509.64	517.28	501.99	129.29	125.48	127.06	123.30
15	1231.17	1,138.29	1,155.36	1,121.21	561.31	512.68	520.37	504.99	130.21	125.83	127.36	123.60
22	1199.22	1,143.75	1,160.91	1,126.59	579.06	516.58	524.33	508.83	131.5	126.06	127.72	123.94
29	1183.29	1,147.01	1,164.22	1,129.81	550.77	518.59	526.37	510.81	129.77	126.24	127.95	124.17
Aug 5	1182.82	1,149.15	1,166.38	1,131.91	542.43	519.99	527.79	512.19	129.09	126.34	128.14	124.35
12	1194.21	1,151.13	1,168.39	1,133.86	539.62	521.15	528.97	513.33	127.94	126.61	128.24	124.45
19	1192.07	1,153.66	1,170.97	1,136.36	533.73	521.89	529.72	514.06	130.88	126.87	128.51	124.71
26	1215.45	1,155.92	1,173.26	1,138.58	532.50	522.51	530.35	514.67	131.07	127.06	128.77	124.97
Sep 2	1239.74	1,159.42	1,176.81	1,142.03	558.94	524.66	532.53	516.79	130.11	127.30	128.97	125.16
9	1225.71	1,164.15	1,181.61	1,146.68	569.66	527.30	535.21	519.39	131.17	127.57	129.21	125.39
16	1255.59	1,167.77	1,185.28	1,150.25	572.73	529.97	537.92	522.02	131.89	127.92	129.49	125.66
23	1233.13	1,172.93	1,190.53	1,155.34	584.33	533.17	541.17	525.17	133.43	128.32	129.84	126.00
30	1272.15	1,176.47	1,194.12	1,158.83	561.58	534.84	542.87	526.82	134.68	128.94	130.24	126.39
Oct 7	1263.52	1,182.10	1,199.83	1,164.37	586.70	537.89	545.96	529.82	138.97	129.44	130.88	127.01
14	1248.88	1,186.89	1,204.59	1,169.09	580.55	540.40	548.51	532.30	137.38	129.99	131.38	127.50
21	1223.48	1,190.54	1,208.59	1,172.68	590.30	543.34	551.49	535.19	138.82	130.54	131.94	128.04
28	1218.29	1,192.47	1,210.36	1,174.59	576.61	545.29	553.47	537.11	139.26	131.01	132.49	128.58
Nov 4	1250.2	1,193.99	1,211.90	1,176.08	586.60	547.72	555.94	539.51	138.58	131.37	132.97	129.04
11	1251.02	1,197.30	1,215.26	1,179.34	595.57	550.54	558.80	542.28	137.09	131.72	133.34	129.40
18	1277.44	1,200.46	1,218.47	1,182.45	606.04	553.80	562.11	545.50	137.33	132.06	133.69	129.74
25	1265.24	1,204.99	1,223.06	1,186.91	610.43	557.13	565.49	548.78	137.52	132.22	134.04	130.08
Dec 2	1260.06	1,208.53	1,226.66	1,190.40	605.29	559.97	568.37	551.57	134.87	132.32	134.21	130.24
9	1242.17	1,211.56	1,229.74	1,193.39	604.91	562.61	571.05	554.17	133.91	131.90	134.31	130.34
16	1250.51	1,213.36	1,231.56	1,195.16	590.15	564.23	572.69	555.77	125.05	131.82	133.87	129.92
23	1258.64	1,215.55	1,233.78	1,197.31	587.26	565.58	574.07	557.10	130.64	131.82	133.80	129.84
30	1211.57	1,218.08	1,236.35	1,199.81	598.59	567.53	576.04	559.01	131.84	131.82	133.80	129.85

Table 5B (cont'd)

Date 1984	DJIA	Exp. Ave. 850.00	+1.5%	-1.5%	Transport	Exp. Ave. 340.00	+1.5%	-1.5%	Utility	Exp. Ave. 105.00	+1.5%	-1.5%
Jan 6-84	1286.64	1,222.11	1,240.45	1,203.78	611.79	570.13	578.68	561.58	134.83	132.00	133.98	130.02
13	1270.1	1,224.94	1,243.31	1,206.56	602.96	572.06	580.64	563.48	134.30	132.13	134.12	130.15
20	1259.11	1,226.95	1,245.35	1,208.54	596.45	573.49	582.10	564.89	130.39	132.03	134.01	130.05
27	1230	1,227.13	1,245.53	1,208.72	567.15	573.12	581.72	564.52	132.66	132.07	134.05	130.09
Feb 3	1197.03	1,225.36	1,243.74	1,206.98	535.37	570.90	579.46	562.34	131.89	132.06	134.04	130.08
10	1160.7	1,221.55	1,239.88	1,203.23	514.55	567.59	576.10	559.07	127.17	131.77	133.75	129.79
17	1148.87	1,217.28	1,235.54	1,199.02	502.31	563.75	572.20	555.29	124.66	131.35	133.32	129.38
24	1165.1	1,214.21	1,232.42	1,196.00	510.89	560.64	569.05	552.23	127.02	131.10	133.06	129.13
Mar 2	1171.48	1,211.70	1,229.87	1,193.52	520.58	558.28	566.66	549.91	129.38	131.00	132.96	129.03
9	1139.76	1,207.46	1,225.58	1,189.35	498.46	554.76	563.08	546.44	125.92	130.70	132.66	128.74
16	1184.36	1,206.11	1,224.20	1,188.01	518.21	552.61	560.90	544.32	127.60	130.52	132.47	128.56
23	1154.84	1,203.09	1,221.14	1,185.04	503.19	549.71	557.95	541.46	126.88	130.30	132.26	128.35
30	1164.89	1,200.84	1,218.86	1,182.83	510.19	547.38	555.59	539.17	126.83	130.10	132.05	128.15
Apr 6	1132.22	1,196.81	1,214.76	1,178.85	484.16	543.66	551.82	535.51	125.43	129.82	131.77	127.88
13	1150.13	1,194.06	1,211.97	1,176.15	497.33	540.94	549.05	532.82	125.34	129.56	131.50	127.62
20	1158.08	1,191.94	1,209.82	1,174.07	500.82	538.58	546.66	530.50	126.69	129.39	131.33	127.45
27	1169.07	1,190.60	1,208.46	1,172.74	497.74	536.18	544.22	528.13	125.39	129.16	131.09	127.22
May 4	1165.31	1,189.11	1,206.95	1,171.28	507.61	534.50	542.51	526.48	126.49	129.00	130.93	127.06
11	1157.14	1,187.23	1,205.04	1,169.42	502.06	532.59	540.58	524.60	129.29	129.02	130.95	127.08
18	1133.79	1,184.09	1,201.85	1,166.33	474.59	529.18	537.11	521.24	127.31	128.92	130.85	126.98
25	1107.1	1,179.56	1,197.25	1,161.87	462.76	525.27	533.15	517.39	123.55	128.60	130.53	126.67
Jun 1	1124.35	1,176.31	1,193.96	1,158.67	478.09	522.49	530.33	514.66	124.37	128.35	130.28	126.43
8	1131.25	1,173.66	1,191.27	1,156.06	477.67	519.86	527.66	512.06	124.37	128.12	130.04	126.20
15	1086.9	1,168.56	1,186.09	1,151.03	458.02	516.22	523.96	508.48	122.25	127.77	129.69	125.86
22	1131.07	1,166.35	1,183.85	1,148.86	475.10	513.80	521.51	506.09	124.37	127.57	129.49	125.66
29	1132.4	1,164.36	1,181.82	1,146.89	474.18	511.47	519.14	503.80	124.28	127.38	129.29	125.47
Jul 6	1122.57	1,161.90	1,179.33	1,144.47	474.69	509.31	516.95	501.67	125.67	127.28	129.19	125.37
13	1109.87	1,158.84	1,176.22	1,141.46	463.27	506.60	514.20	499.00	125.77	127.19	129.10	125.28
20	1101.37	1,155.46	1,172.79	1,138.13	451.75	503.37	510.92	495.82	123.70	126.98	128.89	125.08
27	1114.62	1,153.06	1,170.35	1,135.76	466.60	501.21	508.73	493.69	124.33	126.83	128.73	124.93
Aug 3	1202.08	1,155.94	1,173.28	1,138.60	525.67	502.65	510.19	495.11	126.49	126.81	128.71	124.91
10	1218.09	1,159.59	1,176.99	1,142.20	519.54	503.64	511.20	496.09	128.37	126.90	128.80	125.00
17	1211.9	1,162.67	1,180.11	1,145.23	514.71	504.29	511.86	496.73	128.69	127.00	128.91	125.10
24	1236.53	1,167.02	1,184.52	1,149.51	520.62	505.25	512.83	497.68	129.72	127.16	129.07	125.26
31	1224.38	1,170.39	1,187.95	1,152.83	520.51	506.15	513.74	498.56	129.46	127.30	129.21	125.39
Sep 7	1207.38	1,172.57	1,190.15	1,154.98	507.41	506.23	513.82	498.63	129.26	127.41	129.33	125.50
14	1237.52	1,176.39	1,194.03	1,158.74	526.52	507.42	515.03	499.81	132.80	127.73	129.65	125.82

Date 1984	DJIA	Exp. Ave. 850.00	+1.5%	-1.5%	Transport	Exp. Ave. 340.00	+1.5%	-1.5%	Utility	Exp. Ave. 105.00	+1.5%	-1.5%
21	1201.74	1,177.88	1,195.55	1,160.21	518.69	508.08	515.70	500.46	135.31	128.18	130.10	126.25
28	1206.71	1,179.57	1,197.27	1,161.88	517.61	508.64	516.27	501.01	139.16	128.82	130.76	126.89
Oct 5	1182.53	1,179.75	1,197.44	1,162.05	515.03	509.02	516.65	501.38	138.28	129.38	131.32	127.44
12	1190.7	1,180.39	1,198.10	1,162.69	517.40	509.51	517.15	501.87	140.75	130.05	132.00	128.10
19	1225.93	1,183.07	1,200.82	1,165.32	542.74	511.47	519.14	503.79	144.80	130.92	132.88	128.95
26	1204.95	1,184.36	1,202.12	1,166.59	522.98	512.14	519.83	504.46	141.57	131.54	133.52	129.57
Nov 2	1216.65	1,186.26	1,204.05	1,168.46	532.32	513.33	521.03	505.63	143.82	132.26	134.25	130.28
9	1218.97	1,188.18	1,206.00	1,170.36	532.43	514.45	522.17	506.74	145.77	133.06	135.06	131.06
16	1187.94	1,188.17	1,205.99	1,170.34	516.22	514.56	522.28	506.84	143.77	133.69	135.69	131.68
23	1220.3	1,190.06	1,207.91	1,172.21	532.99	515.64	523.38	507.91	145.72	134.40	136.41	132.38
30	1188.94	1,189.99	1,207.84	1,172.14	522.25	516.03	523.77	508.29	145.62	135.06	137.08	133.03
Dec 7	1163.21	1,188.42	1,206.24	1,170.59	522.70	516.42	524.17	508.68	144.65	135.62	137.66	133.59
14	1175.91	1,187.68	1,205.50	1,169.87	534.99	517.51	525.28	509.75	144.59	136.15	138.19	134.11
21	1198.98	1,188.34	1,206.17	1,170.52	550.38	519.45	527.24	511.66	146.80	136.78	138.83	134.72
28	1204.17	1,189.28	1,207.11	1,171.44	556.91	521.65	529.48	513.83	146.80	137.37	139.43	135.30
Jan 4-85	1184.96	1,189.02	1,206.86	1,171.19	553.03	523.50	531.35	515.64	146.54	137.90	139.97	135.84
11	1218.09	1,190.73	1,208.59	1,172.87	572.52	526.38	534.28	518.48	147.26	138.46	140.53	136.38
18	1227.36	1,192.89	1,210.78	1,174.99	577.72	529.40	537.34	521.46	147.57	138.99	141.08	136.91
25	1276.06	1,197.78	1,215.75	1,179.81	606.73	533.95	541.96	525.94	148.18	139.53	141.62	137.44
Feb 1	1277.72	1,202.48	1,220.52	1,184.44	609.90	538.42	546.49	530.34	148.65	140.07	142.17	137.97
8	1289.97	1,207.63	1,225.74	1,189.51	630.09	543.81	551.97	535.65	150.80	140.70	142.81	138.59
15	1282.02	1,212.00	1,230.18	1,193.82	629.21	548.83	557.06	540.60	150.85	141.30	143.42	139.18
22	1275.84	1,215.76	1,233.99	1,197.52	625.11	553.32	561.62	545.02	149.67	141.79	143.92	139.66
Mar 1	1299.36	1,220.67	1,238.99	1,202.36	635.30	558.14	566.51	549.77	148.80	142.20	144.33	140.07
8	1269.66	1,223.56	1,241.91	1,205.20	615.37	561.51	569.93	553.08	147.77	142.53	144.67	140.39
15	1267.35	1,224.96	1,243.33	1,206.58	602.19	563.90	572.36	555.44	147.00	142.79	144.93	140.65
22	1267.45	1,227.46	1,245.87	1,209.04	594.88	565.72	574.21	557.24	149.26	143.17	145.32	141.02
29	1266.78	1,229.77	1,248.21	1,211.32	603.08	567.92	576.44	559.40	153.01	143.75	145.91	141.59
Apr 5	1259.05	1,231.49	1,249.96	1,213.02	590.79	569.26	577.80	560.73	153.83	144.34	146.51	142.18
12	1265.68	1,233.50	1,252.00	1,216.00	598.21	570.97	579.53	562.40	155.88	145.02	147.20	142.85
19	1266.56	1,235.45	1,253.98	1,216.91	584.92	571.79	580.36	563.21	155.21	145.62	147.81	143.44
26	1275.18	1,237.78	1,256.35	1,219.22	586.25	572.64	581.23	564.05	154.17	146.10	148.32	143.93
May 3	1247.24	1,238.34	1,256.91	1,219.76	584.48	573.34	581.94	564.74	154.95	146.64	148.84	144.44
10	1274.18	1,240.45	1,259.05	1,221.84	617.03	575.91	584.54	567.27	159.75	147.41	149.63	145.20
17	1285.34	1,243.09	1,261.73	1,224.44	622.56	578.65	587.33	569.97	164.75	148.43	150.66	146.21

Table 5B (cont'd)

Date 1984	DJIA	Exp. Ave. 850.00	+1.5%	-1.5%	Transport	Exp. Ave. 340.00	+1.5%	-1.5%	Utility	Exp. Ave. 105.00	+1.5%	-1.5%
24	1301.97											
31	1315.41	1,246.55	1,265.25	1,227.85	627.55	581.53	590.25	572.80	161.98	149.23	151.47	146.99
Jun 7	1316.42	1,250.60	1,269.36	1,231.84	645.16	585.27	594.05	576.49	163.32	150.06	152.31	147.81
14	1300.96	1,254.47	1,273.29	1,235.66	653.45	589.28	598.12	580.44	163.88	150.87	153.14	148.61
21	1324.48	1,257.21	1,276.07	1,238.35	636.94	592.08	600.96	583.20	164.60	151.68	153.96	149.40
28	1335.46	1,261.16	1,280.08	1,242.25	649.58	595.46	604.40	586.53	166.85	152.57	154.86	150.28
Jul 5	1334.45	1,265.53	1,284.52	1,246.55	664.09	599.50	608.49	590.51	164.85	153.29	155.59	151.00
12	1338.6	1,269.59	1,288.63	1,250.54	678.96	604.17	613.24	595.11	166.29	154.06	156.37	151.75
19	1359.54	1,273.65	1,292.75	1,254.54	687.97	609.10	618.24	599.97	168.91	154.93	157.26	152.61
26	1357.08	1,278.70	1,297.88	1,259.52	700.73	614.49	623.71	605.28	166.24	155.60	157.93	153.26
Aug 2	1353.05	1,283.31	1,302.56	1,264.06	688.20	618.83	628.11	609.55	157.42	155.70	158.04	153.37
9	1320.79	1,287.41	1,306.72	1,268.10	699.44	623.57	632.92	614.22	156.85	155.77	158.11	153.44
16	1312.72	1,289.38	1,308.72	1,270.03	679.89	626.88	636.29	617.48	155.06	155.73	158.07	153.39
23	1318.32	1,290.75	1,310.11	1,271.39	666.78	629.23	638.67	619.79	157.21	155.82	158.15	153.48
30	1334.01	1,292.37	1,311.76	1,272.98	686.80	632.62	642.11	623.13	159.21	156.02	158.36	153.68
Sep 6	1335.69	1,294.82	1,314.24	1,275.40	690.66	636.03	645.57	626.49	159.67	156.23	158.58	153.89
13	1307.68	1,297.22	1,316.68	1,277.77	677.55	638.47	648.05	628.90	159.16	156.40	158.75	154.06
20	1297.94	1,297.84	1,317.31	1,278.37	658.47	639.65	649.24	630.05	152.60	156.18	158.52	153.84
27	1320.79	1,299.19	1,318.68	1,279.71	649.34	640.22	649.82	630.62	152.80	155.98	158.32	153.64
Oct 4	1328.74	1,300.93	1,320.45	1,281.42	643.61	640.42	650.02	630.81	150.08	155.63	157.97	153.30
11	1339.94	1,303.23	1,322.77	1,283.68	647.24	640.82	650.43	631.21	155.16	155.61	157.94	153.27
18	1368.84	1,307.09	1,326.69	1,287.48	647.47	641.21	650.83	631.59	154.08	155.52	157.85	153.18
25	1356.52	1,309.99	1,329.64	1,290.34	660.35	642.34	651.97	632.70	154.44	155.45	157.79	153.12
Nov 1	1390.25	1,314.71	1,334.44	1,294.99	665.61	642.76	652.40	633.12	159.16	155.67	158.01	153.34
8	1404.36	1,319.99	1,339.79	1,300.19	678.14	644.11	653.77	634.44	161.78	156.03	158.37	153.69
15	1435.09	1,326.76	1,346.66	1,306.86	684.93	646.11	655.80	636.42	161.93	156.38	158.72	154.03
22	1464.33	1,334.85	1,354.87	1,314.83	682.94	648.39	658.12	638.67	165.78	156.93	159.28	154.58
29	1472.13	1,342.92	1,363.07	1,322.78	690.31	650.42	660.18	640.67	166.14	157.47	159.83	155.11
Dec 6	1477.18	1,350.82	1,371.08	1,330.56	693.59	652.77	662.56	642.98	163.03	157.80	160.17	155.43
13	1535.21	1,361.67	1,382.09	1,341.24	722.61	655.17	665.00	645.34	165.57	158.26	160.63	155.88
20	1543	1,372.33	1,392.92	1,351.75	711.26	659.14	669.02	649.25	168.80	158.88	161.26	156.49
27	1543	1,382.37	1,403.11	1,361.64	708.45	662.20	672.14	652.27	174.96	159.82	162.22	157.43
						664.92	674.90	654.95	172.09	160.54	162.95	158.14

Table 5C details a sample of buy-and-sell signals generated over 15 years. Several months have elapsed since the closing deadline for this chapter and the appearance of *Market Timing with No-Load Mutual Funds* in bookstores. Thus, to collect the data and compute a current exponential moving average for the three Dow Jones indexes would involve considerable time on your part. To simplify these computations, you may re-

Table 5C. Switch dates for 3-A Signal System.

Transaction Date	Transaction Description	Price or Rate
Mar 30 1979	Sell T-Bills	
	Buy Lipper Gr	100.29
May 11 1979	Sell Lipper Gr	99.25
	Buy T-Bills	9.56%
Jun 15 1979	Sell T-Bills	
	Buy Lipper Gr	103.3
Oct 12 1979	Sell Lipper Gr	109.34
	Buy T-Bills	11.35%
Dec 7 1979	Sell T-Bills	
	Buy Lipper Gr	116.97
Dec 31 1979	Year-End Balance	119.09
Mar 7 1980	Sell Lipper Gr	118.98
	Buy T-Bills	15.63%
May 23 1980	Sell T-Bills	
	Buy Lipper Gr	122.42
Dec 31 1980	Year-End Balance	163.47
Jul 2 1981	Sell Lipper Gr	157.71
	Buy T-Bills	14.48%
Dec 4 1981	Sell T-Bills	
	Buy Lipper Gr	153.43
Dec 18 1981	Sell Lipper Gr	151.51
	Buy T-Bills	10.87%
Aug 27 1982	Sell T-Bills	
	Buy Lipper Gr	143.58
Dec 31 1982	Year-End Balance	180.04
Dec 31 1983	Year-End Balance	220.13
Feb 3 1984	Sell Lipper Gr	208.93
	Buy T-Bills	0.0896
Aug 3 1984	Sell T-Bills	
	Buy Lipper Gr	208.92
Dec 31 1984	Year-End Balance	213.98
Sep 6 1985	Last Day of Run	248.76

ceive a free updating of data necessary to follow through on using your own 3-A Signal System by sending a request to Paul A. Merriman & Associates, 1200 Westlake Avenue N., Suite 507, Seattle, WA 98109. Please include a stamped, self-addressed business envelope. An order blank for this information is included on the last page to simplify your ordering.

6

Investing with IRAs and Keoghs

Market timing is a long-term program for building capital. For compound interest to work its wonders, your investments need time to grow and multiply. But what is the biggest hazard to your plans for planting the seeds of capital and allowing them to grow and multiply with the fertilizer of compound interest?

Taxes, of course.

When your money market fund produces its annual yield of 7 percent to 12 percent, that is before taxes. How much is left depends on your marginal tax bracket and whether your state also taxes income. If you are married and filing jointly, and your taxable income ranges from $37,980 to $49,420, you are in the 33 percent marginal tax bracket for 1986. The exemptions and bracket limits are indexed for inflation, so it is likely that both exemptions and bracket limits will increase for 1987 and beyond.

When two income earners pour cash into one annual total, the taxable amount reaches into the upper tax brackets fairly quickly. This means that more of your income flows to the tax collectors. Let us say your money market fund returns an even 10 percent, a nice round number that is easy to use. After deducting 33 percent from the 10 percent yield and another estimated 7 percent for state income taxes, your after-tax or spendable income from the 10 percent yield drops to 6 percent. If inflation continues at recent moderate levels, it might be 4 percent for the year. Thus, the money you invested in a money market fund or other secure opportunity would have lost 4 percent of its ability to buy goods and services. You therefore lose another 4 percent. Now your 10 percent before-tax yield has dwindled to 2 percent in after-tax and after-inflation equivalent value.

The goal of most financial planners is to earn enough on assets to pay taxes and allow for inflation—plus a little bit. Such a goal can be difficult when both interest rates and inflation are high. Interest rates combine a cost for renting money, traditionally 2½ percent to 3 percent, plus an inflation premium. Lenders protect themselves from a loss of purchasing power by charging enough interest to compensate for the effects of inflation. Thus, if inflation is 13 percent and interest rates are 20 percent, as they were in 1981, your equation would look something like this: Federal and state income taxes totaling 40 percent as in the previous example would reduce the before-tax 20 percent to 12 percent. If inflation comes in at 13 percent, your real rate of return drops to a negative 1 percent. Investing within an IRA or a Keogh plan defers the tax on the earnings from your assets and compounds them at tax-free rates.

Here is a briefing on the special conditions and regulations affecting IRA and Keogh plan investment programs. While these two retirement-oriented, tax-deferred programs are similar, there are differences. The following applies to both except where differences are noted.

WHAT ARE IRAS AND KEOGHS?

An Individual Retirement Account (IRA) and a Keogh plan, also known as the HR-10 plan (Eugene Keogh was the congressman who originated it), are tax-deferred savings programs to help individuals set aside money and build an asset base. Income from an asset base can supplement Social Security benefits and possibly a pension after one retires. Payments into an IRA or a Keogh are deductible from income reported each year; that is, your contributions to an IRA or a Keogh are before-tax dollars. This point is critical. You reduce your taxes for each year that you set aside funds to be invested in either plan.

WHO IS ELIGIBLE?

Anyone who earns income from personal services may set up a personal IRA. You may be a participant in a company or public organization pension plan or profit-sharing plan. This does not present a problem; you can still set up a personal IRA. You may be self-employed and have a Keogh plan. There is still no problem; you can still set up a personal IRA. In other words, if you are self-employed, you can contribute to both a Keogh plan and an IRA. You may be employed by a public or nonprofit organization with the opportunity to have a portion of your earnings withheld for inclusion in a tax-sheltered annuity (TSA). No problem; you can still set up a personal IRA.

Personal income is defined as wages, salaries, tips, professional fees, bonuses, and other compensation for providing personal services. Commissions and self-employment income also qualify for inclusion within an IRA. Partnership income may be included within an IRA if you are an active partner and provide personal services. However, if you invest in a partnership but do not provide services, then the partnership income does not qualify for an IRA. Any passive income, such as dividends, rent, and interest, does not count since these sources do not represent income from personal services.

Each year you may contribute any amount up to $2,000. You may contribute this total even if you earn only $2,000 for the year; that is, you can put 100 percent of your earnings into your IRA as long as you earn only $2,000 for the year. But you don't have to put the full $2,000 in each year, and you don't have to put it in all at once. Further, you may establish as many separate IRAs as you wish, although an excessive number of IRAs may be difficult to monitor and manage. You may wish to split your IRA eligibility ($2,000 per year) among three or four different IRAs as a means of diversifying your retirement investment program.

If you are married and your wife does not work outside the home and thus earns no income, you may establish a spousal IRA and contribute a total of $2,250 each year to both your personal and your spousal IRAs. You are permitted to split the $2,250 annual contribution any way you wish as long as not more than $2,000 goes into either IRA. You can, for example, split the $2,250 evenly and put $1,125 in your IRA and $1,125 in your spouse's. Or you may put $250 in yours and $2,000 in your spouse's IRA—or vice versa. IRA accounts must be kept separate to qualify for the full $2,250. You must also file a joint return and take the full amount contributed during the year as a deduction from the joint return. You cannot roll over funds accumulated in your personal IRA into a spousal IRA. You may not continue to contribute to an IRA after you reach age 70½.

Rollover IRAs are different from contribution IRAs. The law permits you to roll over a lump sum received from a qualified pension or profit-sharing plan into a separate rollover IRA. Once you have rolled over the lump sum, all of the income from the assets in the rollover IRA continues to be tax deferred until cash is withdrawn. You must roll over the lump sum into an IRA within 60 days after receiving the distribution. If you were eligible for 10-year averaging when the lump sum was distributed, you lose that option forever when you roll over the pension or profit-sharing distribution into an IRA. Once in an IRA the funds are controlled by the same rules that apply to a contribution IRA. Any amount may be rolled over from a lump sum distribution into a rollover IRA; the $2,000 per year limit that applies to the contribution IRA does not affect rollovers.

Contributions to a Keogh plan by a self-employed person were limited to 15 percent of earnings up to a maximum of $15,000 per year for tax years before 1984. Beginning in 1984, the limits increased to 20 percent of earned income up to a maximum of $30,000 per year. This change was a part of the 1982 tax act and states that the limit is 25 percent of earned income but only after the deduction for the Keogh contribution. Thus, the 20 percent is the effective number for income before the Keogh contribution. For small incomes, the first $750 earned may all be contributed each year as long as the adjusted gross income, including income earned by working for someone else, does not exceed $15,000 for the year. This calculation of adjusted gross income is for each person, however, and is not the total for a couple. A husband might have an earned income of $50,000 and his wife a self-employment income of $5,000 with no other income. She could contribute

$750 of the $5,000 self-employment earnings to her own Keogh plan, and she could contribute another $2,000 to her own IRA.

IRA OPERATIONS

You must establish your IRA or Keogh plan as a trust. Banks, S&Ls, insurance companies, and mutual funds offer plans that comply with IRS regulations.

Self-directed IRAs and Keoghs are also available. These are mainly custodial accounts. An acceptable (to the IRS) trustee takes in your contributions and keeps control of your assets and their earnings, but you make any investment decisions. You may no longer hold gold or silver bullion, coins, or collectibles of any kind in an IRA or a Keogh.

Since this book deals mainly with mutual funds, the possibilities of investing your tax-deferred contributions in an insurance annuity or in individual stocks and bonds through a self-directed IRA or Keogh will not be considered further. Neither will the opportunity to invest in certificates of deposit at your bank, savings and loan association, or credit union be considered. The reasons for selecting mutual funds over fixed-income securities available through banks and similar institutions were considered earlier in chapter 1.

The mechanics of investing your IRA or Keogh funds with a mutual fund are quite simple. You merely request an application for an IRA from the fund of your choice, as detailed in chapter 9. When you receive the IRA or Keogh application, merely fill in the blanks and write a check for the amount you wish to contribute for starters, recognizing any minimum amounts set by the mutual fund. Then send off your application and check to the fund or custodian bank according to the instructions.

Different rules apply for setting up an IRA than for a Keogh. If you have already established either, you may contribute your current year's funds any time prior to filing your income tax return for the year; for example, if you file your income tax return with the IRS for income earned in 1986 on April 15, 1987, you may contribute to your 1986 IRA on the same date or, preferably, the day before. These are contributions to continuing IRAs or Keoghs.

If you are establishing an IRA for the first time, you have until April 15 of the year following the year when earnings were received to establish the IRA. Some investors initiate a new IRA each year as a means of diversifying their retirement investment portfolio.

If you plan to start a Keogh plan, you must set it up before the end of the year during which you earned self-employment income. You may make additional contributions into the new Keogh fund any time up to the time you file your income tax return—including extensions. This rule is different from the one that controls IRAs.

Funding your IRA or Keogh as early in the taxable year as possible will improve the overall performance because the money in the IRA or Keogh earns tax-deferred income up to 15 months longer. You can invest money in your IRA or Keogh on January 1 (actually the second since the first is a holiday) of each year. You don't have to have earned the money before you can invest it. Transferring the full $2,000 for the year into your IRA from a savings or money fund account on January 2 of the taxable year accomplishes two desirable actions:

1. You remove cash from a taxable cash accumulation account, thus reducing your taxes on income from those assets.

2. You start the income ball rolling toward more tax-deferred income within your IRA.

How much does early investing help in building your bag of assets? Table 6A shows one example of the differences between early and last-ditch funding. Contributions of $2,000 to one IRA are deposited at the first of Year No. 1. A second contribution of $2,000 is deposited at the beginning of Year No. 2. By the time the contribution to the second IRA is deposited at the beginning of April in Year No. 2, 15 months after the initial deposit in the first IRA, the first IRA has grown to $4,664. The first IRA has $4,000 of deposits compared to the second IRA with $2,000. If you deduct the second $2,000 to create $2,000 in each, the first IRA is still ahead by $664. At the end of 25 years, the difference is $338,760, after allowing for the $2,000 difference in deposits. That amounts to a 28 percent greater asset accumulation—further testimony to the power of

Table 6A. Effect of IRA investment on January 2 vs. investment on April 1 of following year. Earnings at 20 percent per year.

Year/Month	Annual Amount	Start Balance	Earnings 1.666% / Month	Annual Deposit	Start Balance	Earnings 1.666% / Month
1 1	$2,000	$2,000	$33			
2		$2,033	$34			
3		$2,067	$34			
4		$2,102	$35			
5		$2,137	$36			
6		$2,172	$36			
7		$2,208	$37			
8		$2,245	$37			
9		$2,283	$38			
10		$2,321	$39			
11		$2,359	$39			
12		$2,399	$40			
2 1	$2,000	$4,439	$74			
2		$4,513	$75			
3		$4,588	$76			
4		$4,664	$78	$2,000	$2,000	$33
5		$4,742	$79		$2,033	$34
		$4,821	$80		$2,067	$34
		$4,901	$82		$2,102	$35
		$4,983	$83		$2,137	$36
		$5,066	$84		$2,172	$36
		$5,150	$86		$2,208	$37
		$5,236	$87		$2,245	$37
		$5,323	$89		$2,283	$38
	$2,000	$7,412	$123		$2,321	$39
		$7,535	$126		$2,359	$39
		$7,661	$128		$2,399	$40
		$7,789	$130	$2,000	$4,439	$74
		$7,918	$132		$4,513	$75
		$8,050	$134		$4,588	$76

Year/Month	Annual Amount	Start Balance	Earnings 1.666% / Month	Annual Deposit	Start Balance	Earnings 1.666% / Month
		$1,243,452	$20,716		$968,653	$16,138
		$1,264,168	$21,061		$984,791	$16,407
25 1	$2,000	$1,287,229	$21,445		$1,001,197	$16,680
2		$1,308,674	$21,803		$1,017,877	$16,958
3		$1,330,477	$22,166		$1,034,835	$17,240
4		$1,352,643	$22,535	$2,000	$1,054,076	$17,561
5		$1,375,178	$22,910		$1,071,636	$17,853
6		$1,398,088	$23,292		$1,089,490	$18,151
7		$1,421,380	$23,680		$1,107,641	$18,453
8		$1,445,060	$24,075		$1,126,094	$18,761
9		$1,469,135	$24,476		$1,144,855	$19,073
10		$1,493,611	$24,884		$1,163,928	$19,391
11		$1,518,495	$25,298		$1,183,319	$19,714
12		$1,543,793	$25,720		$1,203,033	$20,043

compound interest. In both cases, a 20 percent annual yield compounded monthly is assumed.

You may not know how much you can contribute to your Keogh fund until your accounting is complete at year's end, but you may estimate annual earnings and deposit a portion of your expected earnings early in the year. Later you can put the final amount into the fund when you know your total earnings for the year.

ADVANTAGES OF TAX-DEFERRED INVESTING

Tax deferral of investment gains in an IRA or a Keogh can help you enjoy a better life-style in retirement. Both IRA and Keogh programs were designed by Congress to encourage savings that would supplement Social Security benefits and pensions after retirement. To discourage any early withdrawals, the laws specify two penalties:

1. The first penalty is an excise tax of 10 percent on any funds withdrawn from either an IRA or a Keogh plan before the owner has reached age $59\frac{1}{2}$, except in the case of death or disability. (For more information on disability, consult IRS Publication 522, "Disability Payments," available free from IRS offices.) The 10 percent penalty applies to partial and complete withdrawals. Thus, if your IRA had built itself to $100,000 and you withdrew $10,000 at age 50, your penalty would be 10 percent, or $1,000, payable along with your income tax payment for the year of withdrawal. The excise tax would increase to 15 percent in proposed tax reform legislation.

2. The second penalty calls for all of the premature withdrawal, before the assessment of the excise tax, to be added to your other gross income for the year in which you withdrew the money. This added cash will then be taxed at your marginal rate.

Despite the two penalties, you can get at the cash if you need it in an emergency. Prohibited transactions include the following actions:

1. You cannot use the funds in your IRA or Keogh as collateral for a loan. That action triggers the same penalties as a premature withdrawal.

2. You cannot borrow directly from IRA or Keogh funds. Any money borrowed is penalized as a premature withdrawal.

3. You may not sell property to the IRA or Keogh trust. Ordinarily, contributions to either an IRA or a Keogh are in cash, but in-kind contributions may be acceptable in rollovers.

WITHDRAWING IRA OR KEOGH CASH

Withdrawals from your IRA or Keogh account(s) without penalty may begin after age 59½. You must begin withdrawing

Table 6B. Life expectancy at age 70½ for men and women plus joint life expectancies when one spouse is 70½ and other spouse is younger or older. Source: IRS Publication 590.

```
        Owner of Individual Retirement
                Arrangement              Multiple

            Female                        15.0
            Male                          12.1

        Two Lives--Joint Life and Last Survivor
                Expected Return Multiples
```

Owner of IRA	Age of Spouse (*)						
	61	62	63	64	65	66	67
Female Mult.	21.63	21.1	20.7	20.3	19.9	19.6	19.2
Male Mult.	23.0	22.4	21.8	21.2	20.7	20.2	19.7

Owner of IRA	Age of Spouse (*)						
	68	69	70	71	72	73	74
Female Mult.	18.9	18.6	18.3	18.0	17.8	17.5	17.3
Male Mult.	19.2	18.7	18.3	17.9	17.5	17.1	16.7

Owner of IRA	Age of Spouse						
	75	76	77	78	79	80	81
Female Mult.	17.1	16.9	16.7	16.6	16.4	16.3	16.2
Male Mult.	16.7	16.1	15.8	15.5	15.2	14.7	14.7

Owner of IRA	Of Spouse (*)			
	82	83	84	85
Female Mult.	16.0	15.9	15.8	15.8
Male Mult.	14.5	14.3	14.1	13.9

```
        * In year owner became 70 1/2
```

the assets by April 15 of the year following the year in which you reach age 70½, and you must withdraw the full amount within your expected life span or the expected joint life span of you and your spouse, a child, grandchild, or another, unrelated person. The IRS publishes the life expectancy of men, women and married couples with varying combinations of ages. Table 6B reproduces the table of life expectancies from IRS Publication 590, "Tax Information on Individual Retirement Arrangements."

Note in table 6B that a male at age 70½ is expected to live another 12.1 years, according to the IRS, and a female will live another 15 years on average. The joint life expectancy of a married couple where both are 70½ extends to about 18 years; that is, one or the other, but not necessarily both, will likely live 18 plus years.

Life expectancies noted in table 6B are important in your planning because they control how you liquidate your IRA. With an IRA you can pull out all of the funds in a lump sum during any year after age 59½ without penalty. Any funds withdrawn must be added to your gross income for the year for tax computations. However, withdrawing all funds from an IRA within one tax year could produce a spike in the tax bill during that year for most people. As noted earlier, favorable 10-year averaging is not available to withdrawals from IRAs, but ordinary income averaging can spread the tax load over four years. The Tax Reform Act of 1984 changed the rules for averaging and makes it harder to benefit from income averaging because the former 120 percent level is now 140 percent, and the base period is now three years rather than the previous four.

Your income planning for the years between 59½ and full retirement will affect the schedule for IRA withdrawals. If you continue to work until age 65, for example, you might prefer to keep the funds within your IRA compounding tax free to build a bigger asset base from which you can withdraw later. You need to program your Social Security benefits into your overall financial plan. You may begin receiving SS benefits at age 62, although they will be reduced by 20 percent compared to the level of benefits you would have received if you were 65. Obviously, your job and how you feel about working will affect your retirement schedule and your withdrawal of IRA funds. But the longer you can leave your IRA funds alone, the more they will continue to build resources you can use for a better lifestyle in retirement.

If you decide to hold off on withdrawals until age 70½, the law requires you to begin taking out the cash at a rate that will deplete the account within your life expectancy or the life expectancy of you and your spouse as noted earlier. But look what happens if you elect the dual life expectancy period. You can expect the balance in your IRA account to be higher at age 71½ than it was at 70½. For minimum withdrawals acceptable to the IRS, the life expectancy period is used as a divisor and the divisor is reduced by one for each passing year. An example will help to explain the process:

Suppose you elect the dual expectancy rate of 18 years (both spouses age 70½). Further, your IRA account is $100,000 at the beginning of the withdrawal period—no later than April 15 following the end of the calendar year in which you reach age 70½. For the first year you divide $100,000 by 18, the divisor for dual life expectancy. Each of the numbers indicating acceptable life expectancy becomes the initial divisor for withdrawals.

Table 6C. Minimum withdrawal amounts from IRA after age 70½ assuming 12 percent earnings on remaining balances (12.1 years is life expectancy for male at age 70½).

Year No.	Begin Balance	Minimum Withdrawal	Remaining Balance	12% Earnings	End Year Balance
1	100,000	8,264	91,736	11,008	102,744
2	102,744	9,256	93,488	11,219	104,706
3	104,706	10,367	94,339	11,321	105,660
4	105,660	11,611	94,049	11,286	105,335
5	105,335	13,004	92,330	11,080	103,410
6	103,410	14,565	88,845	10,661	99,507
7	99,507	16,313	83,194	9,983	93,177
8	93,177	18,270	74,907	8,989	83,896
9	83,896	20,463	63,434	7,612	71,046
10	71,046	22,918	48,128	5,775	53,903
11	53,903	25,668	28,235	3,388	31,623
12	31,623	28,748	2,875	345	3,220
13	3,220	3,228			

It works like this: By the end of the year in which you reach age 70½ (or April 1 of the following year if you choose), you withdraw $5,555.55 or one-eighteenth of $100,000. During the following year, if your assets grow at an annual rate of 12 percent, your $94,444.45 would grow to $105,777.78. By the end of the second year, you withdraw one-seventeenth of the asset base that is now $105,777.78, or $6,222.22, leaving $99,555.56. That asset base then grows another 12 percent during the third year to a total of $111,502.22. Withdraw one-sixteenth or $6,968.89, and you still have $104,613.33—more than your original asset base because you are withdrawing less than the earning capacity of the assets. These are minimum withdrawals.

Table 6C shows the minimum withdrawals for an asset base of $100,000 over a 12.1-year minimum period. Table 6D shows a minimum withdrawal schedule for an 18.3 joint life expectancy. You will see that the asset base remains relatively high when your yield is higher than early withdrawal amounts, as diagramed in figure 6-1. As the divisor becomes smaller each year, however, a larger and larger amount must be withdrawn

Table 6D. Minimum withdrawal amounts from IRA after age 70½ with joint life expectancy of 18.3—man and wife both same age, assuming 12 percent earnings on remaining balances.

Year No.	Begin Balance	Minimum Withdrawal	Remaining Balance	12% Earnings	End Year Balance
1	100,000	5,464	94,536	11,344	105,880
2	105,880	6,120	99,760	11,971	111,731
3	111,731	6,855	104,876	12,585	117,461
4	117,461	7,677	109,784	13,174	122,958
5	122,958	8,598	114,360	13,723	128,083
6	128,083	9,630	118,452	14,214	132,667
7	132,667	10,786	121,881	14,626	136,507
8	136,507	12,080	124,426	14,931	139,357
9	139,357	13,530	125,828	15,099	140,927
10	140,927	15,153	125,774	15,093	140,866
11	140,866	16,972	123,894	14,867	138,762
12	138,762	19,008	119,753	14,370	134,124
13	134,124	21,289	112,834	13,540	126,374
14	126,374	23,844	102,530	12,304	114,834
15	114,834	26,706	88,128	10,575	98,704
16	98,704	29,910	68,793	8,255	77,049
17	77,049	33,499	43,549	5,226	48,775
18	48,775	37,519	11,256	1,351	12,607
19	12,607	12,607			

to stay within penalty-free limits until all the remaining funds are withdrawn during the last year.

The 1984 tax bill liberalized the withdrawal plan to prevent retirees from running out of IRA or Keogh money before their deaths. Even though mortality tables might indicate that the male at age 70½ has 12.1 years remaining on average, few men die strictly on schedule. Under the old rules if a male withdrew all of his IRA or Keogh assets over the 12.1 years as required and was still living, he would be out of cash from that source. If that happened to be his only source of income for retirement, he could end up destitute.

To correct this possibility and to recognize the increasing life spans of both men and women, the tax law now permits you to refigure the minimum withdrawal amounts each year. This al-

Fig. 6-1. Comparison of balances in an IRA between withdrawals at 12.1 years and 18.3 years assuming 12 percent earnings on remaining balances. Note that balances continue to increase after withdrawals begin as earnings exceed withdrawals in early years.

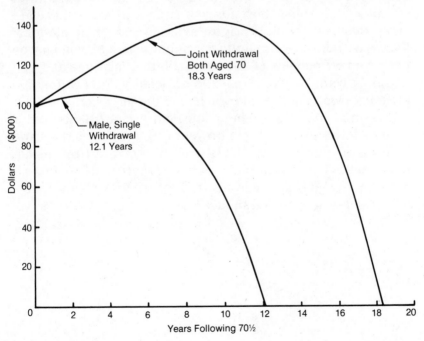

lowance recognizes that the longer a person lives, the longer he or she is likely to live. For example, a man age 45 can look forward to another 34.9 years, according to one mortality table. This means he would live to age 79.9. But if he lives to age 70, he can look forward to another 12 years and live to 82, on average. Under the new rules a man using only his own average life expectancy would begin withdrawing no later than 70½ on a schedule covering 12.1 years. After one or more years he can refigure his life expectancy and use the new rates for minimum withdrawals. Under this new plan he would retain assets in his IRA or Keogh account until death rather than over his expected life span. The IRS has not issued regulations covering this liberalized plan at this writing. They will be published in a future revision of IRS Publication 590, available free from IRS offices.

If you should elect to withdraw more or less than the minimum during any one year, you need to keep track of total withdrawals to avoid the 50 percent penalty. Total withdrawals must equal the total amounts you would have withdrawn over the years if you had adhered to the minimum withdrawal schedule as detailed above for your situation. You will need to make this calculation yearly to avoid excess accumulations. Unless withdrawals equal the minimum schedule, you may be penalized 50 percent of the undistributed amount, and you certainly want to avoid this kind of penalty. Publication 590 includes a worksheet to aid you in making this calculation.

If you and your spouse should die before your IRA account is depleted, the assets will go into your estate, and the rules and regulations that control the distribution of the IRA are detailed in IRS Publication 448, "Federal Estate and Gift Taxes." Your state's regulations may also affect withdrawals and assets left in an estate, and you should investigate state tax laws.

7

Seven-Step Guide to Successful Mutual Fund Switching

Successful investing with market timing in combination with no-load mutual funds will not likely turn you on emotionally. Neither will it offer suitable ear-twitching tidbits of conversation or a succession of "thrill of victory" reports to enable you to attract attention at cocktail parties.

Mutual fund switching is, in a word, dull. If you engage in stock market activities, trading options or commodities, and look for action in every issue of the *Wall Street Journal,* then investing in mutual funds and switching your money from fund to fund on the infrequent signals you or your advisor supplies may not be for you. All you can expect from a program of mutual fund switching are positive results, sleep-easy risks, and little excitement. No market timer can guarantee profits, of course, but you play the game with better odds on your side.

You should understand at the outset that people "play the market" for a variety of reasons. Some fast-track investors like the challenge of going one-on-one with their brokers or competing with their friends. They enjoy the day-to-day mental stimulation of trying to outguess the market, as if the market were some all-knowing individual with a mind of its own. They rise to the lure of trying to outfox the so-called experts. These investors get their jollies from occasional triumphs and may gain mental stimulation from the camaraderie of sharing their "agonies of defeat" with other players.

Many investors are in the market because they think it is the thing to do. After all, "everybody's doing it." They would feel left out if they were not participants. These players may not be into the market deeply enough to understand what is going on. They depend on their brokers and moan when things don't go their way; in fact, many accept reversals almost as if they deserve to lose. None of these players will likely accept the unexciting, strictly disciplined program for market timing with mutual funds. This program differs from some or all of the above for one all-absorbing reason: Market timing with no-load mutual funds makes money! Lots of money.

You have already studied the performance records or analytical simulations of market timers who have been active for 10, 12, 14 or more years. But you must recognize that to achieve the almost unbelievable results noted in chapter 3 you must use a disciplined approach. Discipline is the key.

Here are the seven basic steps you can follow to play this dull, unexciting program that yields excitement at one important location—in your pocket. Market timing with mutual funds produces positive results—more money than you ever thought reasonable from investing in the stock market or mutual funds.

STEP NO. 1: DEFINE YOUR OBJECTIVES

Just because you have been reading about the "hottest fund of the year" or mentally calculating your profits after reading an ad for a mutual fund that outperformed the Dow by 200 percent last year doesn't mean that some highly visible fund is best for you. No market timer can guarantee success, particularly on a short-term basis. Even if you should be "out" of equities during a market downturn and "in" a money market fund earning a reasonable interest, waiting can try your patience. Or you may be disenchanted with your market timer because he missed a couple of minor moves in the market. A market timer working with an aggressive mutual fund may have been whipsawed by short-term market moves that departed from the trend briefly. A market timer working with a conservative equity fund would likely have weathered slight moves.

Or you might have suffered an actual loss, even with market timing. For example, from July 31, 1983, through August 1, 1984, 44 Wall Street Fund declined 58 percent. After a 58 percent decline, remaining assets would have to gain 138 percent to reach their original value. But with PM&A market timing, the client's position declined only 9 percent. Although market timing protected the client from a major loss, the client's position was still down. Losses can occur with market timing, but the difference between a 9 percent loss and a 58 percent loss is monumental, and a 58 percent loss in a buy-and-hold program can be very painful.

With a conservative outlook, timing can produce benefits, as in the Value Line Income Fund over the same period, July 31, 1983, through August 1, 1984. With PM&A timing, the client's position was up about 5 percent. If he had bought and held the position, he would have been down about 13 percent. These results can be compared directly with the results from the aggressive 44 Wall Street Fund above. During the same period a person could have ended up with a gain instead of a loss by using market timing depending on volatility. A conservative fund, such as the Value Line Income Fund, could grow by 30 percent to 40 percent in a strong upward market, but during the same period a volatile growth fund, such as 44 Wall Street Fund, might show gains ranging from 100 percent to 200 percent.

Unless you can look at the long term, you may very well do better in money market funds rather than attempting to dabble in stocks or stock-growth mutual funds. But market timing allows a wider choice for the knowing investor and lower risks overall.

If you are new to market timing, these two examples may help you appreciate the differences between aggressive and conservative funds. You should try to fit your investment objectives to a mutual fund category and use market timing techniques to improve the performance of any fund within that category rather than a buy-and-hold program. Equity mutual funds range in their objectives from aggressive growth to growth, to conservative growth, to income. Fixed-rate income funds invest mainly in bonds. Gold funds form a special group of volatile growth (even speculative) funds. You might consider the gold funds as one form of sector funds—those that focus on specific industries. You should probably consider the gold funds separately from the many equity growth funds because they respond to a different set of market conditions and may move in an opposite direction during some periods and in the same direction in other periods. They, in effect, "march to the beat of a different drummer." If you should elect to move into both general equity growth funds and gold funds, plan to use different indicators to track their position and movements.

Five groups of funds provide opportunities for investors with varying long-term objectives:

Aggressive growth funds (equities) may have one or several of the following characteristics: They aim primarily for capital gains. They invest aggressively in speculative stocks, possibly including the stocks of very small growth companies without much of a track record. Some aggressive fund managers hope to buy into emerging growth companies before they are discovered, when the prices of their shares are cheap. It's called "getting in on the ground floor." Many of the new and emerging companies are thinly capitalized; that is, the founders may keep most of the new shares for themselves and make only a limited number of shares available to the public for trading. Rumors or discouraging reports can play havoc with the prices of a stock when only a relatively few shares trade regularly. While aggressive growth funds tend to do well in up markets when euphoria abounds, they tend to do poorly in down markets; they can go up fast and drop just as fast. One of the reasons for the rapid action is the leverage of some aggressive growth funds. They may borrow in order to buy more shares and thus expand their potential, but just as an upbeat market can prove profitable when buying stocks on margin, a down market can prove disastrous. So it is also with funds that leverage their positions. Some funds may use options either to improve their performance, in the case of an aggressive growth fund, or to increase yield, in the case of an income-oriented fund.

Growth funds are less aggressive than the aggressive growth funds because they tend to invest in companies farther up the growth curve, with a longer track record and with proved management that has positioned the companies in viable markets. They offer growth but are less volatile than the aggressive growth funds that typically go all-out for rapid expansion.

Conservative growth funds primarily emphasize long-term growth and are typically less volatile than either aggressive growth funds or growth funds. Conservative growth funds tend to invest in high-quality, innovative companies with recognized long-term records of steady if not sensational growth. You will recognize IBM, 3M, and General Electric as companies whose stocks show up in conservative growth funds.

You may also get a clue from the size of funds. A billion-dollar fund must invest in major, heavily capitalized companies because it would run out of companies if its charter limits it to owning no more than 5 percent of the stock in any one company. The securities of large growth companies enjoy a wide stock base with substantial liquidity in a downward trending market. These companies and the funds that invest in them do not exhibit the volatility of aggressive growth funds. Funds with much smaller assets enjoy more flexibility and freedom in buying and selling shares, and can invest in smaller, more volatile companies. Large funds with their large block trades would upset prices of shares in thinly capitalized companies.

Growth-income funds (equities) focus their emphasis on a combination of long-term growth and income, and are less volatile than any of the growth funds. In many ways this group has produced the finest risk-adjusted return over time of any fund group. This total performance results from the basic dividends underlying the value of the securities among the funds' portfolios. In declining markets the funds' shares decline less rapidly because of the income floor created by the dividends. On a very long-term basis, market timing of growth-income mutual funds may not produce more than 2 percent or 3 percent plus fees over a buy-and-hold program. It is still important, however, for investors to stay out of major bear markets.

Even these conservative growth-income funds were down as much as 30 percent to 40 percent during the major bear market of 1973–74. Value Line Income Fund, for example, was down 15 percent in 1973 and 16 percent in 1974. Models of PM&A market timing backtested for that period show small gains in each of the two years.

Fixed income funds (bonds) are typically composed of government or corporate intermediate or long-term bonds. Some fixed-income funds are comprised entirely of intermediate- to long-term tax-exempt municipal bonds. Although bond prices fluctuate, their volatility is generally much lower than stocks. Even so, market timing can be used profitably with taxable or tax-exempt bond funds. The marginal or additional return on bond funds with market timing based on a risk-adjusted basis can be phenomenal. Your selection of taxable or tax-exempt bonds will depend on whether you are investing for a qualified plan, such as an IRA or a Keogh, and your marginal income tax bracket. If you are extremely conservative and do not wish to expose your investment to the risks of equities and are in the 20 percent to 30 percent marginal tax bracket, corporate bonds would likely produce a slightly better return than tax-exempt bonds after taxes.

Using market timing techniques in combination with no-load mutual funds holding long-term, very conservative corporate or U.S. Treasury bonds will likely produce far better financial results than buying and holding the bonds themselves or simply putting the money into money market funds. While there is a bit more risk in investing in bond funds rather than in money market funds, even with timing, returns should range from 3 percent to 5 percent greater than money market funds on average. Market timing helps to avoid the long-term risks in holding bonds or funds that invest in bonds due to interest rate cycles. Bond prices correlate inversely with interest rates—rising as interest rates decline and dropping as interest rates rise. Since interest rates tend to cycle up and down over long periods, market timing can easily recognize trend reversals and increase yields without significantly increasing risks. Without market timing during 1978 to 1981, investors saw bond prices decline three years in a row. Conservative investors in retirement could see their pool of funds decline over several years unless market timing got them out of the funds shortly after the decline began.

There is little difference between the trends of taxable and tax-exempt bond funds. There is one difference, however, that can affect comparable yields: When tax-exempt bond funds begin a downward trend and market timing indicators call for switching into money funds, you must choose between switching into a regular money market fund and paying taxes on the income or switching into a tax-exempt money fund and earning a lower yield. Technical differences plus their tax-free status account for the substantial gap in yields between regular and tax-exempt money market funds.

Many buyers of tax-exempt bonds plan to hold them to maturity regardless of what happens to interest rates in the interim. If they can lock themselves into a 12 percent or 13 percent return on tax-exempts by buying bonds during periods of high interest, they will not normally liquidate their holdings during periods of lower interest even though their bonds have appreciated in value. Their answer to the question "Why not sell?" is: "How would I invest the money if I sold?" They may not want to accept the risk of selling and not being able to get back into tax-exempts with those high yields. Market timing holds little appeal to this sizable group of investors.

Gold funds hold stocks of companies involved primarily in the mining and refining of gold. This fund group has been more volatile than most common stock funds. Some precious metal funds may hold stocks of companies that mine and refine silver, platinum, and similar exotic metals anywhere in the world, including South Africa. Many of the stocks held by the gold or precious metal funds are thinly capitalized, and they are susceptible to the sometimes large fluctuations in the prices of gold, silver, and other metals. Since the price swings of precious metal funds are wide and frequent, a buy-and-hold approach is far more dangerous with these funds than with other aggressive growth funds. But if an investor elects to take higher risks, the volatility of gold funds adapts beautifully to market timing.

A number of advertisements appeared about the time the

first edition of this book was being written, asking, "Has your fund gone up 500 percent in the last five years?" If you had invested $10,000 in 1979, it would have been worth about $60,000 by the end of 1983 for a 43 percent rate of growth. Five years earlier the same fund would have had to ask, "Did your mutual fund lose 62 percent over the past five years?" If you had invested $10,000 in 1974, after five years the total value would have dropped to about $3,800. Investors forget that a 62 percent loss requires a 163 percent gain just to get back to even. Market timing could have avoided most of the capital loss by switching to a money fund—but not always. The returns on a buy-and-hold gold fund program are far less than with a market timed gold fund.

Sector funds, which include the group of gold and precious metal funds, have evolved over the past few years to concentrate investor interest in specific markets. Fidelity has been particularly active in developing sector funds that invest in financial institutions, health care, leisure, high technology, and the like. One of the benefits an investor gains from investing in mutual funds is instant diversification. Owning pieces of many companies through a mutual fund is a low-cost way to spread stock risk. Diversification through ownership of mutual fund shares attracts many risk-aversive and conservative investors. Sector funds move away from broad market diversification by concentrating investments in one area of the market. Narrow focusing tends to produce greater volatility and a varying response to market movements. While the overall market may be moving up smartly, one or more sector funds with investments in companies undergoing slow growth or actual declines may be moving in an opposite direction. Thus, general market timing indicators may not work with sector funds. We already know from many years of experience that gold funds do not usually move in concert with general market indicators. Special market timing indicators will be needed to protect investors in sector funds in the same way that special indicators are used in market timing gold funds.

Which Type of Fund for You?

Investing in an aggressive growth fund can be unsettling if you haven't been through enough markets to understand the cyclical nature of prices, trends, and market mentality. Many new investors watching a stock or an aggressive fund drop in price come to believe there is no bottom. They may be scared away from a stock or fund holding just at the wrong time. Clients who see only problems and are not comfortable with any sort of decline should avoid aggressive growth funds. While all mutual funds move up and down on a highly irregular schedule, the aggressive growth funds move in both directions with startling rapidity in certain markets.

Most investors tend to grow more conservative with age, and with good reason. With fewer income-producing years ahead, oldsters wish to conserve as much as possible of what they have accumulated and avoid the risk of losing wealth. Particularly in retirement, loss of capital can be devastating because one is not working to replace the loss. Older investors who wish to earn a fair return with minimum risk should generally avoid the volatile aggressive growth funds.

Younger investors with 30 to 40 years of inflation ahead can afford to take greater risks and, it is hoped, gain a greater return that can compound faster than inflation and taxes. Young investors are frequently told that they cannot afford *not* to take risks. Sticking only with secure minimal-return investments, such as certificates of deposit or Treasury bills, can lead to a negative real rate of return. So-called riskless investment vehicles can lead to guaranteed losses when the gross return fails to compensate for inflation and taxes. Only by assuming more risk, as in aggressive growth funds, is there a chance to avoid the negative real rate of return or guaranteed loss.

Younger clients also tend to be more upbeat and confident. If an aggressive growth fund dips temporarily, they accept the decline because they are confident of a recovery later that will more than compensate for the decline. They know that with market timing they can avoid most of the decline and participate in most of the up moves. Instead of accepting the higher risks they believe are necessary to avoid a negative real rate of return, young, aggressive investors can, with market timing, gain the higher returns they seek while avoiding most of the risks. This is the best of both worlds.

Investment objectives can fit specific groups of mutual funds generally along the following lines: Older, risk-aversive clients can pick growth-income or fixed-income mutual funds along with market timing to improve performance. Younger clients may select aggressive growth funds along with market timing to protect them from disastrous losses. Middle-age clients can get the best combination of growth and compounded income from growth or conservative growth mutual funds, or they can diversify and participate in a variety of mutual funds to gain some degree of risk diversification.

Financial planners faced with the problem of structuring clients' portfolios would likely diversify their holdings according to age, income, and their unique objectives. A 30-year-old client who has at least 30 years to retirement might be advised to keep 10 percent of investable funds in gold funds, 20 percent in bonds, and 70 percent in equities. Perhaps most of the 70 percent allocated for equities can be in very aggressive equities. As people get older, the gold position might remain the same, but the percentages in bonds may increase and the percentage in equities would not only decline but the makeup would become more conservative. Each of the three groups—gold, bond, and equity funds—can be programmed according to age and specific financial objectives to yield far more than a similar program structured for a buy-and-hold approach. One of the areas where market timing is largely ineffective, however, is in real estate. Many aggressive investors become involved directly in income-producing real estate or in limited partnerships that invest in real estate. There is at present little opportunity for market timing of real estate because of its limited liquidity and switching potential.

STEP NO. 2: CHOOSE YOUR FUNDS

Once you have defined your investment objectives and decided which group of funds will most likely meet those objectives, you should begin your search for specific funds within the group or groups. Appendix A lists most of the current no-load mutual funds that are amenable to switching by telephone. Be aware, however, that new funds are being developed regularly. When choosing one or several specific funds, you should resist the temptation to overstep your normal risk/

comfort level. No investment is worth losing sleep over. And while you may be sold on the performance of market timing with mutual funds, underlying risks remain. Prudence calls for starting with a reasonably conservative fund or funds and working with them through at least one up-and-down cycle to gain experience. If you understand and accept the risks and believe you can benefit from a more aggressive approach, then move cautiously toward higher risk and a higher potential profit. But begin conservatively.

Another totally acceptable approach, particularly for younger investors who want to get started on a more aggressive, long-term market timing program, is to diversify among three or possibly four mutual funds at the beginning. If you are in this group, you might pick three funds ranging from a highly aggressive fund, a growth fund, and a conservative growth fund—all set up for market timing. You might pick two different growth funds within one family and the money fund within that family. A third growth fund might be in another family, tying in with the money fund within that family.

You should also avoid the usual tendency of choosing a fund group with a great—even sensational—recent record. You will want to pick a fund family or group of funds with a record of at least five to 10 years of success. Look for a fund or fund family that has been through several bear and bull markets so that you can examine how they react to different conditions. By avoiding new funds you will likely avoid recent funds organized to exploit a current fad or highly publicized niche. Experience indicates that fad funds, whether in medical science, energy, ocean exploration, or other specialties, brought to market with a surge of publicity are unlikely to be profitable long-term holdings.

Several sources are available for studying the objectives and records of possible funds. The Donoghue Organization publishes an annual *Donoghue's Mutual Funds Almanac* that traces performance back 10 years for those funds that have existed that long. The almanac was formerly published by The Hirsch Organization, publisher of the *Stock Trader's Almanac*.

The Handbook for No-Load Mutual Fund Investors is another source of detailed information that is updated annually to provide historical performance data. The publisher also issues a monthly newsletter, *The No-Load Fund Investor*.

The Dow Jones-Irwin *Mutual Fund Yearbook* by William G. Droms contains detailed information on a large number of both load and no-load mutual funds. The information is gleaned from the prospectuses of the individual funds. Each fund's performance history in terms of net asset value is included with each write-up.

Directory—Your Guide to Mutual Funds is an annual publication of the No-Load Mutual Fund Association. It provides neatly organized data about funds that are members of the association but no performance data.

Information about these and other reference materials can be found in the bibliography.

STEP NO. 3: KNOW YOUR FUNDS

Just as you "can't buy the Dow," you can't buy an aggressive growth fund or a conservative growth-income fund. You must pick a specific mutual fund, one that will suit your financial objectives and cooperate with your plans to market time your investment. Once you have decided which objective to pursue, begin to narrow your choices by selecting a family of funds. You would not buy a house without inspecting every little detail about it, neither would you sign a contract committing you to payments for years to come without reading all of the small print. In the same way you should investigate your prospective fund family thoroughly. Here's how:

Examine the mutual fund listings in Appendix A; most of the major fund families are listed. You can use the information gleaned from the sources of performance data noted above to narrow your choice to perhaps half a dozen funds. If you plan to use a market timing adviser, ask for his or her advice. A market timer will generally work most closely with a limited number of funds, possibly no more than five to 10 fund families. Working with a limited number of funds simplifies the paperwork of switching when indicators signal a change.

When you have picked one or several funds, call or write for information. Most no-load funds offer a toll-free (800) number to attract inquiries, thereby saving you time and the inconvenience of writing a letter. Within a few days you will receive a packet of information that includes the required prospectus, an application blank, and various pieces of sales literature. Plan to spend a little time studying and comparing the information for the various funds you are considering.

Recognize that you will be switching from an equity, bond, or gold fund to a money market fund and vice versa from time to time. Therefore, you must pick a fund family that permits switching with little or no added expense. You might be charged a transaction fee of $5 or $10 to cover the cost of the paperwork involved in the switch. That would be acceptable. It might be all right to pay an 8½ percent load commission on interest accumulated during the time your investment was in a money market fund, but only if you prefer to stick with the load fund. Examine the sections of the prospectus headed "Shareholder Services," "Exchange Privilege," "How to Redeem Fund Shares," or some other similar section.

Prospectuses are not written in a style likely to keep you awake late into the night. New, written-in-English prospectuses are easier to understand than the former tomes written in high legalese by attorneys for attorneys. Dreyfus Growth Opportunity Fund offers one example of a new easy-to-read prospectus, and it includes the following under "Shareholder Services": "The Exchange Privilege enables you to purchase shares in any of the other funds in the Dreyfus Family of Funds. These funds have different investment objectives which may be of interest to you if you believe that a transfer between funds is an appropriate investment decision. Many shareholders value this Privilege as an important feature of the Dreyfus Family of Funds."

Since market timing calls for switching between an equity fund and a money market fund, for example, you should look for the equity fund first. All families of funds offer a money market fund, and they tend to operate similarly. The differences between money market fund yields are also minimal. Make sure the mechanics for switching are available at no cost or at a reasonable transaction fee.

You may be surprised to find that some funds are fairly tough on switching but only for telephone switching. The 44 Wall Street Fund charges ¼ of 1 percent of the withdrawal amount when you move money from it to a money market fund by telephone. If you order the move by letter, there is no added cost. Using an overnight letter service, such as Federal Express or the post office's Express Mail, would cost less than the ¼ of 1 percent charge for telephone switching. No fee is charged to move money from a money fund back to 44 Wall by telephone. Even if you use the telephone technique, the round-trip cost is ¼ of 1 percent, so each move figures to be ⅛ of 1 percent.

A number of mutual funds have different rules for IRA and Keogh accounts. The funds' managements figure IRA accounts are more apt to remain for longer terms, and they are willing to establish special rules to entice the very long-term investor. Fidelity presents a different situation. After four switches in any one year, Fidelity charges $50 for each switch. One switch is defined as a round trip. A move from equity to money market fund and then back from money fund to equity fund, for example, is one switch. Now, $50 might not be important for a $500,000 account, but for an IRA account of $5,000, that $50 amounts to a charge of 1 percent.

As you consider different funds, examine a fund's objective as stated in the prospectus and compare it with the size and makeup of its portfolio. You will find a listing of the stocks held in a fund's portfolio at the time the prospectus was prepared. The portfolio changes, sometimes often, and the most recent listing of stocks or other securities held may differ substantially from the listing in a portfolio. If the packet of information you receive from the fund includes a recent quarterly report, examine those securities listed rather than those in the prospectus. The stated objective of Fidelity's Magellan Fund, for example, is to pursue aggressive growth. That objective may have been possible when the fund was smaller, with under $100 million in assets, but how aggressive can growth be when management must handle $5 billion in assets invested in one thousand companies? Fund objectives may change as the fund becomes successful, and the success enjoyed in earlier days may not carry over when the sheer bulk of the fund constrains management decisions.

Examine any size constraints of your fund. If you are depositing directly into an equity fund, look ahead to the money market fund you may be switching to later. Equity funds typically accept smaller initial deposits than money market funds. You should select a fund within a fund family that will accept your initial deposits at both ends, and you may wish to allow a bit extra. The minimum deposit for Value Line Fund is only $250, but the minimum deposit for Value Line Money Market Fund is $1,000. You may want to deposit $1,200, possibly more, in case the capital value declines. The capital value would be unlikely to drop below $1,000 before you switch, but if it did drop, you would have to be within the acceptable limits of the related money market fund. Many mutual funds will bend the minimum investment rules for IRA and Keogh plans. Since IRAs are limited to $2,000 per year, many funds accept that amount while their other account minimums are $2,500 to $5,000 or higher.

The concept of this book is to use no-load mutual funds as the investment vehicles subject to timing strategies. If you are already invested in a load fund, however, you need not liquidate and start over. Neither should you add to the load fund. Most load funds will permit you to switch your money out of a growth or bond fund into the fund family's money market fund at no charge. Even the load fund families operate their money market funds as no-loads. The load funds will also permit switching back from the money market fund into the load fund without paying a new sales charge. There may be one exception worth checking. While your money is in the money market fund, it earns interest. Does your load fund deduct a sales charge on the interest earned in the money market fund when it is switched back to the equity fund? Some load funds do and others do not charge when the added money is switched back. You will know for sure only if you ask your fund's customer service representative.

STEP NO. 4: CHOOSE YOUR TIMER

A selected list of market timing organizations and/or newsletters is given in Appendix B. This list is not intended to be all-encompassing, as timers enter and leave the scene regularly. Information about their timing services is summarized, but you should contact the timing organization directly for more details for these reasons:

1. Operations change, some more frequently than others, so you should get the most recent information before making a choice.

2. Each timer prefers to explain his service and fees in his own manner.

Specific considerations that are important in picking a timer include discipline, communication, and performance. Probably your key question should be: How easy is your timer to work with? If you have to wait for a letter and then act on your own from the instructions in the letter, you may not act quickly, and thus lose some of the benefit of the move. Or you may not move at all. Some timers offer "hotline" telephone updates as often as daily. But, most timers offer these updates on a weekly basis unless some important development, such as a switch signal, needs to be communicated. You must still take the initiative, and usually pay for the cost of the long-distance call, to get the information from the hotline. You may be motivated to do this, but many investors are not. You may be traveling and out of touch, and not get the "word" on a timely basis. In some cases of inadequate communication, you may as well not use a timer at all.

Discipline is all-important. Market timing success depends on moving in and out of funds according to the signals that result from technical analysis. Not moving or delays in moving can definitely affect results. If you are not motivated to act decisively, using the signals communicated to you by any of several means, then you will more likely benefit from private management where the timer actually makes the moves for you. Private management timers typically handle fairly large accounts, and few private managers make their timing signals available to others through a newsletter or other means of communication such as a hotline or Express Mail. Along with the specifics on timing signals, determine whether the importance of discipline is reinforced in all communications.

Timing newsletters should do more than simply communicate facts, figures, and timing signals when they are appropriate. Communications should also repeat the concept of market timing and emphasize the critical importance of discipline. Facts, figures, charts, and analyses can be dull. Newsletters should include some intellectual meat, something of overriding interest to make sure readers actually pay attention to the newsletter when it arrives. Unless readers develop the habit of examining the newsletter the day it arrives, they can easily miss important information or a switch signal. Keeping the newsletter interesting—even compelling— benefits the readers or subscribers because it attracts regular reading.

Evaluating the performance of market timers can be confusing, particularly after a difficult time in the market. Some may rationalize or make excuses, saying something like, "Well, we have changed our method of evaluation for switching signals to a system that will eliminate any repetition of those last four whipsaws. Under our improved system, instead of a sustained loss we would have had a profit." But rarely do timers come up with an analysis that shows how the new system would have fared if they had backtested the new strategy. You must avoid getting fooled by a market timer's fast footwork to adjust the most recent performance in order to make it look good instead of just mediocre. You should be aware of any disastrous periods where people lost lots of money. Being average for periods of time is to be expected. Remember that the key element of market timing strategy is to avoid exposure on a buy-and-hold basis to major declines of the market.

We recommend that you choose a timer that bases his strategy on trend analysis of price reversals to come up with switch signals. This should lead to a more conservative approach, but it won't get you in at the bottom or out at the top. We believe that the best a market timer can do on a consistent basis over several cycles is to fully participate in 65 percent to 70 percent of the up move measured from bottom to top and to avoid 65 percent to 70 percent of the decline from top to bottom. These are reasonable goals. Promising much more than these limits can lead to whipsaws and losses because the timing devices and techniques are inadequate to forecast or signal every change in the market. Using methods other than the price trends and reversals can lead to periods of substantial losses that are difficult for many investors to accept for emotional reasons. When this happens, it is "out of no-loads with market timing and back to the banks for CDs with their mediocre returns for the next 25 years."

When you choose your timer, you should recognize your own attitudes. If you are not willing to sustain some losses, do not select aggressive funds for your market timing program. You should not be using an aggressive market timer either. The attitudes and approaches of market timers vary in much the same manner as the objectives of mutual funds. Some are aggressive. They charge ahead into what might be called high-risk opportunities. Forecasting market timers often attempt to pick exact tops and bottoms. The predictions of bottoms often lead to greater sustained losses, even though the forecaster predicted a turnaround.

Diversification is an important consideration in any investment portfolio, but diversification means more than spreading your investments around in many stocks. You would not expect an aggressive mutual fund to prosper in the same environment as an income-oriented fund, for example. Diversification of risk is another facet of investment strategy. Even in portfolios where stock, bond, or mutual fund choices are keyed to a conservative strategy, some portion, possibly 10 percent to 15 percent, should probably be invested in high-risk, high-profit potential opportunities. You are not deliberately investing to lose but to afford some opportunity to "hit it big." While the whole subject of high-risk investing is beyond the scope of this book, it provides yet another fascinating facet of portfolio planning.

One final consideration in selecting a market timer is how often the timer calls for switching. Past records will disclose a switching pattern that you can forecast for the future of your investments. The average number of switches per year may not be as useful as the variable pattern. A timer may call for eight switches one year and only two the next. While the average is five per year, you may be in trouble if the funds you select limit the number of trades under certain conditions. Fidelity limits the number of round-trip switches to four per year with a substantial penalty of $50 per switch over that limit. The transaction costs of too many switches could limit overall performance.

The important consideration is how well the market timer performs: What has been his track record for producing gains and profits over the years? This should be your main concern, and you should look to go with a winner. *The Hulbert Financial Digest* reports on timer performance and is one key in selecting a timer, as noted earlier.

STEP NO. 5: AUDIT YOUR FUNDS

Like everyone else in this imperfect world, the people who manage mutual funds can and do make mistakes. You need to pay attention to what is happening with your invested cash in any fund. Auditing is a simple process, but it does require discipline. As you do with your personal checkbook, you need to balance and reconcile your funds' transactions. One report indicates that as many as 10 percent to 15 percent of mutual funds' transactions are in error. This is a high number, and we have not experienced such inaccuracies in dealing with the funds that qualify for private management with PM&A. The problems are not with the ubiquitous computer—they are universally used; the problems are with people. People make the errors; computers simply carry out the errors quickly.

Auditing transactions begins with a telephone call. Today, almost all transactions are handled by telephone, and the calls are recorded. Even so, when you call in instructions, record the date and time along with the person's name that you spoke to. Generally, the person answering the phone will give his or her name at the outset, possibly so quickly that you cannot catch it clearly. Ask again to be sure you know with whom you are speaking.

When the confirmation comes in the mail, compare it with your notes of the telephone transaction. Note too if the net asset value (NAV) recorded as the transaction price on the confirmation sheet is the same as the NAV recorded in the newspaper for that date. Check to be sure that the account name is correct. In the database for a mutual fund of any size, there may be many accounts with the same last name, possibly even with the same first name and middle initial. After checking your name, check the account number. Your name and account number should check out with your older records. If any of these facts do not agree with your notes, contact the fund immediately to correct the records. Do not wait until you are ready to switch. Remember, we are working at building a $1 million retirement fund for you, and some of the responsibility remains on your shoulders. Although not necessary in all cases, some clients send a confirming letter after transacting their business on the telephone.

STEP NO. 6: REVIEW YOUR FUNDS

Mutual funds change. A particular fund may grow beyond its original size and thus lose flexibility, or the fund's management may change and bring in a different approach. Or your investment objectives may change. None of these changes is likely to occur over a few weeks or months, but over a year or more any of numerous changes may occur that can leave your objectives out of sync with those of the funds where your money is deposited. Further, the economy or the investment climate can and does change, and not always for the better. You must maintain surveillance of your fund or funds, not on a daily basis necessarily but at specific checkpoints during a year.

Funds change their character as time goes by and the size of their asset base grows. Magellan Fund established itself as a dynamic growth fund through its policy of selecting small, emerging companies that offered a promise of rapid growth. Magellan could function with a free hand when it was managing $100 million in assets. The fund's market moves had little effect on share prices. There were many small, aggressive companies around, and opportunities for picking prospective growth situations were everywhere. But as a fund with $5 billion of assets to invest and monitor, Magellan Fund is now different from its younger and smaller days. Investors may expect too much of the fund based on its earlier, headier days of growth. Magellan is different, not necessarily better or less desirable, but different.

Many changes can affect a fund over time. The management may grow stale, or the capable team that brought it to prominence may disband or be spread around to manage several funds. The talent that was evident earlier may no longer be associated with it, and you may not be aware of this change unless you read the quarterly and annual reports. Monitor articles about the funds in publications such as the *Wall Street Journal, Forbes,* and *Money.*

Your objectives may change over time as well. As your retirement nears, you will likely become more conservative; most of us do. A fund that you considered dynamic, growing, volatile, and promising at an earlier stage might be considered too venturesome later. You may prefer to take fewer chances even though the downside market risk is minimized through market timing. You may change to a less volatile, more predictable fund, possibly one aimed at producing more income to suit your different objectives. Although your financial advisor may suggest regular reviews, you can keep up with changes yourself, since you are likely to be tuned to anything that affects your funds or your investments in them.

STEP NO. 7: REVIEW YOUR MARKET TIMER

Track the activities of your market timer much as you do the progress of your funds. The key factor in a timer's success, and your success along with his, is discipline. You won't benefit if your fund has grown large under the timer's direction and you give it all back during a big market decline. Over several cycles you will come to know about how much of a setback you can expect before your market timer signals a switch from an equity or bond fund into a money market fund. If actions appear to be following a different turn, you might question what is happening. Because you are not privy to the inside workings of your market timer's organization, you are not likely to know whether or not there has been some change of technique or a refinement of strategy. If you have any question about possible changes in technique or the timing of switching signals and discipline, talk with your timer—and then talk some more. It's your money! It's your retirement. No one has a greater stake in the activities of your fund than you do. Pay attention. The opportunities for building your retirement fund to a million dollars is there, but you need to devote some time and effort to monitoring your market timer's actions and discipline. You are always in control, but control is meaningless unless you exercise it.

You may have to fire your timer for any of several reasons. You can usually change timers or discontinue the market timing activity at your discretion and without penalty. One of the big factors to watch for is a large and continuing market slide without a sell signal from your timer. The essence of market timing is avoiding losses. If your market timer allows your holdings to decline substantially over a period of time, then you might want to consider changing timers. You certainly should be asking questions, for this is part of your surveillance activities. You can probably avoid the big split if you pay attention to his performance during earlier market slides. If you notice that your timer's sell discipline is not sensitive to trend reversals on the down side, check out your suspicions then rather than later, after a major decline in your holdings. No investment strategy can be ignored, and market timing is no different. For your own peace of mind and for the benefit of your asset base, keep track of what is going on with your funds and with your market timer.

Table 7A. Fund performance: Buy-and-hold vs. PM&A's Market Timing 1984-1985.

	Since Inception (7/31/83)		12 Months Ending (11/29/85)	
	BUY/HOLD	TIMING	BUY/HOLD	TIMING
AGGRESSIVE GROWTH				
Columbia Growth	+ 21.1%	+ 31.6%	+ 29.5%	+ 25.8%
IDS Growth Fund	- 6.5	+ 13.6	+ 31.2	+ 25.3
IDS Discovery Fund	- 11.7	+ 14.9	+ 25.3	+ 24.7
IDS Progressive Fund	+ 15.4	+ 28.6	+ 29.5	+ 25.4
Kemper Summit	+ 8.0	+ 20.7	+ 25.6	+ 22.2
Oppenheimer AIM	+ 3.5	+ 26.1	+ 41.3	+ 36.3
Oppenheimer Directors	- 12.3	+ 28.0	+ 21.0	+ 21.1
Lord Abbett Developing Growth	- 20.6	+ 4.2	+ 11.3	+ 12.2
Putman Voyager	+ 19.6	+ 33.4	+ 33.8	+ 29.0
Stein Roe Special	+ 26.9	+ 30.0	+ 28.5	+ 25.0
Value Line Special Situations	- 19.3	+ 4.7	+ 22.0	+ 17.2
USAA Mutual Fund-Sunbelt ERA	- 10.7	+ 24.2	+ 21.6	+ 21.9
GROWTH				
Boston Co. Capital Appreciation	+ 44.9%	+ 39.7%	+ 33.7%	+ 26.7%
Dreyfus Growth Opportunity	+ 13.1	+ 19.3	+ 28.4	+ 24.8
Dreyfus Leveraged Fund	+ 46.1	+ 43.3	+ 29.4	+ 23.3
Dreyfus Third Century	+ 30.0	+ 37.4	+ 29.0	+ 26.4
IDS New Dimensions	+ 17.1	+ 25.9	+ 35.5	+ 32.2
Loomis-Sayles Capital Development	+ 25.6	+ 30.0	+ 46.1	+ 31.9
Kemper Growth	+ .8	+ 21.0	+ 11.0	+ 23.9
Putnam Growth	+ 11.6	+ 29.8	+ 23.7	+ 17.5
Safeco Growth	+ 4.4	+ 24.5	+ 16.4	+ 19.6
Value Line Leveraged Growth	+ 5.3	+ 26.2	+ 28.0	+ 24.1
Value Line Fund	+ 5.9	+ 21.1	+ 35.1	+ 26.0
GROWTH-INCOME				
American Mutual	+ 33.3%	+ 40.6%	+ 29.8%	+ 25.3%
Financial Industrial Income	+ 42.6	+ 39.9	+ 27.7	+ 24.1
Investment Company of America	+ 40.3	+ 35.8	+ 28.4	+ 23.2
Oppenheimer Equity Income	+ 34.5	+ 42.6	+ 30.7	+ 27.0
Dreyfus Fund	+ 37.6	+ 34.6	+ 25.8	+ 21.7
Value Line Income	+ 13.3	+ 29.5	+ 20.9	+ 13.7
Safeco Income Fund	+ 45.7	+ 46.4	+ 28.9	+ 26.7

Table 7A *(cont'd)*

	Since Inception (7/31/83)		12 Months Ending (11/29/85)	
	BUY/HOLD	TIMING	BUY/HOLD	TIMING
FIXED INCOME TAXABLE				
Dreyfus A Bonds Plus	+ 40.6%	+ 39.2%	+ 20.3%	+ 13.4%
Kemper High Yield	+ 38.1	+ 43.2	+ 17.0	+ 19.4
Oppenheimer High Yield	+ 42.9	+ 35.2	+ 16.0	+ 16.0
Value Line Bond Fund	+ 45.4	+ 41.0	+ 21.7	+ 17.5
FIXED INCOME TAX-EXEMPT				
Dreyfus Tax-Exempt Bond Fund	+ 31.8%	+ 33.7%	+ 18.2%	+ 17.9%
Financial Tax-Free Income	+ 23.8	+ 28.9	+ 15.3	+ 15.0
GOLD				
Golconda Investors Ltd.	- 30.1%	- 5.0%	- 4.0%	- 2.9%
International Investors	- 26.6	- 5.6	- 9.4	- 8.5
United Services Gold Shares	- 50.2	- 36.0	- 50.0	- 33.8
Franklin Gold Fund	- 33.8	- 15.2	- 14.6	- 13.4
SUMMARY				
Aggressive Growth Funds	+ 1.1%	+ 21.3%	+ 26.7%	+ 23.8%
Growth Funds	+ 18.6	+ 28.9	+ 28.8	+ 25.1
Growth-Income Funds	+ 35.3	+ 38.5	+ 27.5	+ 21.1
Fixed Income Taxable Funds	+ 41.8	+ 39.7	+ 18.8	+ 16.6
Fixed Income Tax-Exempt Funds	+ 27.8	+ 31.3	+ 16.8	+ 16.5
Gold Funds	- 35.2	- 15.5	- 19.5	- 14.7

8

Risk and Market Timing

Risks are always with us. When we enter an automobile and drive out of our garage, we may encounter a variety of risks. We may be struck by another vehicle as we enter the street or pass the next street corner. Our car could suddenly quit, or we could strike a pedestrian or another vehicle.

So it is with investing. No system of investing avoids risks completely. Even the so-called risk-free, insured savings accounts or government securities incur risks related either to inflation or interest rates. Market timing can and does help to minimize risks, but it does not *eliminate* risks. To help you understand the concept of relative risk, we must first define risks and help you recognize those risks that are acceptable in market activities.

A term heard often is "risk/return ratio." This concept attempts to relate the degree of risk with the potential return. There is little point to assuming a substantial risk if the potential gain is minimal. Or you may look at risk/return another way: Suppose two alternative investments promise a like return. If one alternative appears less risky, then the risk/reward ratio is better even though the reward potential is the same.

Another concept heard frequently is that "risk is reflected in the price." Bond prices are particularly sensitive to risks, and bonds offering the same coupon rate may carry higher or lower prices than other bonds with the same coupon rate. When the price is higher (yield lower), the risk is perceived to be less. Part of the lower price for a comparable bond is perceived to be a premium for assuming a higher risk. So-called "junk bonds" pay handsome returns because buyers perceive them to be high-risk investments. Prices attached to certain bonds, for example, represent the sum total of investor perceptions regarding the risk of those particular bonds.

CATEGORIES OF RISK

Risk is not an all-inclusive term. There are different kinds of risks, and some are more important than others as they relate to your investments.

Capital risk involves your capital's safety. Will your capital be returned to you? Will its value decline? Is it liquid and readily available? An easy way to visualize the concept of capital risk is to think of making a loan to a friend. Will your friend repay the loan under the agreed terms? You assume a similar risk when you buy a bond. Will the borrower of your money pay you back at the agreed time in full? If the company issuing the bond should go bankrupt, you would not likely receive the full value of your bond. This is capital risk.

Stocks are a bit different; here the asset value of your capital is still involved. Instead of a corporation paying you in full for the value of your stock at some future date, as in the case of a bond or other debt instrument, you may be concerned about the future value of your shares in the marketplace. Will you be able, at some future date, to recover the capital value of your stock?

Yield risk involves the return you expect from the capital you invest. Will the income from your capital be paid on time and will it match or surpass the yield from alternative investments? When you buy a bond, for example, you agree to a fixed return that is spelled out at the time of the purchase by the coupon rate and the price. A $1,000 bond may carry a coupon rate of 12 percent or $120 (different bonds denote the return either as a percent of the par value or as a specific number of dollars to be paid annually). You would know that your return is 12 percent of the money invested. If the $120 coupon rate is purchased at some value other than its face or par value, however, the yield will be different. If the $1,000 face value bond should sell at a discount price of $900, then the $120 of annual interest yields a 13.33 percent return on your invested funds. If the bond should sell at a premium (that is, at a price higher than the $1,000 face value), then the $120 of annual interest would yield a lower return than the nominal 12 percent.

The yield risk is composed of two parts:

1. The risk associated with that specific bond and the issuer of the bond. A corporation with an unblemished record of paying interest on its bonds when due and with a reputation for being a well managed, prosperous corporation would be more credit worthy (less risk) than a struggling corporation. This portion of the risk is associated with specific issues of bonds and how investors perceive the credit rating of the issuer.

2. The interest environment that affects all issues of bonds whether government, corporate, or municipal. While some classes of bonds with specific risks may move up or down at different rates, all bonds reflect the general level of interest rates that change daily.

Negotiable bonds move up or down in value inversely with interest rates; that is, as the general level of interest rates rises, bond prices decline, and vice versa. Thus, when a $1,000 face value bond sells at a discount of $900, the yield will be higher, but as long as you own that bond, the yield remains constant because the coupon rate doesn't change. Recognize here that we are talking only of the current yield. Any bond purchased at a discount will return a higher yield-to-maturity (YTM) because the bond will be paid off at face value by the issuing organization at maturity. The yield risk you assume when buying a bond is the variability of the current yield. If you pay $1,000 for a bond that later declines in price to $900, you retain the $120 of interest (following the same example), but you have lost the opportunity to invest the same capital for a higher return. Yield risk is always with us and is the primary reason behind the volatile nature of bond prices today. During previous periods bonds were perceived as stable, practically risk-free investments.

Inflation risk is all-pervasive and is a risk that is difficult to anticipate or to cope with. Inflation risk involves the variability of purchasing power and is related to the "money illusion." Inflation is perceived by many to be the rising level of prices we all pay for goods and services. This is how we see the pace of inflation: The Consumers Price Index (CPI) is the most visible index of inflation, although there are others. The CPI is popularly known as the "cost of living" index. In its inexorable upward path, the CPI records the overall increase in the cost of living along with the components that make up the overall index. The money illusion leads us to focus on prices rather than on what is really happening—the decreasing value of our U.S. dollar.

When the CPI increases 10 percent, we must spend $110 to buy the goods and services that $100 would have bought in the base period. When you must pay more dollars to buy a fixed bag of goods and services, the purchasing value of each dollar has declined. The money illusion would have us believe that the dollar is a constant and prices vary. Actually, the value of goods and services, while certainly not constant, varies relatively little; it is the dollar that changes in value.

Gold is a much more stable arbiter of value than the dollar or any other modern currency. The value of gold has been regularly devalued or revalued. Prior to 1934 an ounce of gold was valued at $22.42. In 1934 the price of a troy ounce of gold was restated as $35. In 1972 the price of gold was again devalued to $38, and in 1973 the price was again officially revalued to $44.22, where it remains today. At about that time the two-tier price structure of gold was recognized. One tier was the official price of $44.22, a meaningless figure since dollars and gold are never interchanged at that price today. The second tier is the world price of gold that changes minute by minute at different exchanges around the world. Recent prices for gold (January 1986) were in the $340-$360 range. Yet the cost of a pound loaf of bread in New York City in 1900 was almost exactly the same as a similar loaf of bread in 1985 when stated in terms of gold. Thus, gold has remained remarkably stable in terms of its purchasing power while growing many times over in value relative to the dollar—or any other national currency.

Monetarists, led by Nobel Laureate Milton Friedman, equate the loss of the dollar's purchasing power to the expansion of the money supply. The monetarists cite the logic that "more dollars available means each of those dollars is worth less." Further, the monetarists have studied the relationship of an expansion of the money supply and found that prices rise (dollar value declines) about 18 to 24 months following the expansion of the money supply. In the United States the Federal Reserve System attempts to control the money supply as measured by three levels of monetary aggregates, known generally as M1, M2, and M3. Numerous tools may be used to control the money supply, but the controls are seldom precise and the money supply tends to vary more widely than the Fed would like. Many investors, and others who may not have known there was such a thing as the money supply, now watch the mounting numbers as eagerly as they watch the results of T-bill auctions each Monday. Whatever the cause—and economists debate inflation and its causes constantly—inflation remains a dominant factor in investment strategy. It is a fact of your investment life that you ignore at your peril.

Inflation risk in investment terms is what happens to the value of your capital or yield relative to the purchasing power of your investment. Take bond interest rates as an example. Over the past several hundred years, interest rates have generally ranged from $2\frac{1}{2}$ percent to 3 percent. This is true interest, known in financial circles as the rental cost for money. When you borrow money, you agree to pay back the full amount plus the rent. The rental cost is expressed as interest and is figured in different ways. Simple or bank interest is the rental cost for borrowing money after one year. The true interest rate may fluctuate according to the supply and demand for money, but it assumes a constant value of money. Thus, a lender may assume that $100 after one year will buy the same bag of goods and services as the original $100 did at the time it was borrowed. The lender gains the value of interest.

Inflation alters this simple arrangement. The interest rate you see in long-term government bonds or Treasury bills now includes at least two elements. The first is the long-term rental cost of money, and the second is an inflation allowance or bias to account for the diminishing purchasing power of money over time. The inflation element of interest attempts to compensate for the declining value of the dollars to be paid back after an interval of time. If you assume that inflation will continue at 10 percent per year, then the interest rate will likely be somewhere around 13 percent—10 percent to account for the decline in purchasing power of the original capital, and 3 percent for rent (true interest). There may be another element in the overall interest rate to account for possible capital risk or yield risk. The inflation element states, in effect, that "$110 (the original $100 of capital plus $10 in interest) will buy essentially the same bag of goods and services one year hence that $100 would buy today."

If this simplistic relation actually exists, then why are interest rates on T-bills in the 7 percent to 8 percent range when inflation is about 3 percent to 3½ percent? If the inflation factor is 3½ percent and the long-term rental cost of money is 2½ percent, the overall rate for a risk-free investment in a U.S. Government security should be 6 percent—not 7 percent or 8 percent. The answer relates not to the actual inflation rate, as reported monthly by the Bureau of Labor Statistics, but to the inflation expectations of lenders. They are saying, in effect, "We believe inflation will likely be higher a year from today, and we want to make sure our money doesn't lose its buying power. We therefore require a higher rate of interest as a hedge against the inflation we see coming."

MUTUAL FUND RISKS

All of the risks noted above are reflected in the prices and yields from mutual funds in ways that are far from precise. In fact, there is no method or system of relating so-called fundamental risks to the actual prices of mutual fund shares. Mechanically, the net asset values (NAV) of mutual fund shares reflect the underlying value of the stocks in the funds' portfolios as calculated at the end of each business day. This definition begs the question, however, because the values investors place on the underlying stocks result from myriad factors.

Emotion and perceptions affect the market values of shares and, thereby, the NAV of mutual fund shares in so many ways that accurate forecasts of market movements have never been available. If we could accurately forecast the direction of the market, there would be no need for market timing. But changes do occur, apparently with little rhyme or reason. Stock market followers claim that the price of a particular corporation's stock results from the sum total of all investors' perceptions and knowledge of that corporation and its share prices. Obviously, for every sale there must be a buyer, and these differences of opinion when summed at the close of a market day are reflected in the value of those shares.

Why the prices of shares change is open to as many opinions as there are analysts or observers. One wizened veteran of the market, when asked the question of why stocks declined, summed it all up by saying, "More sellers than buyers."

Market timing reduces the risks of investing in the market by lessening your exposure to conditions that change prices. Using a buy-and-hold strategy, let us say you own shares in XYZ no-load mutual fund. Over a period you will likely experience up and down movements of the NAV. These changes in the NAV reflect all of the factors that could affect the value of those shares: yield, capital gains, recognized or not, the changing makeup of the fund's portfolio, management's perception of the economy, and many others. The fact is that the NAV of XYZ fund will likely cycle up and down either about a stable mean or an ascending or descending trend line.

Your risk in remaining with any fund relates to the nature of the fund. An aggressive fund will cycle up and down over a wide range of NAV values, possibly over short periods. A conservative income-oriented fund, on the other hand, will likely cycle up and down more slowly and over a far narrower range of NAV values. This difference in variability or volatility has a name: beta.

The concept of beta was developed by Value Line in relation to individual stocks, but it is equally applicable to mutual funds. Beta is basically a numerical measure of a stock's volatility and is reported in the Value Line Survey. The base is 1.00, defined as the average volatility of the Standard & Poor's Index of 500 Stocks. A stock with a beta of 1.00 would cycle up and down with the same volatility as the S&P 500 index. A stock that cycles up and down with a volatility 20 percent greater than the S&P 500 base would have a beta of 1.2, meaning that if the S&P 500 rose by 10 percent, the stock's price would rise by 12 percent. Stocks with a beta higher than 1.00 move up faster than the base S&P 500 and decline faster. Thus, beta represents a numerical value of volatility that you can use to compare stocks in a reasonable manner.

Aggressive stocks are known as high-beta stocks. Conversely, conservative or income stocks may carry a beta lower than 1.00. Utility common stocks, for example, typically carry beta designations of .6 or .7. Risk is associated with beta, and high-beta stocks tend to be more risky. Because of their volatility (high-beta) characteristics, aggressive stocks may decline faster than the overall market. You could therefore lose money quicker, and this is a form of stock risk.

The concept of beta may also be applied to mutual funds. A mutual fund with an NAV that cycles up and down in concert with the S&P 500 could be given the base value of 1.00, as with individual stocks. Aggressive mutual funds that move up and down at a faster rate than the S&P 500 would have betas higher than 1.00. Slower moving mutual funds would have betas lower than 1.00. Understanding the concept of beta may be easy, but computing the numbers is difficult. Statistics on beta are available in yearly editions of *The Individual Investor's Guide to No-Load Mutual Funds* published by the American Association of Individual Investors and in *The Handbook for No-Load Mutual Fund Investors*.

The concept of beta and how it relates to risk and the reduction of risk through market timing is a valuable tool, and you can use it in your investment planning. An example will help to explain how market timing dramatically reduces the risks of investing in no-load mutual funds.

BETA AND MARKET TIMING RISK

Money market mutual funds are designed to maintain constant share values at $1 per share. The fixed rate on money market instruments held in the portfolios of money market funds and their extremely short maturity help money fund managers maintain the NAV of money fund shares at a constant $1 value. Since there is no volatility, money market funds carry a beta of 0.

Aggressive no-load mutual funds are known to have betas higher than 1.00. Suppose, for this example, that you invest in ABC Fund that carries a beta of 1.5. This is a fairly aggressive fund that will rise 50 percent faster than the overall market and sink half again as fast as the market during a bear phase. With market timing you can buy into ABC Fund at some point on a rising trend. As the overall market rises, ABC Fund rises 50 percent faster (beta = 1.5). When the market stumbles and begins to trend down, however, your market timer calls for switching out of ABC Fund into a money market fund. Such a move preserves the capital accumulated during the bull phase of the market. Your capital remains in the money market fund until the market reverses its down cycle and begins trending upward again. Your market timer then signals for a switch back to ABC Fund from the money market fund.

What has happened to risk over a complete switching cycle? If you assume that you were in ABC Fund for half the time and in the money market fund half the time, you have cut your risk in half. The overall beta of your investment is .75. Half the time your investment rated a beta of 1.50, and half the time your investment rated a beta of 0. Thus, the average beta is half of 1.50, or .75—even using an aggressive growth fund.

MARKET AND SECURITY RISKS

Two additional risks pose hazards for the stock or mutual fund investor. Market risk involves the happenings in the overall market. Generally, a rising market will affect all shares. Some stocks may decline, but they will probably decline less in a rising market than in a bear market. The Wall Street maxim that "a rising tide lifts all boats" stems from this concept of overall market movement. Various averages attempt to measure overall market motion. The Dow Jones Industrial Average is the longest running indicator of general market activity even though it includes stocks of only 30 major corporations. The Standard & Poor's Index of 500 Stocks offers a broader measure. The New York Stock Exchange's Composite Index of all stocks is an even broader indicator of activity among those stocks listed on the NYSE. Similar indexes relate to American Stock Exchange issues and to those traded over the counter.

Any investor holding individual stocks incurs a measure of market risk. The issues he or she holds may rise or fall in concert with the overall market or at least be influenced by the overall market's direction. Market timing reduces the market risk by getting investors out of the equity market during downturns and getting them back into the market following the beginning of upturns. During downturns, your investment funds are safely parked in a money fund drawing market rates of interest.

Security or stock risk is narrower and relates to a specific stock. Although an individual stock's price will likely be affected by the overall market—as much as 70 percent, according to some observers—individual issues react to different factors. Even in a rising market, a disappointing earnings report can cause a corporation's stock to drop. The announcement of a big new strike by an oil company can send its shares sharply up even in an overall market that declined for the day or is in a declining trend. While analysts attempt to discover good opportunities in individual stocks through a variety of stock picking techniques, their record is mixed.

The conservative investor is likely to avert stock risk through diversification. Investors with large assets available for investing can buy stocks in a variety of companies to achieve a diversified portfolio, one that reduces stock risk by investing in many issues. Small investors with limited funds can achieve equivalent or even greater diversification by buying shares in a mutual fund. They can even diversify their holdings among several no-load mutual funds with a variety of objectives—and a corresponding variety of betas.

While there is no way to avoid all risks, the use of market timing to minimize market risk and no-load mutual funds to minimize security or stock risk offers an unbeatable combination for investors.

9

Market Timing Transactions

Now it's crunch time. Getting involved in market timing requires you to take some action if you expect to profit. You know about market timing organizations. You are familiar with the basic concept of market timing. You understand the rudiments of indicators that tell you when to switch from the potentially profitable equity funds to the defensive money funds, and vice versa. It's time to put your know-how to work. It's time for action.

You can elect any of several routes or combinations to put your profit-generating plan into action, but they boil down to two fundamental alternatives:

MARKET TIMING ON YOUR OWN

You can do it yourself; that is, you can calculate your own indicator, as detailed in chapter 5, or by some other system. You would transfer funds between equity and money funds according to those signals. If you are not comfortable with or do not have the time to develop and monitor your own indicators, you can retain the switching activity but rely on a newsletter, hotline, or other source of signals. In any case, you must take the initiative to get things under way. If you are a natural self-starter, you will be comfortable operating in this mode. If you elect the do-it-yourself approach, and you may very well profit from this method of operation, you can choose either of two routes for putting your system into effect: You can work with the funds of your choice directly (later in this chapter we will detail the steps you must follow in effecting the necessary transactions), or you can execute your trades through Charles Schwab Mutual Fund Marketplace. Either way you should be aware of the hazards of the do-it-yourself approach. Procrastination and not being on top of the market at all times may be your biggest problems.

MARKET TIMING BY PRIVATE MANAGEMENT

You need not do any of the above to gain the investment opportunities of market timing. You can simply turn over the operation of your market timing program to an organization that will pick the funds to be used, generate the switching indicators, make the switches as needed, and keep you apprised of the results. A private market timing organization will charge a fee ranging from 1 percent to 3 percent of the assets under management. Further, the minimum account size may be upward of $2,000—and frequently begins at $100,000. The management fee is much like a tax; it comes every year and reduces the net compounding rate for building your assets. Market timing offers such major investment benefits that paying for private management is still preferable, on average, to working with a broker or management firm. Two forms of private management are in general use:

1. In one plan you turn over your funds to the management firm for total control. You should ask about safeguards in case the organization misappropriates funds or goes under with your funds and others. Ordinarily, a market timing organization will not provide Securities Investor Protection Corporation (SIPC) protection for funds under its control in the way a brokerage firm will. Turning over complete control of your assets under a discretionary management agreement without some insurance or other protection should be avoided.

The private management organization of your choice will then select the mutual funds to be used. Your risk tolerance, age, and investment objectives should be considered. This part of the private management program is very important and should not be short-circuited. The management firm will then buy shares for your account in the mutual funds selected and the firm will keep you advised on the progress, but it may or may not advise you of each move.

2. In the second plan you deposit cash with a mutual fund (in your name or jointly with your spouse or other person). You may choose the mutual fund or follow the recommendation of the market timing organization. When you have established your accounts, you provide a limited power of attorney to the timer. This authorizes the market timer to switch funds between equity and money market funds on his signals, but he cannot withdraw money or change the mutual funds other than switching between the funds you have designated. This program leaves you in complete control of your investments. Even with the limited power of attorney in effect, you can withdraw funds from the mutual funds at any time. The amount of information provided to you under this limited management arrangement depends on the firm.

Your primary benefit from using a management organization is the discipline it provides to switch on signal and avoid procrastination. Turning the switching over to a specialized management organization also protects your investments if you should be traveling on business, out of contact on vacation, or unavailable for any other reason. Market timing requires quick, direct action to take full advantage of the changes in the market that generate switching signals. Failure to act promptly can negate part or all of the benefits inherent in the program.

There are, obviously, pluses and minuses with each of these approaches. If you elect to develop your own indicators and switch between equity or bond funds and money funds on the basis of those signals, you retain complete control. You also avoid the expense of newsletter subscriptions or management fees, but you incur costs for your time and effort. If the concept intrigues you and you accept the challenge of jousting with professionals, you may very well profit from the do-it-yourself approach.

And you would not be alone. Many thousands of investors take a serious interest in the growth of their financial resources. They willingly spend the time necessary to make sure their assets are growing apace or ahead of the market. After all, nobody has the intense personal interest in your own investments that you have. Intense personal interest may compensate for a lack of expertise.

On the other hand, you may have little time and/or interest in the details of investing through market timing of no-load mutual funds. You may be too busy doing your own thing to "bother with your investments." We all have different attitudes toward money and how to manage it. So, being "too busy" can be a valid concern. You may then choose to turn over the responsibilities for managing your assets to another and pay a price for your actions, with the price varying according to how many of the activities you delegate.

DEVELOPING YOUR OWN INDICATORS

You may decide to take on the whole ball of wax—developing your own switching signals, switching assets between the funds of your choice on signal, and continually monitoring results. For any successful market timing system to work, reliable indicators are essential as the first step.

The level of technical expertise required to develop and implement your own indicators ranges from a "keep it simple" moving-average system to a multiple-indicator approach with appropriate filtering. A relatively simple system is detailed in chapter 5. Purveyors of switching signals operate with organizations peopled with specialists who use highly refined computer models and constantly check and recheck their results. They can and do develop useful data and translate their findings into signals you can use for market timing. Some of the market timers have better track records than others, but nowhere is it written that what has worked best in the past will continue to work in the future.

Relying on others for switch signals involves one basic fault: You are not alone. You are one of a crowd—perhaps large, perhaps small, but a crowd nevertheless. When your source calls for a switch, many others will likewise be switching. How serious is this fault? No one really knows at this juncture because market timing with no-load mutual funds has not been around long enough to provide an answer. So far there is no indication that the market has been upset or influenced by large switches within a short time frame.

Your big benefit from developing your own switching signals may be the loneliness of your position. Whatever you elect to do will likely have no effect on others or on the market. And that can be good—if your research is good. With such a program you may be ahead of the pack.

A number of books may help you educate yourself. One of the best is *Stock Market Trading Systems* by Gerald Appel and Fred Hitschler (Dow Jones-Irwin, 1980). Another is the *Dow Jones-Irwin Guide to Mutual Funds* by Donald D. Rugg and Norman B. Hale (Dow Jones-Irwin, revised edition, 1985). A strong background in statistics will be helpful. Further, a computer will simplify handling the calculations involved and greatly speed up your analyses. Make no mistake: Developing and monitoring the data needed to make your signals reliable can be time-consuming. It also offers a fascinating challenge.

TRADING WITH OTHERS' INDICATORS

If you decide to gain the benefits of market timing but do not have the time or inclination to develop your own market timing indicators, look for a timing service to provide the signals. You may receive the signals by mail, a hotline, or a direct telephone call. Using that information, do your own switching.

Six distinct steps are required for this mode of operation:

1. Select a market timer.
2. Select the mutual funds to be used in your switching program.
3. Set up your mutual funds to permit switching on signal.
4. Deposit the cash you wish to invest and inaugurate your switching program.
5. Switch assets between funds according to the switching signals from your market timer.
6. Monitor your progress and keep records to enable you to file timely tax returns. Monitoring your market timing program may call for comparing its progress with a buy-

and-hold program. Or you may compute a return on assets from your record of gains and losses during a year.

Appendix B lists representative market timers with established records from which you can choose. This is not intended to be either a complete list or a recommended list. Ask one or several timers for information to help you decide. The information should include his *modus operandi*, how he would operate with you, a fee schedule, and the forms or agreements you would have to sign. From these data and the information on evaluating market timers in chapter 7, choose your timer.

Your market timer may select the mutual funds for you or strongly recommend that you select the mutual funds he normally works with. He may provide signals applicable to several funds and leave the choice up to you.

Select specific mutual funds to match your investment objectives and risk tolerance. The mutual funds you are considering must permit switching. Be sure you select your equity, equity-income, or bond fund in the same family as a money market mutual fund.

Request prospectuses from all of the funds you are considering. Since most mutual fund families offer one or more money market mutual funds, select the equity, equity-income, or bond fund first. Open accounts in both funds—equity, bond, or gold, and a money market fund in the family. Accounts must be established to permit switching by telephone.

Check out by telephone the operations of the mutual funds you expect to use. Most no-load funds offer toll-free (800) numbers for practically all transactions. As part of their procedures, you will find your telephone conversation is recorded. The beeps every so often remind you that the recorder is on. Getting through to the fund can be a problem at times, and if the problem persists through several attempts, you may want to consider another fund family. But there are some tricks to getting through: Try calling early in the morning, remembering the time zone of the fund's office, or call late in the afternoon. Calling before 4:00 P.M. Eastern time means your switching instructions will probably be implemented the same day, at that day's closing net asset value; otherwise, you will take the closing NAV of the following day. If your signal says "trade immediately,'' don't be put off. If you must get through and the toll-free numbers are constantly busy, call the fund's normal business number. Call collect to save money.

GETTING STARTED

Opening your account begins by filing an application blank and enclosing a check for the initial deposit. Surprisingly enough, investors who have dealt mainly with stockbrokers or banks are often concerned about this simple task. Most application blanks require only minimal information, and the forms are easy to complete. Remember, no-load mutual funds do almost all of their business by mail. They have designed their paperwork to be as simple as possible. Reproduced in figure 9-1 is a sample application blank, with the important blanks noted. You will have several options, including whether you wish the account to be in your name alone or jointly with your spouse or other person. If there is a blank on the form asking your intentions about possible switching to another mutual fund within the family, be sure to indicate yes by checking the box provided or filling in the blank. Sign up for check-writing privileges. Also, note your bank's name and address and your checking account number for possible future use in wire transfers. Sign your name; both parties should sign if it is a joint account. That's about it. Simple, huh? You must open two accounts—one for the growth (equity) fund and one for the money market fund within the same family. The names must be identical on both funds to permit switching by telephone.

Deposit your initial check in the money market fund to protect your investment against a decline in value while your check clears. Some funds will not permit a switch until an account is open 15 to 30 days. As an option, you can wire the money to the fund and have it working the next business day. You can easily figure the value of wiring your deposit versus sending a check and waiting for it to clear. Time is worth money, and the value depends on the interest rate. Suppose, for example, that the money fund of your choice is paying 12 percent; the daily rate of interest is therefore .000329 (.12 divided by 365). If the cost of a wire deposit from your bank to

Fig. 9-1. Sample application form for use in investing in no-load mutual fund.

Dreyfus
OPEN ACCOUNT APPLICATION
Do not use for Keogh or I.R.A. Plans which require special forms available upon request.
PLEASE PRINT ALL ITEMS EXCEPT SIGNATURES

① TO ESTABLISH AN ACCOUNT —I am enclosing a check payable to The Bank of New York, as my initial investment in the Fund(s) checked below, whose current prospectus(es) I have received:

Check One
or More — Amount of Investment

[A]	☐ DREYFUS TAX EXEMPT BOND FUND	$_____ (Minimum $2,500) (Complete Sections ②, ③, ⑥ and ⑦)
[B]	☐ DREYFUS TAX EXEMPT MONEY MARKET FUND	$_____ (Minimum $5,000) (Complete Sections ②, ③, ⑤, ⑥ and ⑦)
[C]	☐ DREYFUS ...	$_____ (Minimum $2,500) (Complete Sections ②, ③, ⑥ and ⑦)
[D]	☐ DREYFUS ... PLUS	$_____ (Minimum $2,500) (Complete Sections ②, ③, ⑥ and ⑦)
[E]	☐ DREYFUS ... CIAL INCOME FUND	$_____ (Minimum $2,500) (Complete Sections ②, ③, ⑥ and ⑦)
[F]	☐ DREYFUS NUMBER NINE	$_____ (Minimum $2,500) (Complete Sections ②, ③, ⑥ and ⑦)
[G]	☐ DREYFUS THIRD CENTURY FUND	$_____ (Minimum $2,500) (Complete Sections ②, ③, ⑥ and ⑦)

Check Box to Select Fund **Indicate Amount of Deposit** **Check to** → ... the Bank of New York)

Total $_____

② REGISTRATION —THE SHARES SHOULD BE REGISTERED AS FOLLOWS:
(No stock certificate will be issued unless requested in writing by the Shareholder.)

Your Name
Print Applicant's Name. For clarity, please skip a space where appropriate.
Joint Owner's Name (If Any)
Print Joint Owner's Name. If joint ownership presumed, unless tenancy in common is indicated.)
Address & Phone
PRINT STREET ADDRESS _____ CITY _____ STATE _____ ZIP CODE
Home Phone No. _____ (Include Area Code) Business Phone No. _____ (Include Area Code)
U.S. CITIZEN ☐ Yes ☐ No (If "No," indicate country of citizenship _____)

③ FOR ALL FUNDS EXCEPT DREYFUS LIQUID ASSETS
DISTRIBUTIONS (Check one box only for each fund account you are opening)

Tax Exempt | Tax Exempt Money Market | A Bonds Plus | Special | Number Nine | Third Century

Select Reinvestment of Earnings ... all dividends and distributions, without a sales charge.
or Pay Dividends in Cash ... REINVESTMENT—Reinvest distributions of realized securities profits only, ... les charge; income dividends are to be paid in cash.
CASH—Pay all income dividends and distributions from realized securities profits in cash.

④ FOR DREYFUS LIQUID ASSETS ONLY
MONTHLY OR QUARTERLY DISTRIBUTION PLANS Please redeem on the first business day of each month or calendar
YES NO quarter all shares purchased during the preceding month or quarter for the investor's account through
(Check one box) ☐ Monthly ☐ Quarterly reinvestment of dividends and distributions and MAIL the proceeds to the investor's address.
(Check one box ONLY if "Yes" is checked)

⑤ FOR DREYFUS LIQUID ASSETS AND/OR DREYFUS TAX EXEMPT MONEY MARKET FUND
[A] CHECK REDEMPTION PRIVILEGE
YES NO I hereby request The Bank of New York ("Bank") to honor checks drawn by me against my Company(s) account subject to
(Check one box) ☐ ☐ **Check Box for Check Writing Privileges** ...

[B] EXPEDITED REDEMPTION PAYMENTS
YES NO **Check Box for Wire Transfer** ... quickly, amounts of $1,000 or more will be sent ONLY ...
(Check one box) ☐ ☐

FILL OUT THE REST OF THIS BOX ONLY IF "YES" IS CHECKED NEXT TO EXPEDITED REDEMPTION PAYMENTS

Name _____
Bank Data for Wire Transfer
Account Name _____ Account Number _____
Address of Bank _____ City _____ State _____ Zip Code _____

[C] STATUS OF ACCOUNT TELEPHONE CONSENT —The investor hereby authorizes The Bank of New York ("Bank") to
YES NO **Check Box for Telephone Query** ... but not limited to the number of shares held.
(Check one box) ☐ ☐ The Bank shall ... remain in effect until the Bank has received written revocation.

⑥ [A] TELEPHONE EXCHANGE PRIVILEGE (Available For All Funds)
[B] TELEPHONE **Telephone Exchange & Redemption** Dreyfus Tax Exempt Bond Fund and
Dreyfus ...
☐ Check this box only if you wish to have a Telephone Authorization form sent to you.

⑦ SIGNATURE—By the execution of this Application, the investor represents and warrants that he has full right, power and
authority, and, if a natural person, is of legal age in his state of residence, to make the investment applied for pursuant to this
Application, and the person or persons, if any, signing on behalf of the investor represent and warrant that they are duly
authorized to sign this Application and to purchase or redeem shares on behalf of the investor. If applicable, the investor
hereby appoints The Bank of New York as its agent to receive dividends and distributions for their automatic reinvestment
in additional shares of the Fund(s). **Signatures**

SIGNATURE OF APPLICANT _____ DATE _____ SIGNATURE OF JOINT REGISTRANT, IF ANY _____
SS Number
TAXPAYER IDENTIFICATION NUMBER _____ NAME OF TAXPAYER WHOSE NUMBER APPEARS AT LEFT _____

Mail this form with your check payable to The Bank of New York to: P1P-9-A
THE BANK OF NEW YORK, DREYFUS SERVICE CORPORATION, P.O. BOX 12118, NEWARK, NEW JERSEY 07101

the fund is $6, then you can deposit $18,237 and regain the interest for one day. But if the fund declares that it will hold your deposit for 10 business days (at least 12 calendar days), then the break-even deposit drops to $1,529. If your deposit exceeds that break-even amount, you will earn money by paying your bank's wire transfer fee and wiring the cash to the fund.

If you send a check and wait for it to clear through normal channels, you will lose interest. More important, by wiring your initial deposit, you can enter your equity or income fund directly, knowing that you can switch out of it at any time. If you decide to wire your cash to the fund and you do not have an account established, call the fund for explicit instructions. You will be given an account number and told exactly how to instruct your bank to wire transfer your cash.

TAX EFFECTS

Retain all of the confirmations and reports from the fund for reference. If you switch from your money market fund into an equity fund, note exactly how much interest was earned during the time your funds were on deposit in the money market fund. The interest received will always be taxed at ordinary income rates.

Switches out of an equity or equity-income fund need to be monitored for any capital gains or losses, including those taken by the fund and distributed to you. If you owned the equity shares for at least 31 days, any capital gains distributed to you or reinvested for additional shares would be reported as long-term capital gains. The mutual fund will usually net out the gains by subtracting any losses from recognized gains.

If you owned the shares in the equity fund for less than six months, any gain or loss in the NAV would be short-term and would be reported as ordinary income or loss. Switching after holding the equity shares for longer than six months entitles you to a long-term gain if the shares sell for more than the price you paid. When your mutual fund switching program is invested in an IRA or a Keogh, you need not concern yourself about the long- or short-term effects of trades.

The terms "buy" and "sell" in a market timing program refer to the prices and dates at which you switch funds. Switching out of an equity fund into a money market fund, for example, is considered a sale of your equity fund shares. Switching from a money market to an equity fund is a "buy." Recognize, too, that a capital gain or loss resulting from the sale of a mutual fund that invests in municipal tax-free bonds will also affect your taxes according to how long you owned the shares. Income from tax-free bonds is not taxable at the federal level, but capital gains are taxed. Whether you incur state taxes on the income depends on other factors beyond the scope of this book. Check with your accountant for any possible tax impact.

Use your records to compare your program's progress with that of other timers. You might also use the data you collect to modify your own indicators.

10

Using Margin to Increase Performance

You may margin your no-load mutual funds to gain an added measure of performance. Charles Schwab & Co. is the largest service currently offering margin accounts for a wide selection of no-load mutual fund shares. At this writing, Schwab permits trading in about two hundred different mutual funds. Jack White & Co. (La Jolla Gateway Bldg., Suite 220, 9191 Towne Center Drive, San Diego, CA 92122; (800) 233-3411 national or (800) 542-6188 in California) offers margin accounts with no-load funds. Fidelity permits margining shares of their own funds, but at this writing its margin program does not extend to the trading of non-Fidelity fund shares. Indications are that this limit may be lifted. Schwab's Marketplace program affords the aggressive investor the opportunity of leveraging no-load mutual fund accounts and increasing the rate of return—if the market responds positively.

Paul A. Merriman & Associates (PM&A) ran a simulation of a program comparing their three nonleveraged models with leveraged programs for three levels of volatility. The conditions assumed that the shares would be fully margined to the limit of 50 percent. When switching from an equity fund into a money fund, Schwab offers a choice of three Kemper money market funds: Kemper Cash Equivalent Fund, Kemper Tax-Exempt Fund, and Kemper Government Securities Portfolio.

With or without market timing, past results of mutual fund performance are only hypothetical when projected into the future. Unfortunately, looking backward is the only way to determine what might be reasonable in the future. The following comments and assumptions are important when reviewing the comparisons of results with an aggressive mutual fund without timing, with timing, and with timing on margin:

Paul A. Merriman & Associates started managing funds with the Merriman Equity Switch Model on July 31, 1983, so all prior timing dates are strictly hypothetical. The Merriman Equity Switch Model is hypothetically applied to the fund from January 1970 through July 31, 1983. The original investment in the simulation was $10,000. Average 90-day Treasury bill rates are assumed while the account is in money market funds. The only time the account borrows on margin is while it is invested in the equity fund. Borrowing at a 50 percent margin assumes an interest rate 3 percent above average T-bill rates.

Table 10A. Performance of buy-and-hold investment program as a base compared with market timing with and without margin in Value Line Special Situations Fund.

	Buy/Hold		Market Timing Without	Margin	Market Timing Without	Margin
	% Change	Value	% Change	Value	% Change	Value
1970	- 34.4	$6,560	+ 10.5	$11,050	+ 16.8	$11,680
1971	+ 17.6	$7,715	+ 35.9	$15,017	+ 61.0	$18,805
1972	- 11.0	$6,866	- 4.5	$14,341	- 17.6	$15,495
1973	- 45.5	$3,742	- 1.6	$14,112	- 10.4	$13,884
1974	- 29.5	$2,638	+ 7.1	$15,114	+ 7.1	$14,870
1975	+ 47.0	$3,878	+ 34.0	$20,252	+ 45.8	$21,680
1976	+ 52.7	$5,922	+ 57.8	$31,958	+106.8	$44,834
1977	+ 12.3	$6,650	+ 3.5	$33,077	- .5	$44,609
1978	+ 21.2	$8,060	+ 17.0	$38,700	+ 24.2	$55,404
1979	+ 43.6	$11,574	+ 26.0	$48,762	+ 33.9	$74,186
1980	+ 54.4	$17,870	+ 79.4	$86,991	+144.6	$181,459
1981	- 2.2	$17,477	+ 8.5	$94,385	+ 8.2	$196,339
1982	+ 23.1	$21,514	+ 30.7	$123,361	+ 41.5	$277,819
1983	+ 19.4	$25,688	+ 21.4	$149,761	+ 23.5	$343,106
1984	- 25.5	$19,138	- 5.7	$141,224	- 24.5	$259,045
1985	+ 21.1	$23,176	+ 21.1	$171,023	+ 28.7	$333,391
(1)	+ 5.4%		+ 19.4%		+ 24.5%	
(2) (10)	+ 31.2%	(14)	+ 27.2%	(12)	+ 45.2%	
(3) (5)	- 24.7%	(3)	- 3.9%	(4)	- 13.3%	

(1) Compound Rate of Return
(2) Average Rate of Return for Profitable Years--(No. of Years)
(3) Average Rate of Return for Unprofitable Years--(No. of Years)

The simulation includes Schwab commissions. Results do not include any allowance for taxes or PM&A annual fees.

Investing in securities on margin represents additional risk and may not be appropriate for every investor. Results of the simulated comparison of market timing with margin and without margin in Value Line Special Situations Fund are shown in table 10A. Results of the simulated comparison of market timing with margin and without margin in Value Line Fund are shown in table 10B and in Value Line Income Fund in table 10C. Charts graphically displaying these differences are shown in figures 10-1, 10-2, and 10-3. Recognize, however, that you cannot margin an IRA or a Keogh retirement account. You are encouraged to compare the results of these three approaches: buy-and-hold with and without market timing, and margining with market timing. The results are indeed startling.

Table 10B. Performance of buy-and-hold investment program as a base compared with market timing with and without margin in Value Line Fund.

	Buy/Hold		Market Timing Without Margin		Market Timing With Margin	
	% Change	Value	% Change	Value	% Change	Value
1970	- 25.1%	$7,490.00	+ 9.8%	$10,980.00	+ 10.5%	$11,050
1971	+ 16.8	$8,748.00	+ 27.3	$13,978.00	+ 48.7	$16,431
1972	+ 10.5	$9,667.00	+ 4.9	$14,663.00	+ .2	$16,464
1973	- 29.7	$6,796.00	+ 2.5	$15,030.00	- 3.3	$15,921
1974	- 22.4	$5,274.00	+ 7.1	$16,097.00	+ 7.1	$17,051
1975	+ 39.0	$7,331.00	+ 20.2	$19,349.00	+ 26.0	$21,484
1976	+ 43.0	$10,483.00	+ 45.1	$28,075.00	+ 80.1	$38,693
1977	+ 9.5	$11,479.00	+ 1.1	$28,356.00	- 6.8	$36,062
1978	+ 19.3	$13,694.00	+ 12.3	$31,844.00	+ 15.0	$41,471
1979	+ 44.1	$19,733.00	+ 32.1	$42,066.00	+ 46.7	$60,838
1980	+ 41.6	$27,942.00	+ 57.4	$66,212.00	+100.7	$122,102
1981	+ 2.4	$28,613.00	+ 5.2	$69,655.00	+ 6.1	$129,550
1982	+ 28.1	$36,653.00	+ 23.5	$86,024.00	+ 31.0	$169,711
1983	- 1.7	$36,030.00	- .6	$85,508.00	- 7.1	$157,662
1984	- 15.2	$30,553.00	+ 1.6	$86,876.00	- 10.6	$140,950
1985	+ 34.6	$41,124.00	+ 33.0	$115,545.00	+ 53.8	$216,781
(1)	+ 9.2%		+ 16.5%		+ 21.2%	
(2) (11)	+ 26.3%	(15)	+ 18.9%	(12)	+ 35.5%	
(3) (5)	- 18.8%	(1)	- .6%	(4)	- 7.0%	

(1) Compound Rate of Return
(2) Average Rate of Return for Profitable Years (No. of Years)
(3) Average Rate of Return for Unprofitable Years (No. of Years)

CHARLES SCHWAB MUTUAL FUND MARKETPLACE

Rather than deal directly with each of the mutual funds and gain the privilege of margining your mutual fund shares, you may decide to use the flexible program offered by Charles Schwab & Co. While there is a fee charged on each trade (switch), offsetting advantages may make the cost worthwhile. You can do a number of things through the Schwab Marketplace that you cannot do directly with the funds. These advantages may very well be worth the cost of trading. A summary of the differences between using the Schwab Marketplace and dealing directly with the mutual funds of your choice are as follows:

1. A wide selection of mutual funds of all types can be traded or switched through a Schwab account. Currently about two hundred no-load mutual funds can be accessed directly through the Schwab Marketplace. Recognize the advantage of

Table 10C. Performance of buy-and-hold investment program as a base compared with market timing with and without margin in Value Line Income Fund.

		Buy/Hold	Market Timing Without	Margin	Market Timing With	Margin
	% Change	Value	% Change	Value	% Change	Value
1970	+ 6.7%	$10,670	+ 19.3%	$11,930	+ 29.5	$12,950
1971	+ 13.5	$12,110	+ 19.4	$14,244	+ 40.0	$18,130
1972	+ 5.1	$13,212	+ 2.0	$14,529	- 6.6	$16,933
1973	- 15.9	$11,111	+ 8.8	$15,808	+ 9.2	$18,491
1974	- 16.1	$9,322	+ 7.1	$16,930	+ 7.1	$19,804
1975	+ 41.7	$13,209	+ 22.3	$20,705	+ 32.4	$26,220
1976	+ 34.5	$17,766	+ 29.2	$26,751	+ 48.0	$38,806
1977	+ 1.8	$18,086	+ 4.2	$27,875	- .5	$38,612
1978	+ 11.1	$20,094	+ 16.5	$32,474	+ 23.4	$47,647
1979	+ 27.6	$25,640	+ 15.5	$37,507	+ 13.9	$54,270
1980	+ 26.0	$32,512	+ 35.0	$50,634	+ 55.8	$84,553
1981	+ 16.4	$37,844	+ 6.2	$53,773	+ 13.6	$96,052
1982	+ 29.7	$49,084	+ 20.6	$64,850	+ 25.3	$120,353
1983	+ 6.5	$52,274	+ 8.4	$71,381	+ 10.1	$132,509
1984	+ 2.7	$53,685	+ 14.1	$81,446	+ 14.8	$152,120
1985	+ 23.9	$66,516	+ 20.6	$98,224	+ 39.7	$212,511
(1)	+ 12.6%		+ 15.3%		+ 21.2%	
(2) (14)	+ 18.8%		(16)+ 15.6%		(14) + 25.9%	
(3) (2)	- 16.0%		(0) 0		(2) - 3.6%	

(1) Compound Rate of Return
(2) Average Rate of Return for Profitable Years (No. of Years)
(3) Average Rate of Return for Unprofitable Years (No. of Years)

this feature. Earlier we said that you should select your equity, gold, or bond fund and the money market fund in the same fund family. Otherwise, switching by telephone would not be possible. With the Schwab Marketplace, this requirement is no longer limiting. You may switch from one no-load mutual fund to any other fund in the Schwab Marketplace. This feature alone may be worth the fee. As an example, if you find that Equity Fund A is no longer on the high growth track that originally induced you to buy it, at the next switch signal, to get back into a rising market, you easily switch funds into Equity Fund B. If you decide that the volatility of the original Equity

Fig. 10-1. Graphic comparison of investment results between buy-and-hold and market timing with and without using margin in Value Line Special Situations Fund.

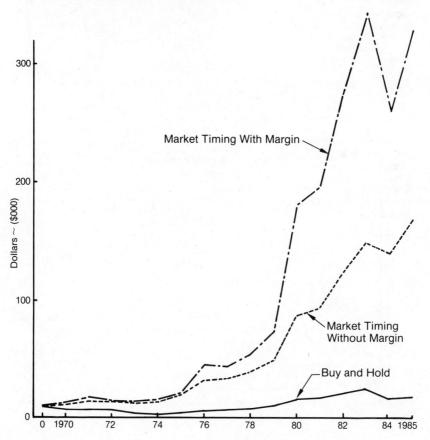

Fund A was a bit too risky for your taste, the next time you switch back into equities, choose a more conservative equity fund with a lower beta.

2. All of your dividend and capital gains distributions will be reinvested automatically. If you prefer to have the income from the funds sent to you by check, that option is also availa-

Fig. 10-2. Graphic comparison of investment results between buy-and-hold and market timing with and without using margin in Value Line Fund.

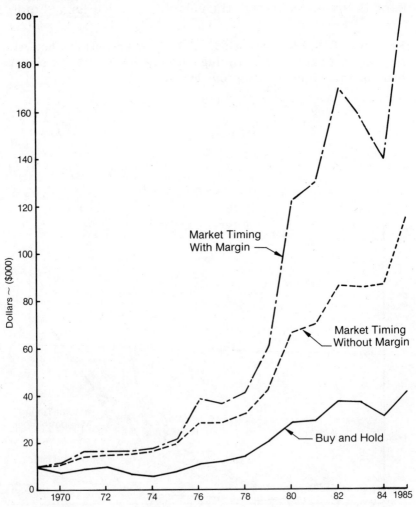

ble. All of the records to be kept for tax and investment monitoring will be shown on monthly reports.

3. Transaction fees for the Schwab Marketplace are less than the discounted fee schedules for trading stocks. Further, switching from one fund to another incurs only one fee—not a sales fee plus a buying fee, as is usual with stocks or bonds. The transaction fees for Schwab Marketplace are as follows:

Dollar Range for Transaction	*Transaction Fee*
0–$3,000	$12 + 8/10 of 1% of principal amount
$3,001–$7,000	$24 + 4/10 of 1% of principal amount
$7,001–up	$38 + 2/10 of 1% of principal amount

(Some funds may also charge sales and/or redemption fees. Read the prospectus for each mutual fund for details. The transaction fees listed above are charged by Charles Schwab & Co., Inc., and not by the funds or their underwriters.)

Fig. 10-3. Graphic comparison of investment results between buy-and-hold and market timing with and without using margin in Value Line Income Fund.

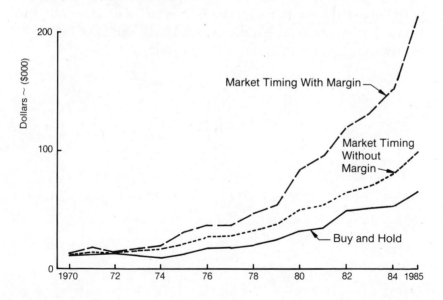

While the fee schedule appears reasonable, considering the features, recognize that frequent switches can run up your expenses. Further, as a retirement program builds its asset base, you could be in for higher fees. Switching $100,000 from an equity fund to a money market fund would involve a fee of $38 plus .002 percent of $100,000, or a total of $238. Three switches during one year would reduce your overall gain by about seven-tenths of 1 percent. On the other hand, margining your account during one of the upswings could more than offset the cost.

IT'S YOUR MOVE

As the saying has it, the ball is now in your court. You understand the concept of market timing with no-load mutual funds. You are aware of the details on how to initiate a program—either under your direction or under the management of a specialist organization. Now it's up to you to take action or forget the whole idea and return to what you have been doing. We have provided what we believe is uncontestable evidence that market timing can build your assets quicker and with less risk than any other program we know. If this evidence has not motivated you to act, then . . . But procrastination might be your biggest threat. Don't let the failure to act scuttle your opportunity to gain wealth and financial independence before it even begins. As we said, the ball is in your court.

APPENDIX A

Mutual Funds Suitable for Market Timing

Following is a listing of mutual fund managers and the mutual funds they manage that allow switching for investors who adapt their investment strategy to market timing. The listing is designed to provide information on the funds' basic operating policies, not their specific historical performance. (See Appendix B for a list of timing organizations and newsletters that publish mutual fund performance data. Also, see Appendix C for a list of no-load mutual funds that can be margined through Charles Schwab & Co. for specific performance data over recent three-month, one-year, and five-year periods.) The listing of mutual funds suitable for timing is not intended to supply complete information. You should always refer to a fund's prospectus or contact the fund directly for specific and up-to-date information.

The information provided in the following listing has been obtained from fund prospectuses, through direct conversations with mutual fund managers, and from various trade sources. We believe the information to be accurate at the time it was obtained and published. The authors are not responsible for inadvertent errors or changes in the information, which is intended to be used in the broad selection of funds and not for the actual purchase. The authors recommend that you carefully review a fund's prospectus before purchasing shares.

The information on fund performance that is shown in the listing in brief form does not take into consideration income taxes. Listings do not imply recommendations. The material does not purport to comply with the Statement of Policy of the Securities and Exchange Commission and may not be used by any issuer, underwriter, dealer, or any other representatives or employees to promote the sale of fund shares. Past results are no guarantee of future profits.

The following information explains the various categories noted in the listings:

Fund Objectives: Investment categories are based on what Paul A. Merriman & Associates perceives to be their historic investment objective and volatility rating. These categories may not agree with those stated in the individual fund's prospectus. The fund categories used within this list are as follows:

Aggressive Growth Funds (equities) aim for capital gains and invest aggressively in speculative stocks. They may use speculative investing techniques, such as margining the portfolio and options, and they tend to be relatively volatile.

Growth Funds (equities) primarily emphasize long-term growth and are typically less volatile than Aggressive Growth Funds. Conservative growth funds are included within this group.

Growth-Income Funds (equities) focus their emphasis on a combination of long-term growth and income, and are less volatile than Growth Funds.

Fixed-Income Funds (bonds) typically invest in government or corporate intermediate- to long-term bonds. Some bond funds invest only in municipal (tax-free) bonds. Although bond prices fluctuate, their volatility is generally much lower than stock prices.

Gold Funds (equities) invest in companies involved primarily in the mining and refining of gold. Some so-called gold funds may also invest in silver or other precious metal mining companies. This group tends to be more volatile than most common stock funds.

Manager: A list of the fund managers appears ahead of the fund listings. These managers are numbered, and their numbers appear on the charts for reference. To obtain a copy of the prospectus for a fund or to ask specific questions of any particular fund, contact the fund manager.

Switches: This column notes the number of switches the fund permits each year. A switch is defined as a round-trip involving two transactions—either a move from a money fund to an equity or bond fund and back to the money fund, or a move from an equity or bond fund to a money fund and back to the equity or bond fund. Specific information on special switch restrictions, if any, may be obtained directly from each fund. You should know the exact rules for each particular fund before you invest.

Switch Fee: This is the charge that a fund levies for each switch. It is important to note that qualified plans (IRA/Keogh) may be exempt from a switch fee. You should study the prospectus carefully before investing. Some funds charge switch fees for telephone switching but do not impose a fee on written switching, and some funds impose a fee when switching in one direction but not in the opposite direction.

Sales Fee: In this column, N denotes that the fund is a no-load; that is, there are no sales fees or commissions charged to buy into the mutual fund. An L indicates that the fund is loaded, and you will be charged a commission or sales fee to purchase shares in the fund.

Written Exchange: In this column, Y for Yes indicates that the fund will accept a letter from you as authorization to transfer your investment between an equity or bond fund and a money fund. Many funds require that your signature be guaranteed. You should read the prospectus carefully for any special rules governing these types of transactions and acceptable signature guarantees.

Telephone Exchange: In this column, Y for Yes and N for No indicate whether the fund will allow you to switch between equity or bond funds and a money market fund in either direction by calling on the telephone. Almost every fund requires you to file a special telephone exchange authorization form with the fund prior to entering any of these transactions.

Five-Year Average Return: The approximate five-year average (not compound) rates of return listed in these columns assume the reinvestment of all interest, dividends, and capital gains without considering taxes. Results are based on buy-and-hold. With a timing strategy, many of the poorer performances are improved considerably.

Size: For the purpose of this listing, the following symbols denote the relative size in terms of assets of each fund, as of September 30, 1985:

S	up to $50 million		
M	$50 million	to	$200 million
L	$200 million	to	$500 million
XL	$500 million	to	$1 billion
G	$1 billion	or greater	

MUTUAL FUND MANAGERS

Following is a list of mutual fund managers. The addresses and telephone numbers listed for these companies can be used for requesting prospectuses and information. Also included is the name of one money fund offered by each fund family. Additional money market funds may be available, as some fund families offer more than one. Each of the money market funds offers check-writing privileges, which is important because it allows you to liquidate portions of your funds immediately simply by writing a check.

1. AIM Management, 107 N. Adams St., Rockville, MD 20850; (800) 638-2042; *Short Term Yield Securities.*
2. American Funds Distributors, 333 S. Hope St., Los Angeles, CA 90071; (800) 421-9900; *Cash Management Trust of America.*
3. American Investors, P.O. Box 2500, Greenwich, CT 06836; (800) 243-5353; *American Investors Money Fund.*
4. AMEV Investors, P.O. Box 64284, St. Paul, MN 55125; (800) 328-1064; *AMEV Money Fund.*
5. Axe-Houghton Securities, 400 Benedict Ave., Tarrytown, NY 10591; (800) 431-1030; *Axe-Houghton Money Market Fund.*
6. Benham Capital Management, 755 Page Mill Rd., Palo Alto, CA 94304; (800) 227-8380; *Capital Preservation Fund.*
7. BLC Equity Services Corp., 711 High St., Des Moines, IA 50307; (515) 247-5711; *BLC Cash Management Fund.*
8. Boston Co. Capital Group, One Boston Place, Boston, MA 02108; (800) 343-6324; *Boston Co. Cash Management Fund.*
9. Bull and Bear Group, 11 Hanover Square, New York, NY 10005; (800) 431-6060; *Bull and Bear Dollar Reserves.*
10. Calvin Bullock, 40 Rector St., New York, NY 10006; (800) 221-5757; *Equitable Money Market Account.*
11. Calvert Group, 1700 Pennsylvania Ave., N.W., Washington, DC 20006; (800) 368-2747; *Money Management Plus.*
12. Cigna Securities, Hartford, CT 06152; (800) 225-5151; *Cigna Money Market Fund.*
13. Colonial Investment Services, 75 Federal St., Boston, MA 02110; (800) 225-2365; *Colonial Money Market Trust.*
14. Columbia Management Co., 1301 S.W. 5th Ave., P.O. Box 1350, Portland, OR 97207; (800) 547-1037; *Columbia Daily Income.*
15. Country Capital Management Co., P.O. Box 2222, Bloomington, IL 61701; (309) 557-2444; *Country Capital Money Market Fund.*
16. Criterion Distributors, 333 Clay St., Suite 4300, Houston, TX 77002; (713) 751-2400; *Current Interest Money Market Fund.*

17. Dean Witter Reynolds, One World Trade Center, New York, NY 10048; (800) 221-2685; *Active Assets Money Trust.*
18. Delaware Distributors, 10 Penn Center Plaza, Philadelphia, PA 19103; (800) 523-4640; *Delaware Cash Reserve.*
19. Delfi Capital Sales, Greenville Center C-200, Wilmington, DE 19802; (800) 441-9490; *Sigma Money Market Fund.*
20. Dreyfus Service Corp., 600 Madison Ave., New York, NY 10022; (800) 645-6561; *Dreyfus Liquid Assets.*
21. Eaton Vance Distributors, 24 Federal St., Boston, MA 02110; (800) 225-6265; *Eaton Vance Cash Management Fund.*
22. Equity Services, National Life Drive, Montpelier, VT 05604; (800) 233-4332; *Sentinel Cash Management Fund.*
23. Federated Securites Corp., 421 Seventh Ave., Pittsburgh, PA 15219; (800) 245-2423; *High Yield Cash Trust.*
24. Fidelity Distributors Corp., 82 Devonshire St., Boston, MA 02109; (800) 544-6666; *Fidelity Cash Reserves.*
25. Financial Programs, P.O. Box 2040, Englewood, CO 80201; (800) 525-8085; *Financial Daily Income Shares.*
26. First Investors Management Co., 120 Wall St., New York, NY 10005; (800) 223-6300; *First Investors Cash Management Fund.*
27. 44 Securities, One State Street Plaza, New York, NY 10004; (800) 221-7836; *Reserve Fund.*
28. John Hancock Distributors, P.O. Box 111, Boston, MA 02117; (800) 225-5291; *John Hancock Cash Management Trust.*
29. E. F. Hutton and Co., One Battery Park Plaza, New York, NY 10004; (800) 468-8614; *Hutton AMA Cash Fund.*
30. IDS/American Express, IDS Tower, Minneapolis, MN 55474; (800) 328-8300; *IDS Cash Management.*
31. Janus Fund, 100 Fillmore St., Suite 300, Denver, CO 80206; (800) 525-3713; *Kemper Money Market Fund.*
32. Kemper Sales Co., 120 S. LaSalle St., Chicago, IL 60603; (800) 621-1048; *Kemper Money Market Fund.*
33. Legg Mason Wood Walker, P.O. Box 1476, Baltimore, MD 21203; (800) 492-7777; *Legg Mason Cash Reserve.*
34. Lexington Management Corp., P.O. Box 1515, Saddle Brook, NJ 07662; (800) 526-0057; *Lexington Money Market Trust.*
35. Lord Abbett and Co., 63 Wall St., New York, NY 10005; (800) 223-4224; *Lord Abbett Cash Reserve Fund.*
36. Merrill Lynch Funds Distributor, 633 Third Ave., New York, NY 10017; (212) 692-8159; *Merrill Lynch Ready Assets Trust.*
37. Murphey-Favre, Seafirst Financial Center, 9th Fl., Spokane,

WA 99201; (800) 541-0830, (509) 624-4101; *Composite Cash Management.*

38. Mutual of Omaha Fund Management, 10235 Regency Circle, Omaha, NE 68114; (800) 228-2499; *Mutual of Omaha Cash Reserve.*

39. National Securities and Research Corp., 605 Third Ave., New York, NY 10158; (800) 223-7757; *National Cash Reserves.*

40. Nationwide Financial Services, One Nationwide Plaza, Columbus, OH 43216; (800) 848-0920 *Nationwide Money Market Fund.*

41. NEL Equity Services, 501 Boylston St., Boston, MA 02117; (800) 343-7104; *NEL Cash Management Trust Money Market Series.*

42. Neuberger and Berman Management, 342 Madison Ave., New York, NY 10173; (800) 367-0770; *Neuberger & Berman Government Fund.*

43. Oppenheimer Investor Services, 2 Broadway, New York, NY 10004; (800) 525-7048; *Oppenheimer Money Market Fund.*

44. Paine Webber, 1285 Ave. of the Americas, 15th Fl., New York, NY 10020; (800) 223-3402; *Paine Webber Cash Fund.*

45. Phoenix Equity Planning Corp., One American Row, Hartford, CT 06115; (800) 243-4361; *Phoenix Money Market Fund.*

46. Prescott, Ball and Turben, 230 W. Monroe St., Chicago, IL 60606; (800) 621-7321; *Prescott Money Market Fund.*

47. PRO Services, P.O. Box 1111, Blue Bell, PA 19422; (800) 523-0864; *PRO Money Fund—Treasury.*

48. Prudential-Bache, One Seaport Plaza, New York, NY 10292; (800) 872-7787; *Command Money Fund.*

49. Putnam Financial Services, One Post Office Square, Boston, MA 02109; (800) 225-1581; *Putnam Daily Dividend Trust.*

50. Safeco Securities, Safeco Plaza, Seattle, WA 98185; (800) 426-6730, (206) 545-5530; *Safeco Money Market Fund.*

51. Seligman Marketing, One Bankers Trust Plaza, New York, NY 10006; (800) 221-2450; *Seligman Cash Management Fund Prime.*

52. Sentry Equity Services, 1800 N. Point Drive, Stevens Point, WI 54481; (800) 826-0266; *Sentry Cash Management Fund.*

53. Smith Barney, Harris Upham & Co., 333 W. 34th St., New York, NY 10001; (212) 613-2631; *National Liquid Reserves.*

54. State Bond Sales Corp., Investment Dept., 100-106 N. Minnesota St., New Ulm, MN 56073; (800) 328-4735; *State Bond Cash Management Fund.*

55. Stein Roe and Farnham, P.O. Box 1162, Chicago, IL 60690; (800) 621-0320; *Stein Roe Cash Reserves.*
56. Unified Management Corp., 600 Guaranty Bldg., Indianapolis, IN 46204; (800) 862-7283; *Liquid Green Trust.*
57. United Services Advisors, P.O. Box 29467, San Antonio, TX 78229; (800) 824-4653; *United Services Treasury Securities.*
58. USAA Transfer Services, P.O. Box 33277, San Antonio, TX 78265; (800) 531-8181; *USAA Money Market Fund.*
59. Value Line Securities, 711 Third Ave., New York, NY 10017; (800) 223-0818; *Value Line Cash Fund.*
60. Waddell and Reed, 2400 Pershing Rd., P.O. Box 1343, Kansas City, MO 64141; (800) 821-5664; *United Cash Management.*

The following listing of mutual funds (pages 168–177) is organized by Fund Objective. The listed funds are known to have liberal switching policies. With the exception of Tax-Exempt Fixed-Income Funds, all of the funds offer qualified IRA and Keogh plans and have the ability to automatically deduct fixed amounts on a regular basis from your checking accounts (Automatic Contributions).

Aggressive Growth Funds

	Mgr.	Switches	Switch Fee($)	Sales Fee	Written Exch.	Tel. Exch.	5-Year Aver.	Assets
AMEV Capital	4	8	0	L	Y	Y	N/A	S
AMEV Growth	4	8	0	L	Y	Y	21.1	M
AMEV Special	4	8	0	L	Y	Y	18.7	S
Cigna Aggressive Growth	12	UNL	5	L	Y	Y	N/A	S
Constellation Growth	46	UNL	0	N	Y	Y	4.1	M
Dean Witter Developing Growth	17	UNL	0	L	Y	Y	N/A	M
Delta Trend Fund	18	UNL	5	L	Y	Y	21.0	M
Dreyfus Leverage	20	UNL	0	N	Y	Y	15.3	L
Fairfield Fund	39	UNL	5	L	Y	Y	9.7	S
Fidelity Discoverer Fund	24	8	0	N	Y	Y	20.2	M
Fidelity Freedom Fund	24	8	0	N	Y	Y	N/A	XL
Fidelity OTC Portfolio	24	8	0	L	Y	Y	N/A	M
Fidelity Special Situations	24	8	0	N	Y	Y	N/A	S
Financial Dynamics	25	8	0	N	Y	Y	11.1	M
First Investors Discovery	26	UNL	5	L	Y	N	10.0	S
44 Wall Street Equity	27	UNL	1/4 of 1%	N	Y	Y	-3.7	S
44 Wall Street Fund	27	UNL	1/4 of 1%	N	Y	Y	-13.9	S
Greenway Fund	1	UNL	0	L	Y	Y	8.7	S
Hutton Invest. Emerging Growth	29	UNL	5	L	Y	Y	N/A	M
IDS Discovery Fund	30	UNL	0	L	Y	Y	N/A	L
IDS Progressive Fund	30	UNL	0	L	Y	Y	21.3	M
IDS Strategy-Aggress. Equity	30	UNL	0	N	Y	Y	N/A	S
Janus Fund	31	8	5	N	Y	Y	26.2	L
Leverage Fund of Boston	21	UNL	5	L	Y	N	8.6	S
Lord Abbett Dev. Growth	35	UNL	0	L	Y	N	7.6	L
Lowry Market Timing	16	UNL	5	L	Y	Y	N/A	M
Oppenheimer Challenger	43	UNL	5	L	Y	N	N/A	S
Oppenheimer Directors	43	UNL	5	L	Y	N	10.9	L
Oppenheimer Regency	43	UNL	5	L	Y	N	N/A	M

	Mgr. Switches	Switch Fee($)	Sales Fee	Written Exch.	Tel. Exch.	5-Year Aver.	Assets
Oppenheimer Target	43	UNL	5	L	Y	N	N/A	M
Oppenheimer Time	43	UNL	5	L	Y	N	16.5	M
Phoenix Stock	45	UNL	0	L	Y	Y	32.0	M
Pilot Fund	16	UNL	5	L	Y	Y	10.0	M
Putnam Capital	49	UNL	5	L	Y	N	10.4	S
Putnam Vista Fund	49	UNL	5	L	Y	N	22.3	M
Putnam Voyager Fund	49	UNL	5	L	Y	N	15.8	L
Sigma Capital Shares	19	UNL	0	L	Y	Y	26.0	M
Sigma Venture Shares	19	UNL	0	L	Y	Y	15.2	S
Stein Roe Discovery	55	UNL	0	N	Y	Y	N/A	M
Stein Roe Special Fund	55	UNL	0	N	Y	Y	20.1	L
Stein Roe Universe Fund	55	UNL	0	N	Y	Y	N/A	S
United New Concepts	60	UNL	0	N	Y	N	N/A	S
USAA Sunbelt ERA	58	UNL	5	N	Y	Y	N/A	M
Value Line Leverage Growth	59	UNL	0	N	Y	Y	16.0	M
Value Line Special Situations	59	UNL	0	N	Y	Y	4.4	L

Growth Funds

	Mgr.	Switches	Switch Fee($)	Sales Fee	Written Exch.	Tel. Exch.	5-Year Aver.	Assets
AMCAP Fund	2	UNL	0	L	Y	Y	19.7	S
American Investors	3	UNL	0	N	Y	Y	-.6	M
AMEV Capital	4	8	0	L	Y	Y	21.8	M
Axe-Houghton Stock	5	UNL	0	L	Y	N	9.7	M
BLC Growth Fund	7	UNL	0	L	Y	Y	11.4	S
Boston Co. Capital Appreciation	8	UNL	0	N	Y	Y	15.3	L
Boston Co. Special Growth	8	UNL	0	N	Y	Y	N/A	S
Bull & Bear Capital Growth	9	UNL	0	L	Y	Y	7.5	M
Bullock Aggressive Growth	10	UNL	0	N	Y	Y	N/A	S
Calvert Equity Fund	11	UNL	0	L	Y	Y	N/A	S
Cigna Growth Fund	12	UNL	5	L	Y	Y	12.1	M

Growth Funds *(cont'd)*

	Mgr.	Switches	Switch Fee($)	Sales Fee	Written Exch.	Tel. Exch.	5-Year Aver.	Assets
Colonial Growth Shares	13	UNL	5	L	Y	N	11.4	M
Columbia Growth	14	UNL	0	N	Y	N	20.9	M
Country Capital Growth	15	UNL	0	L	Y	Y	14.7	M
Dean Witter Ind. Valued Secs.	17	UNL	0	L	Y	Y	8.8	S
Dreyfus Growth Opportunity	20	UNL	0	N	Y	Y	5.8	L
Dreyfus Third Century Fund	20	UNL	0	N	Y	Y	9.4	M
Eaton Vance Growth	21	UNL	5	L	Y	N	16.7	M
Eaton Vance Special Equities	21	UNL	5	L	Y	N	14.5	S
Federated Growth	23	UNL	0	L	Y	Y	N/A	S
Fidelity Contra Fund	24	8	0	N	Y	Y	13.4	M
Fidelity Destiny Fund	24	8	0	L	Y	Y	27.3	XL
Fidelity Magellan Fund	24	8	0	L	Y	Y	46.1	G
Fidelity Mercury Fund	24	8	0	L	Y	Y	N/A	M
Fidelity Trend	24	8	0	N	Y	Y	12.2	XL
First Investment Fund for Growth	26	UNL	5	L	Y	N	2.0	M
Growth Fund of America	2	UNL	0	L	Y	Y	16.9	XL
Hutton Investment Basic Value	29	UNL	5	L	Y	Y	N/A	M
Hutton Investment Growth	29	UNL	5	L	Y	Y	N/A	XL
ICA	2	UNL	0	L	Y	Y	21.7	G
IDS Growth Fund	30	UNL	0	L	Y	Y	16.1	XL
IDS New Dimensions	30	UNL	0	L	Y	Y	21.8	L
Kemper Growth Fund	32	UNL	0	L	Y	Y	14.1	L
Kemper Summit Fund	32	UNL	0	L	Y	Y	16.6	M
Legg Mason Value Trust	33	8	0	L	Y	Y	27.2	L
Lexington Growth Fund	34	UNL	5	N	Y	Y	2.2	S
Lexington Research Fund	34	UNL	5	N	Y	Y	12.8	M
Loomis-Sayles Capital	41	UNL	0	L	Y	Y	35.8	M
Lord Abbett Value Appreciation	35	UNL	0	L	Y	Y	N/A	L
Merrill Lynch Fund for Tomorrow	36	UNL	0	L	Y	N	N/A	L
Merrill Lynch Special Value	36	UNL	0	L	Y	N	9.2	M
Mutual of Omaha Growth	38	UNL	0	L	Y	Y	11.5	S
National Growth Fund	39	UNL	5	L	Y	Y	3.7	M

Fund								
Nationwide Growth	40	UNL	0	L	Y	N	24.9	M
NEL Growth Fund	41	UNL	0	L	Y	Y	30.8	M
New Economy Fund	2	UNL	5	L	Y	Y	N/A	L
Oppenheimer Fund	43	UNL	5	L	Y	N	4.7	L
Oppenheimer Special	43	UNL	5	L	Y	N	10.4	XL
Paine Webber Olympus	44	UNL	0	L	Y	Y	N/A	S
Phoenix Growth	45	UNL	0	L	Y	Y	32.9	M
PRO Fund	47	UNL	0	L	Y	Y	8.7	S
Prudential-Bache Equity	48	UNL	0	L	Y	Y	N/A	M
Prudential-Bache Growth Oppor.	48	UNL	0	L	Y	Y	N/A	M
Prudential-Bache Research	48	UNL	5	N	Y	Y	N/A	XL
Putnam Investors Fund	49	UNL	0	L	Y	Y	13.4	M
Safeco Growth Fund	50	UNL	0	L	Y	Y	13.5	S
Selected Special Shares	46	UNL	0	L	Y	Y	10.8	S
Sentinel Growth Fund	22	UNL	0	L	Y	Y	17.5	S
Sentry Fund	52	UNL	10	L	Y	Y	10.5	M
Sigma Special Fund	19	UNL	5	L	Y	N	11.5	S
Smith Barney Equity	53	UNL	5	L	Y	N	13.2	S
State Bond Common Stock Fund	54	UNL	0	N	Y	N	6.3	M
State Bond Progress Fund	54	UNL	0	N	Y	N	9.1	L
Stein Roe Capital Opportunity	55	UNL	0	L	Y	Y	4.9	S
Stein Roe Stock Fund	55	UNL	5	L	Y	Y	8.5	M
Summit Investors	1	UNL	0	N	Y	N	N/A	L
Sunbelt Growth Fund	16	UNL	0	L	Y	N	N/A	S
Unified Growth Fund	56	UNL	5	N	Y	Y	14.5	M
United Accumulative Fund	57	UNL	0	L	Y	N	22.0	S
United Services Growth	57	12	5	N	Y	Y	N/A	XL
United Vanguard Fund	57	UNL	0	L	Y	N	24.6	S
USAA Mutual + Growth Fund	58	UNL	5	N	Y	Y	8.9	L
Vance Sanders Special	21	UNL	5	L	Y	N	7.7	M
Washington Mutual Investors	2	UNL	0	L	Y	Y	27.2	XL

Growth-Income Funds

	Mgr. Switches	Switch Fee($)	Sales Fee	Written Exch.	Tel. Exch.	5-Year Aver.	Assets
Affiliated Fund	35	UNL	0	L	Y	Y	18.5	G
American Leaders	23	UNL	0	L	Y	Y	26.1	M
American Mutual Fund	2	UNL	0	L	Y	Y	24.3	G
BLC Income Fund	7	UNL	0	L	Y	N	26.4	S
Bull & Bear Equity Income	9	UNL	0	N	Y	Y	13.1	S
Bullock Dividend Shares	10	UNL	0	L	Y	Y	19.8	L
Bullock Growth Fund	10	UNL	0	L	Y	Y	13.2	M
Cigna Value Fund	12	UNL	5	L	Y	Y	N/A	S
Colonial Corporate Cash I	13	UNL	5	L	Y	N	N/A	L
Colonial Corporate Cash II	13	UNL	5	L	Y	N	N/A	M
Composite Fund	37	UNL	0	L	Y	N	20.5	S
Dean Witter Div. Growth	17	UNL	0	L	Y	Y	N/A	L
Decatur Income Fund	18	UNL	5	L	Y	Y	22.4	XL
Delaware Fund	18	UNL	5	L	Y	Y	23.4	L
Div./Growth Dividend Series	1	UNL	10	N	Y	Y	14.9	S
Dreyfus Fund	20	UNL	0	N	Y	Y	16.4	G
Eaton & Howard Stock	21	UNL	5	N	Y	N	15.8	M
Eaton Vance Tax-Mgt. Trust	21	UNL	5	L	Y	N	N/A	XL
Federated Stock Trust	23	UNL	0	N	Y	N	N/A	L
Fidelity Equity Income	24	8	0	N	Y	Y	31.5	G
Fidelity Fund	24	8	0	N	Y	Y	19.7	XL
Fidelity Puritan	24	8	0	N	Y	Y	29.2	G
Financial Industrial Fund	25	8	0	N	Y	Y	12.0	L
Financial Industry Income	25	8	0	N	Y	Y	19.2	L
Fundamental Investors	2	UNL	0	L	Y	Y	21.3	L
Hamilton Funds	43	UNL	5	L	Y	N	10.0	L
IDS Equity	30	UNL	0	L	Y	Y	11.8	L
IDS Managed Retirement	30	UNL	0	L	Y	Y	N/A	M
IDS Stock Fund	30	UNL	0	L	Y	Y	12.7	G

	Mgr. Switches	Switch Fee($)	Sales Fee	Written Exch.	Tel. Exch.	5-Year Aver.	Assets
IDS Strategy-Equity	30	UNL	0	L	Y	Y	N/A	S
Income Fund of America	2	UNL	0	L	Y	Y	27.9	L
Merrill Lynch Basic Value	36	UNL	0	L	Y	N	23.6	L
Merrill Lynch Capital	36	UNL	0	L	Y	N	22.8	L
National Stock Fund	39	UNL	5	L	Y	N	14.0	L
Nationwide Fund	40	UNL	0	L	Y	N	18.3	L
NEL Equity Fund	41	UNL	0	L	Y	Y	18.3	S
NEL Retirement Equity	41	UNL	0	L	Y	N	19.6	M
Oppenheimer Equity	43	UNL	5	L	Y	N	26.3	M
Paine Webber Am. Fund	44	UNL	5	L	Y	Y	N/A	M
Prudential-Bache Utility	48	UNL	5	L	Y	N	N/A	M
Putnam Fund, Growth & Income	49	UNL	15	L	Y	N	17.4	XL
Safeco Equity Fund	50	UNL	0	N	Y	Y	12.6	S
Safeco Income Fund	50	UNL	0	N	Y	Y	24.3	S
Selected American Shares	46	UNL	0	N	Y	Y	22.7	M
Sentinel Common Stock	22	UNL	0	L	Y	Y	23.3	L
Sigma Investment Shares	19	UNL	10	L	Y	Y	18.5	M
Smith Barney Income & Growth	53	UNL	5	L	Y	N	24.7	M
Value Line Fund	59	UNL	0	N	Y	Y	6.8	L
Value Line Income	59	UNL	0	L	Y	N	23.0	XL

Fixed-Income—Taxable Funds

	Mgr. Switches	Switch Fee($)	Sales Fee	Written Exch.	Tel. Exch.	5-Year Aver.	Assets
Bullock High Income Shares	10	UNL	0	L	Y	Y	17.3	M
Bullock Monthly Income Shares	10	UNL	0	L	Y	Y	20.7	S
Bullock U.S. Government Income	10	UNL	0	L	Y	Y	N/A	S
Calvert Income	11	UNL	5	N	Y	Y	N/A	S
Cigna High Yield Fund	12	UNL	5	L	Y	Y	22.1	M
Cigna Income Fund	12	UNL	0	N	Y	Y	18.7	L
Columbia Fixed Income	14	UNL	0	L	Y	Y	N/A	M
Colonial Enhanced Mortgage	13	UNL	5	L	Y	N	N/A	S

Fixed Income—Taxable Funds (cont'd)

	Mgr.	Switches	Switch Fee($)	Sales Fee	Written Exch.	Tel. Exch.	5-Year Aver.	Assets
Colonial Govt. Securities Trust	13	UNL	8	L	Y	N	N/A	G
Colonial High Yield Fund	13	UNL	5	L	Y	N	20.8	M
Colonial Income Fund	13	UNL	5	L	Y	N	19.3	M
Composite Income Fund	37	UNL	0	L	Y	Y	19.1	S
Composite U.S. Govt. Securities	37	UNL	0	L	Y	Y	N/A	S
Country Capital Income	15	UNL	0	L	Y	Y	16.6	S
Dean Witter High Yield Sec.	17	UNL	0	L	Y	Y	20.6	XL
Dean Witter U.S.Govt. Sec. Trust	17	UNL	0	L	Y	Y	N/A	XL
Delchester Bond Fund	18	UNL	5	N	Y	Y	20.4	M
Dreyfus A Bond Plus	20	UNL	0	N	Y	Y	18.6	M
Eaton Vance Govt. Obligations	21	UNL	5	L	Y	N	N/A	L
Federated GNMA Trust	23	UNL	0	N	Y	Y	N/A	L
Federated High Income	23	UNL	0	N	Y	Y	20.6	L
Federated Income Trust	23	UNL	0	N	Y	Y	N/A	L
Fidelity Corporate Bond	24	8	0	N	Y	Y	16.5	L
Fidelity Government Securities	24	8	0	N	Y	Y	16.7	M
Fidelity High Income	24	8	0	N	Y	Y	24.5	M
Fidelity Mortgage Securities	24	8	0	L	Y	Y	N/A	L
Fidelity Thrift Trust	24	8	0	N	Y	Y	19.6	L
First Investors Fund for Income	26	UNL	5	L	Y	N	14.2	G
First Investors Government	26	UNL	5	L	Y	N	N/A	M
Fund for U.S. Govt. Securities	23	UNL	0	N	Y	Y	18.9	L
High Yield Securities	1	UNL	0	L	Y	Y	37.9	M
Hutton Investment Bond	29	UNL	5	L	Y	Y	N/A	L
Hutton Investment Government	29	UNL	5	L	Y	Y	N/A	G
IDS Bond Fund	30	UNL	0	L	Y	Y	21.4	G
IDS Federal Income	30	UNL	0	L	Y	Y	N/A	S
IDS Selective Fund	30	UNL	0	L	Y	Y	22.3	XL
IDS Strategy-Income	30	UNL	0	L	Y	Y	N/A	S
Investment Port.-Govt. Plus	32	UNL	0	L	Y	Y	N/A	XL
Investment Port.-High Yield	32	UNL	0	L	Y	Y	N/A	S
Kemper High Yield Fund	32	UNL	0	L	Y	Y	25.5	L
Kemper Income & Cap. Preserv.	32	UNL	0	L	Y	Y	20.3	M
Kemper U.S. Govt. Securities	32	UNL	0	L	Y	Y	16.5	XL

Fund	#	Type						Return	Size
Lexington GNMA Income Fund	34	UNL	5	N	Y	Y	Y	13.6	M
Lord Abbett Bond Debenture	35	UNL	0	L	Y	Y	Y	19.1	L
Merrill Lynch Federal Sec.	36	UNL	0	L	Y	N	Y	N/A	L
Merrill Lynch High Income	36	UNL	0	L	Y	N	Y	19.7	L
Merrill Lynch High Quality	36	UNL	0	L	Y	N	Y	N/A	M
Merrill Lynch Intermediate	36	UNL	0	L	Y	N	Y	N/A	S
Mutual of Omaha America	38	UNL	5	L	Y	Y	Y	14.7	S
National Bond Fund	39	UNL	5	L	Y	Y	Y	17.9	L
National Federal Sec. Trust	39	UNL	5	L	Y	Y	Y	N/A	S
National Preferred Fund	39	UNL	0	L	Y	N	Y	22.0	S
Nationwide Bond Fund	40	UNL	5	L	Y	Y	Y	16.8	L
NEL Income Fund	41	UNL	5	L	Y	N	Y	17.3	S
Oppenheimer High Yield	43	UNL	5	L	Y	N	Y	16.9	S
Oppenheimer Ret. U.S. Govt.	43	UNL	5	L	Y	N	Y	N/A	G
Oppenheimer U.S. Govt. Trust	43	UNL	5	L	Y	Y	Y	N/A	M
Paine Webber GNMA	44	UNL	5	L	Y	Y	Y	N/A	M
Paine Webber High Yield	44	UNL	5	L	Y	Y	Y	N/A	S
Paine Webber Invest. Grade	44	UNL	5	L	Y	Y	Y	N/A	S
Phoenix High Quality Bond	45	UNL	0	L	Y	Y	Y	19.5	S
Phoenix High Yield	45	UNL	0	L	Y	Y	Y	14.8	XL
PRO Income Fund	47	UNL	0	L	Y	Y	Y	N/A	G
Prudential-Bache Adj. Rate Pref.	48	UNL	0	L	Y	Y	Y	19.8	L
Prudential-Bache High Yield	48	UNL	0	L	Y	Y	Y	N/A	S
Prudential-Bache Quality Income	48	UNL	0	L	Y	Y	Y	N/A	S
Putnam High Income Govt.	49	UNL	5	L	Y	N	Y	22.0	XL
Putnam High Yield Trust	49	UNL	5	L	Y	N	Y	N/A	G
Putnam U.S. Govt. Guar. Sec.	49	UNL	0	L	Y	N	Y	17.7	L
Sentinel Bond Fund	22	UNL	5	L	Y	Y	Y	18.9	S
Sigma Income Shares	19	UNL	10	L	Y	Y	Y	N/A	S
Smith Barney U.S. Govt. Sec.	53	UNL	5	L	Y	N	Y	17.4	M
Stein Roe Bond Fund	55	UNL	0	L	Y	N	Y	21.1	L
United Bond Fund	57	UNL	0	L	Y	N	Y	N/A	M
United Government	57	UNL	0	L	Y	N	Y	21.0	XL
United High Income	57	UNL	0	N	Y	N	Y	20.2	M
USAA Income Fund	58	UNL	5	N	Y	Y	Y	N/A	M
Value Line Bond Fund	59	UNL	0	L	Y	Y	Y	N/A	M

Fixed-Income—Tax-Exempt Funds

	Mgr.	Switches	Switch Fee($)	Sales Fee	Written Exch.	Tel. Exch.	5-Year Aver.	Assets
Benham Calif. Tax-Free	6	UNL	0	N	Y	Y	N/A	M
Bullock Tax-Free Shares	10	UNL	0	L	Y	Y	16.5	M
Cigna Municipal Bond	12	UNL	5	L	Y	Y	15.6	M
Composite Tax-Exempt Bond	7	UNL	0	L	Y	Y	15.3	M
Dean Witter Tax-Exempt	17	UNL	0	L	Y	Y	18.5	L
Dreyfus Calif. Tax-Exempt	20	UNL	0	N	Y	Y	N/A	XL
Dreyfus NY Tax-Exempt	20	UNL	0	N	Y	Y	N/A	XL
Dreyfus Tax-Exempt Bond	20	UNL	0	N	Y	Y	16.4	G
Eaton Vance Municipal	21	UNL	0	L	Y	N	18.2	S
Federated Tax-Free Income	23	UNL	0	N	Y	Y	16.2	M
Fidelity High Yield Municipal	24	8	0	N	Y	Y	18.4	G
Fidelity Municipal Bond	24	8	0	N	Y	Y	15.9	XL
Financial Tax-Free Income	25	UNL	0	N	Y	Y	N/A	M
Hancock Tax-Exempt	28	UNL	0	L	Y	N	14.9	L
IDS Tax-Exempt Bond	30	UNL	0	L	Y	N	17.5	XL
Kemper Municipal Bond	32	UNL	0	L	Y	Y	19.4	XL
Merrill Lynch High Yield Muni	36	UNL	0	L	Y	Y	18.8	XL
Mutual of Omaha Tax-Free	38	UNL	0	L	Y	Y	15.0	M
National Tax-Exempt Bonds	39	UNL	5	L	Y	Y	16.1	M
Oppenheimer Tax-Free Bonds	43	UNL	5	L	Y	N	21.0	M
Prudential-Bache High Yield Muni	48	UNL	0	L	Y	N	18.8	XL
Putnam Tax-Exempt	49	UNL	5	L	Y	N	22.5	L
Quality Tax-Free Bond	16	UNL	5	L	Y	Y	N/A	S
Safeco Municipal Bond	50	UNL	0	N	Y	Y	N/A	M
Stein Roe Tax-Exempt Bond	55	UNL	0	N	Y	N	20.9	L
Tax-Exempt Bond Fund	2	UNL	0	L	Y	Y	17.5	M
USAA Tax-Exempt	58	UNL	3	N	Y	Y	N/A	XL

Gold Funds

	Mgr. Switches	Switch Fee($)	Sales Fee	Written Exch.	Tel. Exch.	5-Year Aver.	Assets
Fidelity-Precious Metals	24	0	L	Y	Y	N/A	M
Golconda	9 UNL	5	N	Y	Y	-6.5	S
International Investors	5 UNL	0	L	Y	Y	-3.1	XL
Lexington Gold	34 UNL	5	N	Y	Y	N/A	S
United Services Gold	57 UNL	5	N	Y	Y	-7.2	L
United Services Prospector	57 UNL	2%	L	Y	Y	N/A	M

APPENDIX B

Market Timing Organizations and Newsletters

Following are survey results from active market timers who responded to a standard inquiry. The results are presented in two parts. Part One is a tabular review of important data that is available at a glance. From this first review you may wish to examine other timing organizations noted in Part Two. Each timer's response is summarized to show the significant differences in the services offered and the methods of operation. Following the summary of survey results is a list of other known market timers. This list is not intended to be a complete list of newsletter publishers or organizations that offer timing services or private management. Further, new timing organizations join the ranks from time to time.

PART ONE

Name of Service	Newsletter Rated By:			Switching Signals Sent By						Timing Signals For Types of Funds							
	Hulbert	Timer Digest	Other	Hot-Line	Newsletter	Telephone	Letter	Mailgram	Other	Aggressive Growth	Conservative Growth	Tax-Exempt Bond	GNMA	Internationanal	Other Sector	Growth/Income	Corporate Bond
Shoal P. Berer Assoc., Inc. Pittsburgh, PA										●	●	●				●	●
Covato/Lipsitz, Inc. Pittsburgh, PA				●	●	●	●	●		●	●				●	●	
George Dagnino Akron, OH	●		●	●		●					●	●	●			●	●
The Donoghue Organization Holliston, MA					●					●	●						
Peter G. Eliades Los Angeles, CA	●	●	●	●	●					●							
The Garside Forecast Santa Ana, CA	●	●	●	●	●					●	●						●
Growth Fund Guide Rapid City, SD	●				●					●	●			●	●	●	
Institute of Wall Street Studies Boca Raton, FL	●	●	●				●			●	●					●	
Investment Timing Service Pittsburgh, PA										●		●	●	●		●	●
Lowry Management Corporation North Palm Beachj, FL										●	●						
David H. Menashe Co. Woodland Hills, CA	●		●	●	●		●			●	●			●	●	●	●
Paul A.Merriman & Associates Seattle, WA	●	●	●	●	●	●	●			●	●	●	●			●	●
Mutual Fund Management Systems Pittsburgh, Pa					●		●			●	●					●	
Mutual Fund Strategist Burlington, VT	●	●	●	●						●	●			●	●	●	
New Classics Library Gainesville, GA	●	●	●	●	●				●								
NoLoad Fund X San Francisco, CA	●				●					●	●	●	●	●	●	●	●
Professional Timing Service Missoula, MT	●	●		●	●		●			●	●						
PSM Investors, Inc. Carlisle, MA										●	●				●	●	
Schield Management Co. Denver, CO								●	●	●	●					●	
Signalert Corporation Great Neck, NY	●	●		●	●					●	●	●			●	●	
James B. Stack Kalispell, MT	●	●		●	●					●	●						
Timer Digest, Inc. Ft. Lauderdale, FL		●		●	●										●		
Time Your Switch Andover, MA			●	●			●	●		●	●				●	●	
Wellington Capital Honolulu, HI	●				●				●	●	●	●	●	●	●	●	●

(cont'd)

Name of Service	Timing Signals for Types of Funds			Average Number of Trades					Types of Funds Under Management							
	CA T-E NY T-E	Gold	Funds on Margin	Equity	Gold	Other	Bonds	Sector	Aggressive Growth	Growth/ Income	Tax-Exempt Bond	Gold	Conservative Growth	Corporate Bond	CA T-E NY T-E	Private Management
Shoal P. Berer Assoc., Inc. Pittsburgh, PA	●	●		3	3		2		●	●	●	●	●	●	●	Y
Covato/Lipsitz, Inc. Pittsburgh, PA									●	●			●			Y
George Dagnino Akron, OH		●		8	2		6									Y
The Donoghue Organization Holliston, MA				2												N
Peter G. Eliades Los Angeles, CA				6												N
The Garside Forecast Santa Ana, CA		●		6	3		1									N
Growth Fund Guide Rapid City, SD		●		1				1								N
Institute of Wall Street Studies Boca Raton, FL														●		N
Investment Timing Service Pittsburgh, PA	●	●		3	4		4		●	●	●		●	●	●	Y
Lowry Management Corporation North Palm Beachj, FL				2 1/4					●				●			Y
David H. Menashe Co. Woodland Hills, CA		●		4	**				●	●			●			Y
Paul A.Merriman & Associates Seattle, WA	●	●	●	4	3		7		●	●	●	●	●	●	●	Y
Mutual Fund Management Systems Pittsburgh, Pa		●	●	3.48	7				●	●			●			Y
Mutual Fund Strategist Burlington, VT		●	●	5-10		1	10-2									N
New Classics Library Gainesville, GA					*											N
NoLoad Fund X San Francisco, CA	●	●		2					●	●	●		●	●	●	Y
Professional Timing Service Missoula, MT				4												Y
PSM Investors, Inc. Carlisle, MA			●	3-5					●	●			●			Y
Schield Management Co. Denver, CO				3					●	●			●			Y
Signalert Corporation Great Neck, NY		●		14			5	10	●	●			●			Y
James B. Stack Kalispell, MT		●		1	1											N
Timer Digest, Inc. Ft. Lauderdale, FL								4	●							Y
Time Your Switch Andover, MA		●		3-4			4-6									N
Wellington Capital Honolulu, HI	●	●	●	1	0-1	1	1-2		●	●			●			Y

PART TWO

Shoal P. Berer Associates, Inc.
717 Grant Street, Suite 1001
Pittsburgh, PA 15230
(412) 471-6226

Principals: Shoal P. Berer, President; Joseph R. Pankowski, Executive Vice President; Mary C. Scarry, Secretary-Treasurer.

All timing accounts are under the firm's discretionary management.

Current model began October 1968. Simulation testing for two years prior. Model is proprietary. Signals provided for both load and no-load funds. All switches are 100 percent in or out. Switch dates are documented with a mailgram to attorney's office. Timing model is based on a strict formula with no subjective analysis. Model is based 30 percent on forecasting, 70 percent on trend following.

Annual reports on results of timing strategies versus buy-and-hold.

Management fee structure: 2 percent on first $500,000, 1½ percent on next $500,000, and 1 percent over $1 million. Negotiable over $3 million. Minimum account size: $10,000, except for qualified plans at $2,000. No setup, extra maintenance, or termination fees. Fees are billed annually or semiannually; annually at client's request. Currently managing between $50 million and $100 million.

Member of Pittsburgh Securities Association and International Association of Financial Planners. Author of "Market Timing with Mutual Funds" in *Financial Planning Encyclopedia* and two magazine articles.

Covato/Lipsitz, Inc.
1910 Cochran Road
Pittsburgh, PA 15220
(412) 341-1144

Principals: Phillip Covato, President; Alfred Lipsitz, Vice-President.

Issues *TAP* report twice monthly on average, at cost of $12,000 to $50,000 per year for institutional portfolio managers. Renders buy/sell recommendations and other technical advice.

Trial subscriptions are sometimes for up to six months to institutional clients. *TAP* report published since 1971.

Current model or system tested for two years. Timing signals for load and no-load funds. Timing model is 10 percent proprietary and 90 percent disclosed. Not all switches are 100 percent— typically 50 percent. Switch dates are documented by CPA. Timing model is 80 percent formula, 20 percent judgment. System is trend following. Provides results of timing versus buy-and-hold strategies.

Offers private management. Minimum managed account size is negotiable. Setup fee: $50 for accounts under $25,000; $100 for accounts over $25,000. Annual fees range from 2 percent for accounts up to $499,999 to ½ percent for accounts of $5 million or more. No extra annual maintenance fee and no termination fee. Quarterly billing. Monthly letters sent to managed accounts. Number of accounts and assets under management not available.

Member of NASD, IAFP, Market Technicians Association, and Society for Investigation of Recurring Events.

George Dagnino
65 Lakefront Drive
Akron, OH 44319
(216) 644-2782

Principal: George Dagnino, Ph.D., Publisher and Editor.

Publishes *The Peter Dag Investment Letter* at three-week intervals. Cost: $250 per year. Trial subscription: $75 for three months. Sample copy free.

Timing signals rated in *Hulbert Financial Digest* and *Hard Money Digest*. Current model began January 1979. Backtested for two years. Model developed with both fundamental and technical analyses. Proprietary, with 10 percent to 20 percent retained on switches. Switch dates are published on record. Model depends on formula and subjective analysis. Model depends on forecasting with no trend following. Results of timing versus buy-and-hold strategy published in every issue of newsletter.

Offers private management with fee less than 1 percent of assets. Minimum account size not available. No setup, maintenance, or termination fees. Clients are billed quarterly. Managed accounts do not receive newsletter.

Author of "Business and Financial Cycles—A System Approach to Forecasting and Decision Making." Publisher not noted.

The Donoghue Organization, Inc.
Box 540
Holliston, MA 01746
(800) 343-5413

Principal: William E. Donoghue, President.

Publishes *Donoghue's Moneyletter*, 24 issues a year at $87 per year. Trial subscription: six months at $49. Sample copy free. Newsletter published since 1980. Recommends specific funds to buy.

Timing model began January 1983. Backtested for 12 years. Provides signals for no-load funds only. Switches are 25, 50, 75, or 100 percent depending on interest rates. Model based primarily on technical analysis, with some fundamental analysis included, and is fully disclosed. Switch dates are documented in newsletter. Model depends on strict formula but with some subjective analysis. System is both forecasting and trend following. Provides results of timing versus buy-and-hold strategies.

Does not offer private management.

Author of *William E. Donoghue's Complete Money Market Guide* (1981), *William E. Donoghue's No-Load Mutual Fund Guide* (1983), *William E. Donoghue's Guide to Finding Money to Invest* (1985), and *Donoghue's Investment Tips for Retirement Savings* (1986). Publishes *Donoghue's Mutual Funds Almanac* (Annual).

Peter G. Eliades
2260 Cahuenga Blvd., Suite 305
Los Angeles, CA 90068
(213) 465-6601
Principal: Peter G. Eliades, sole proprietor.

Publishes newsletter, *Peter Eliades' Stockmarket Cycles*, every three weeks. Subscription $198 per year without daily quotes or $480 per year with daily phone quotes. Trial subscription: two issues with updates, $60. Sample copy free. Newsletter published 10 years.

Rated by *Hulbert Financial Digest, Timer Digest,* and *Stock Selectors* (Sacramento, CA).

Recommends specific funds to buy.

Current switching model began January 1984. Model based on technical analysis but is not a strict formula. Some subjective analysis applied. Provides signals for load and no-load funds. All switches are 100 percent. Switch dates are documented in *Timer Digest*.

Results of timing strategies are documented in *Timer Digest*.

Does not offer private management.

Author of *Encyclopedia of Stock Market Techniques*, published by Investor Intelligence, and *Using Cycles for Price Projections*.

The Garside Forecast
P.O. Box 1812
Santa Ana, CA 92701
(714) 259-1670
Principal: Ben C. Garside, Editor and Publisher.

Publishes *The Garside Forecast*, bimonthly at $125 per year. No trial subscriptions but sample copy free on request. Newsletter published for 16 years. Rated in *Hulbert Financial Digest, Timer Digest,* and *Select Information Exchange.*

Experienced in market timing for 30 years but just starting in mutual funds. Provides signals for load funds only. Uses technical analysis, and model is proprietary. Switches may be one-third in or out, typically. Switch dates are not documented. Analysis is subjective; depends on forecasting and is not trend following. No specific results of timing strategies versus buy-and-hold.

Does not offer private management.

Growth Fund Guide
P.O. Box 6600
Rapid City, SD 57709
(605) 341-1971

Principals: Walter J. Rouleau, President; William H. Rouleau, Vice-President.

Publishes *Growth Fund Guide* monthly at $85 per year. Trial subscription: $49 for six months. Sample copy free on request. Newsletter published for 18 years. Rated in *Hulbert Financial Digest.*

Operates several models with backtesting to 1966. Timing signals only for no-load funds. Model is based on both fundamental and technical analyses and is fully disclosed. Switches are usually 100 percent. Switch dates have been documented since 1977. Model is based on formula with "a bit" subjective. Model depends on both forecasting and trend following.

Does not offer private management.

Has written and published 30 books and special reports on market timing since 1968. Many reports sent free to subscribers.

Institute of Wall Street Studies
1200 N. Federal Highway
Boca Raton, FL 33432
(800) I-LETTER

Principals: Peter Bruno, Publisher/President; Thomas Ardiff, Associate Publisher.

Publishes *Investment Strategy & Market Timing Update* newsletter monthly at $145 per year. Trial subscription: three months for $50. Sample copy free on request. Newsletter published since July 1984. Rated in *Hulbert Financial Digest, Timer Digest,* and *Rating the Stock Selectors.* The editor of the newsletter is Bob Brinker, financial broadcaster on WMCA in New York; he has provided timing signals for the past five years.

Model provides signals for no-load funds only. It is proprietary. No information on analytical methods. Switch dates are documented in newsletter. Publishes results of timing strategies versus buy-and-hold.

Does not offer private management.

Investment Timing Services, Inc.
2600 Boyce Plaza Road
Pittsburgh, PA 15241
(412) 257-0100

Principals: Walter A. Stenger, President; Jon W. Erdner, Executive Vice-President.

Does not publish a newsletter.

Timing model began in 1978; backtested to 1973. Provides signals for load and no-load funds. Timing model depends on both fundamental and technical analyses and is proprietary. Switches are always 100 percent. Switch dates are documented in a mailgram. Model is based predominantly on formula with subjective analysis applied. Is predominantly trend following. Publishes results of timing versus buy-and-hold strategies.

Offers private management with minimum account size of $5,000. Fee structure is 2 percent for accounts $5,000 to $500,000; 1½ percent for $500,000 to $1 million; and 1 percent for accounts over $1 million. There are no setup, extra maintenance, or termination fees. Clients are billed annually.

Published article, "Market Timing: A New Name for an Old Technique," *The Financial Planner* (May 1981) and "Market Timing: A Flexible Approach for Stock Market of the 1980's," *The Financial Planner* (June 1983).

Lowry Management Corporation
701 N. Federal Highway
North Palm Beach, FL 33408
(305) 863-7990

Principals: Paul F. Desmond, Chairman; John R. Smith, President; John H. Amann, Secretary-Treasurer.

Affiliate corporation publishes *Lowry's Reports*, but this service publishes no newsletter and does not provide timing signals on a subscription basis.

Provides timing signals for load and no-load funds. Uses technical analysis, and model is proprietary. Switches 100 percent "in nearly all cases." Switch dates are documented in published reports. Model is based on a strict formula with no subjective analysis and is trend following. Publishes results of timing versus buy-and-hold strategies.

Offers private management. Minimum account size, $100,000. Fee structure is on a sliding scale from 2 percent to .75 percent. There are no setup, extra maintenance, or termination fees. Clients are billed annually. Currently manages over $100 million in assets.

Published numerous magazine articles.

Member of Market Technicians Association and International Association for Financial Planning.

David H. Menashe & Co.
P.O. Box 663
Woodland Hills, CA 91365
(818) 346-5637

Principal: David H. Menashe, sole proprietor.

Publishes *Fundline* twice monthly at $97 per year. Trial subscription: one month for $9. No sample copies. Has published newsletter since March 1968. Rated in *Hulbert Financial Digest* and *Rating the Stock Selectors*.

Timing model began in 1968. Provides signals for no-load funds only. Model depends on technical analysis and is proprietary. Amount of assets switched on signals varies. Model depends somewhat on subjective analysis in addition to formula. System is forecasting.

Offers private management with minimum account size of $50,000. Fee structure is on a sliding scale starting at 2 percent and moving down to 1 percent. Breakpoints not noted. Setup fee of $100 but no extra maintenance or termination fees. Clients are billed quarterly. Managed accounts receive newsletter.

Paul A. Merriman & Associates
1200 Westlake Ave. N., Suite 507
Seattle, WA 98109
(206) 285-8877

Principal: Paul A. Merriman, President.

Publishes *The Fund Exchange* monthly at $125 per year. Trial subscription: six months for $49. Sample copy free on request. Newsletter published for three years. Rated in *Hulbert Financial Digest* and *Timer Digest*. Timing model began July 1983 but backtested to 1970. Timing signals for load and no-load funds. Model depends on technical analysis and is proprietary. All switches 100 percent. Switch dates are audited by Touche, Ross & Co., CPA. Model is based on strict formula with no subjective analysis. System is only trend following. Publishes results of timing versus buy-and-hold strategies. Recommends specific funds.

Offers private management with no minimum account size. Fee structure varies from 2 percent to 1 percent depending on size of account, as follows: For equity or gold funds, portfolio values up to $5,000, annual fee of $100 per year; $5,000 to $100,000, 2 percent per year; $100,000 to $250,000, 1.75 percent per year; $250,000 to $500,000, 1.5 percent per year; over $500,000, 1 percent per year. For bond fund, from $10,000 to $100,000, 1.5 percent per year; over $100,000, 1 percent per year. Charges setup fee of $25 but no extra maintenance or termination fees. Clients billed quarterly. Managed accounts receive newsletter. Currently manages over $25 million.

Author of special reports, "Rags or Riches; The Market Timer's Guide to Gold Funds," "How to Build a Million-Dollar IRA," and "How to Double Your Profits Buying No-Load Funds on Margin." Writes monthly column, "The Market Timer," for *Personal Investing*.

Member of No-Load Mutual Fund Association, International Association for Financial Planning, and Advisory Board of Investors Club of the Air.

Mutual Fund Management Systems, Inc.
P.O. Box 13161
Pittsburgh, PA 15243
(412) 563-1816

Principal: Pritt Galford, President.

Publishes *MFMS* letter, monthly with interims as necessary, at $100 per year. Trial subscription: three months for $20. Sample copy at $10 with five-year track record plus other information. Letter published since October 1, 1983. Recommends specific funds to buy.

Timing model began October 1983; backtested for five years. Timing signals for no-load funds only. Switches are always 100 percent. Switch dates are documented in five-year track record. Model based on strict formula; no subjective analysis, and is mostly trend following. Results of timing versus buy-and-hold strategy published in five-year track record plus updates with each issue.

Offers private management with minimum account of $5,000. Fee structure: 2 percent up to $100,000; 1.75 percent to $500,000; and 1.5 percent beyond. No setup, extra maintenance, or termination fees. Clients are billed quarterly. Sends newsletter to privately managed accounts over $25,000. Manages less than $5 million.

The Mutual Fund Strategist
P.O. Box 446
Burlington, VT 05402
(802) 658-3513

Principal: Charlie Hooper.

Publishes monthly newsletter, *The Mutual Fund Strategist*, at $127 per year. Trial subscription: six months at $80. Free sample on request. Letter published for three and a half years; rated in *Hulbert Financial Digest, Timer Digest*, and *Rating the Stock Selectors*. Recommends specific funds to buy.

Timing model depends on technical analysis, provides signals for no-load and low-load funds, and is 100 percent in or out. Switch dates are documented in newsletter. Model uses subjective analysis and is both forecasting and trend following.

Does not offer private management.

New Classics Library, Inc.
P.O. Box 1618
Gainesville, GA 30503
(404) 536-0309

Principal: Robert R. Prechter, Jr., President; Robin Prechter, Vice-President.

Publishes monthly newsletter, *The Elliott Wave Theorist*, at $233 per year. Trial subscription: two months for $55. Sample back issues at $5 or current issue at $20. Letter published since April 1979 and is rated by *Hulbert Financial Digest, Timer Digest, Rating the Stock Selectors, Commodity Traders Consumer Report* (hotline). Does not recommend specific funds to buy.

Timing model began April 1979. Provides signals for load and no-load funds. Model depends on technical analysis and is fully disclosed. Switches may be from 50 percent to 100 percent. Switch dates are documented in newsletter. Model depends on subjective analysis and is strictly forecasting. Results of timing versus buy-and-hold strategies available through rating services.

Does not offer private management.

**NoLoad Fund*X
235 Montgomery Street, Suite 839
San Francisco, CA 94104
(415) 986-7979

Principals: Burton Berry, Publisher; Janet Brown, Managing Editor.

Publishes monthly newsletter, **NoLoad Fund*X*, at $95 per year. Trial subscription: three months at $27. Sample copy free on request. Provides performance data only for 370-plus no-load funds and some low-load funds. Newsletter published for 10 years and is rated in *Hulbert Financial Digest*. Recommends specific funds to buy.

Timing signals via recommended (starred) funds in all categories except funds on margin. System began August 31, 1976. System is trend following. Not specifically a switching system, but plan for upgrading investments in best performing funds. Results of upgrading versus buy-and-hold reported in newsletter.

Offers private management with minimum account of $400,000. Fee structure is 1 percent for first $250,000, .75 percent for next $750,000, and .5 percent to $3 million. No setup, extra maintenance, or termination fees. Clients are billed annually. Currently manages $25 million to $50 million in assets.

Burton Berry is the author of *Loaded Questions on NoLoad Funds*.

Professional Timing Service

P.O. Box 7483
Missoula, MT 59801
(406) 543-4131

Principal: Curtis J. Hesler, Owner and Publisher.

Publishes newsletter, *Professional Timing Service*, twice a month at $185 per year. Trial subscription: $50. Sample copy free on request. Newsletter published for eight years. Rated in *Hulbert Financial Digest* and *Timer Digest*. Recommends specific funds to buy.

Timing model began in 1962. Model provides signals for load and no-load funds. Model depends on technical analysis and is proprietary. Percentage of position switched varies with market. Switch dates are documented in track record. Model is based on strict formula and is forecasting. Does not provide annual results of timing versus buy-and-hold strategies.

Offers private management by arrangement, with minimum account of $25,000. Fee schedule is by arrangement. No setup, extra maintenance, or termination fees.

Published articles, "The Magic of Ringing," "Zero Balance," and "Three Signals of Dynamic Price Movement."

PSM Investors Inc.

121 Judy Farm Road
Carlisle, MA 01741
(617) 369-0033

Principal: Stan Lipstadt, President.

Provides timing signals exclusively to clients under private management. Model began in 1979 and was backtested for two prior years. Provides signals for load and no-load funds. Model is largely technical and is proprietary. Switches are usually 100 percent except when market is very volatile. Switch dates are documented in confirmations to clients. Model based mainly on strict formula and is trend following. Provides results of timing versus buy-and-hold strategies to clients.

Offers only private management, with minimum account of $75,000. Fee structure is 2 percent on first $500,000. No setup, extra maintenance, or termination fees. Clients are billed quarterly. Newsletter is sent to managed accounts quarterly.

Author of two articles in *Market Technicians Association Journal*. Currently manages $50 million to $100 million of assets in 75 accounts.

Schield Management Company
1610 Wynkoop Street
Denver, CO 80202
(303) 592-1545

Principals: Marshall L. Schield, President; Michael Schield, Treasurer; Karen Oliver, Secretary.

Publishes a bimonthly newsletter exclusively for clients and their brokers. Newsletter not priced separately from managed account fees. Switch signals instituted by the company as a service to clients. Operating since 1972.

Specific funds are not selected by service. A client and broker select fund. Schield Management retained to apply risk management to the investment. Works with aggressive and conservative growth funds and growth/income funds. Averages three switches per year.

Current models applied to individual portfolios since 1972 and to mutual funds since 1982. Signals provided for load and no-load funds. Model depends on technical quantitative analysis and is proprietary. Switches are always 100 percent. Switch dates are documented by Deloitte, Haskins & Sells, CPAs. Model based on strict formula and is strictly applied without subjective input. Model is trend following. Results provided on timing versus buy-and-hold strategies.

Provides private management. Minimum account of $10,000 except for IRAS and other retirement plans. Fee structure is 2 percent, billed annually, with half reverting to referring broker. Setup fee of $50. Maintenance fee of $25 billed annually. No termination fee, although 30 days' notice is required. Fees are billed quarterly or annually.

Member of Investment Company Institute and is a registered investment advisor with SEC.

Signalert Corporation
150 Great Neck Road
Great Neck, NY 11021
(516) 829-6444

Principals: George Appel, President; Judith Appel, Vice-President.

Publishes newsletter, *Systems and Forecasts*, since 1973; 24 issues a year at $160. Trial subscription: three issues for $25. Free sample copy on request. Newsletter rated in *Hulbert Financial Digest* and *Timer Digest*. Service recommends specific funds to buy.

Current model began 1980, backtested to 1966. Provides signals for load and no-load funds. Model depends on technical analysis and is fully disclosed. Percentage of trades varies from 50 percent to 80 percent of assets. Switch dates are documented in public announcements. Model based on strict formula and is both forecasting and trend following. Results of timing versus buy-and-hold strategies are not compared.

Offers private management; minimum account of $50,000. Fee schedule is 2 percent of first $100,000; 1 percent above that. No setup, extra maintenance, or termination fees, but requires 30-day notification. Clients are billed quarterly.

Author or coauthor of numerous books, including *Stock Market Trading Systems* (with Fred Hitschler), referenced in other sections of this book, *The Moving Average Convergence-Divergence Trading Method, Time-Trend . . . The Advanced Time-Trend-Momentum Intermediate Term Trading System,* and *The Big Move . . . How to Trade for the Really Big Market Swings Using the Big Move Composite Trading Index .* Write for titles to others.

James B. Stack
522 Crestview Drive
Kalispell, MT 59901
(406) 755-8527

Principal: James B. Stack.

Publishes newsletter, *InvesTech Market Letter*, twice monthly at $185 per year. Trial subscription: three months for $55. Free sample on request. Published since 1980. Rated in *Hulbert Financial Digest* and *Timer Digest*. Recommends specific funds to buy.

Current timing model began May 1984 and backtested for 20 years. Provides signals for no-load funds only. Model depends on technical analysis and is proprietary. Switch amounts vary. Switch dates are documented in newsletter. Model based on strict formula without subjective input. System is forecasting. Results of timing versus buy-and-hold strategies are provided.

Does not offer private management.

Author of "Development & Debiasing of a Relational Oscillator," "Tick & Trim & Timing," "Money-Supply-itis," and "Escaping Options Expiration." These special reports are available free to subscribers.

Timer Digest, Inc.
333 Sunset Drive, Suite 202
Ft. Lauderdale, FL 33301
(305) 764-8499

Principals: Robert E. James, President; Joan W. Rosenthal, Vice-President.

Publishes newsletter, *Timer Digest*, 18 issues a year at $150. Occasionally offers trial subscription: two months at $20. Free sample copy on request. Newsletter published four years. Recommends specific funds to buy.

Current model began August 1985 and was backtested for two years. Model depends on technical analysis and is proprietary. Switches are 100 percent. Switch dates are documented in newsletter. Model is based on strict formula with "a little" subjective input. Model is mostly trend following. Provides results of timing versus buy-and-hold strategies.

Offers private management with minimum account of $2,000. Fee schedule is 3 percent from $2,000 to $15,000; 2 percent to $100,000; 1 percent above $100,000. No setup, extra maintenance, or termination fees. Clients are billed quarterly, but less frequently on small accounts. Newsletter provided to clients with accounts over $50,000.

Time Your Switch
P.O. Box 673
Andover, MA 01810
(617) 470-3511

Principals: Fred W. Hohn, Editor; Marcia Drew, Circulation Manager.

Publishes newsletter, *Time Your Switch*, 26 issues a year at $94.

Trial subscription: four issues for $22. Latest sample issue, $7; includes additional background information. Newsletter published two years. Rated in *Rating the Stock Selectors*. Recommends specific funds to buy.

Current timing model began January 1, 1985; was backtested for three years. Provides signals for load and no-load funds. Based on technical analysis and is fully disclosed. Partial switches 50 percent to 60 percent. Switch dates are documented. Model depends on both technical analysis and chart interpretation and is a combination of forecasting and trend following, heavily influenced by chart reading and chart trends. Reports annual results of timing versus buy-and-hold strategies.

Does not offer private management.

Author of *The Best from Garfield A. Drew*.

Wellington Capital, Inc.

733 Bishop Street, Suite 1800
Honolulu, HI 96813
(808) 524-8063

Principal: Bert Dohmen-Ramirez, President.

Publishes monthly newsletter, *Worry-Free Investing*, at $129 per year. Trial subscription: three months for $44. Sample back issue, $5. Sample current issue, $20. Newsletter gives automatic buy-or-sell point for each fund. Newsletter published since September 1983. Rated in *Hulbert Financial Digest*. Recommends specific funds to buy.

Current timing model began November 1983; was backtested for 10 years. Provides signals for load and no-load funds. Model based on technical analysis and is proprietary. Partial switches are typically 50 percent. Switch dates are documented in newsletter. Model based on strict formula, although "on rare occasions, we will override a weak signal." Model is partly forecasting, mostly trend following.

Offers private management; minimum account of $100,000. Fee schedule: .7 percent per quarter scaling down to .2 percent per quarter depending on account size. No setup, extra maintenance, or termination fees, but 30 days' written notice is required. Clients are billed quarterly. Newsletter sent to private management clients.

Other Known Market Timers

The Hulbert Financial Digest
663 South Carolina Avenue, S.E.
Washington, DC 20003

**Johnson's Investment
Company Charts**
Johnson's Charts, Inc.
1800 Rand Building
Buffalo, NY 14203

**Lipper—Mutual Fund
Performance Analysis
Lipper—Fixed-Income Fund
Performance**
Lipper Analytical Services, Inc.
5 Carol Road
Westfield, NJ 07090

Mutual Funds Forum
Published quarterly by the
Investment Company Institute
1775 K Street, N.W.
Washington, DC 20006

The Mutual Fund Specialist
Royal R. LeMier & Co.
P.O. Box 75, Wall Street Station
New York, NY 10005

**Newgate's Fund Letter
The Mutual Fund Monitor**
Newgate Management
Corporation
P.O. Box 628
Northampton, MA 01061

The No-Load Fund Investor
P.O. Box 283
Hastings-on-Hudson, NY 10706

Portfolio Timing, Inc.
American Federal Building,
Suite 828
Tacoma, WA 98402

**Retirement Fund Advisory
Switch Fund Advisory**
Schabacker Investment
Management
8943 Shady Grove Court
Gaithersburg, MD 20877

Smart Money
The Hirsch Organization, Inc.
Six Deer Trail
Old Tappan, NJ 07675

United Mutual Fund Selector
United Business Service
212 Newbury Street
Boston, MA 02116

**Weisenberger Current
Performance & Dividend
Report
Weisenberger Management
Results**
Warren, Gorham and Lamont,
Inc.
210 South Street
Boston, MA 02111

APPENDIX C

Marginable Mutual Funds

The following funds are available for margined purchases through the Schwab Mutual Fund Marketplace. These notes will help you to read this guide:

Fund Name: Funds are listed alphabetically within the following categories: Aggressive Growth, Growth, Growth & Income, Option/Income, Income, Tax-Exempt, Balanced, Special Purpose, and Bond. The symbol # next to the fund name indicates that the fund is a low-load fund. The symbol () indicates the fund is closed to new accounts. An asterisk * indicates that lower minimums are available for Keogh and/or IRA accounts. N.A. indicates information or data not available.

Purchase Minimum Requirements: Gives the minimum amount required for initial and subsequent investments in the fund through Schwab. If an asterisk (*) appears next to the initial investment amount, a lower minimum is available for IRA and/or Keogh accounts.

Total Return Percentage Changes: Gives the percentage of change for the total return of the fund during two one-year periods, August 14, 1981, to August 13, 1982 (a bear market) and August 13, 1982, to August 12, 1983 (a bull market). The total return treats dividend and capital gain payments as reinvested at the end of the periods shown. These figures can be used to compare past performance in different types of markets.

Five Years: Gives the percentage of change for the fund's total return for the five-year period ending June 30, 1985, treating dividend and gain payments as reinvested in the fund. Reflects the fund's past performance over the long term.

One Year: Gives the percentage of change for the fund's total return for the one-year period ending June 30, 1986, treating dividend and capital gains as reinvested in additional shares.

Three Months: Gives the percentage of change for the fund's total return for the three-month period ending June 30, 1985, treating dividend and capital gains as reinvested in additional shares.

Yield: Gives the percentage yield, based on dividends paid, for the one-year period ending June 30, 1985.

General Notes: Historical financial data should be evaluated in relation to each fund's stated investment objective. No fund is right for every investor, and a fund that is right for you today may not meet your needs tomorrow.

These listings may not contain all the information necessary to evaluate a fund or family of funds. Additional sources of information are noted in the bibliography. Past performance is not necessarily an indication of future returns. For more complete information, including management fees and expenses, consult each fund's prospectus and read it carefully before you invest or send money.

Information presented in the following listings is believed to be reliable, but its accuracy is not guaranteed. The list is subject to change without notice. An appearance on the listings is not to be considered a recommendation. Historical financial data were provided by DAL Investment Co., publisher of the monthly *NoLoad Fund X*, 235 Montgomery Street, San Francisco, CA 94104.

AGGRESSIVE GROWTH FUNDS

FUND NAME	PURCHASE MINIMUM REQUIREMENTS Initial	Subsequent	BEAR MARKET 8/14/81-8/13/82 %	BULL MARKET 8/13/82-8/12/83 %	5 Yr to 12/31/84 %	1 Yr to 2/28/85 %	3 Mo to 2/28/85 %	YIELD % Annual Div to 2/28/85
American Investors Fund, Inc.	$ 400	$ 250	-55.5	83.4	-0.5	-7.8	8.1	1.9
Bull & Bear Capital Growth Fund	1,000	*	-28.4	67.8	61.7	19.3	15.7	0.9
Dreyfus Growth Opportunity Fund	1,000	*	-33.1	73.5	48.6	-2.6	6.7	1.6
Fidelity Freedom Fund, Inc.	500	250	n.a.	n.a.	21.9	21.8	12.2	1.8
Fidelity Magellan Fund, Inc.#	1,000	250	-8.0	109.5	221.9	19.8	14.4	0.9
Fidelity Mercury Fund, Inc.#	1,000	250	n.a.	n.a.	n.a.	27.0	21.0	0.5
Fidelity OTC Portfolio#	2,500	*	n.a.	n.a.	n.a.	n.a.	n.a.	0.0
Fidelity Select Portfolios, Inc.#								
Defense & Aerospace	1,000	250	n.a.	n.a.	n.a.	11.2	21.1	0.0
Energy	1,000	250	n.a.	65.3	n.a.	11.2	12.3	0.2
Financial Services	1,000	250	n.a.	74.0	n.a.	32.2	43.6	0.4
Health Care	1,000	250	n.a.	86.5	n.a.	29.1	23.6	0.2
Leisure & Entertainment	1,000	250	n.a.	n.a.	n.a.	n.a.	25.9	0.0
Precious Metal & Minerals	1,000	250	n.a.	111.3	n.a.	-37.2	-15.4	1.6
Technology	1,000	250	n.a.	177.7	n.a.	12.5	17.9	0.0
Utilities	1,000	250	n.a.	30.1	n.a.	28.7	6.6	1.1
Financial Group Portfolios								
Energy	1,000	250	n.a.	n.a.	n.a.	-1.8	6.4	1.6
Gold	1,000	*	n.a.	n.a.	n.a.	-47.6	-18.0	1.4
Health & Sciences	1,000	*	n.a.	n.a.	n.a.	18.8	19.2	0.3
Leisure	1,000	*	n.a.	n.a.	n.a.	22.8	17.7	0.6
Pacific Basin	1,000	*	n.a.	n.a.	n.a.	-8.0	7.2	1.2
Technology	1,000	*	n.a.	n.a.	n.a.	-6.1	30.3	0.2
Founders Special Fund, Inc.	500	500	-25.4	104.2	87.5	13.2	14.4	2.2
Hartwell Leverage Fund	2,000	250	-34.0	130.8	70.3	-3.7	27.4	0.0
Janus Fund, Inc.	1,000	250	-6.3	78.1	129.4	13.0	8.8	10.2
Lehman Capital Fund	2,500	1,000	-5.1	92.4	116.2	12.7	17.2	3.8
Omega Fund	1,000	250	-40.9	65.0	33.0	20.8	13.3	1.0
Rainbow Fund	300	250	-30.6	48.9	31.6	11.6	4.5	1.0
T.Rowe Price New Horizons Fund	1,000	*	-25.1	100.0	78.2	19.4	18.0	1.9
Scudder Capital Growth Fund	1,000	*	-12.2	73.3	90.8	21.8	16.1	1.4
Scudder Development Fund, Inc.	1,000	*	-17.1	66.9	91.0	15.8	18.2	0.9
Sherman Dean Fund, Inc.	1,000	*	-46.4	79.0	-13.3	-23.1	16.4	0.9
Sierra Growth Fund, Inc.	250	250	-22.8	58.3	6.3	-7.2	16.4	1.3
Stein Roe & Farnham Cap. Opprtn.	2,500	*	-29.3	112.8	69.9	11.4	19.0	1.2
Stein Roe Special Fund, Inc.	2,500	*	-20.2	99.3	104.2	26.8	17.1	0.7
Value Line Lvrgd. Growth Inv.	250	250	-5.8	41.2	60.9	17.9	15.8	0.1
Value Line Special Situations	250	250	-17.2	75.4	62.8	-3.4	19.8	1.1
Vanguard Explorer Fund	3,000	*	-17.5	106.6	109.8	7.0	20.4	1.1

AGGRESSIVE GROWTH FUNDS (cont'd)

FUND NAME	PURCHASE MINIMUM REQUIREMENTS		TOTAL RETURN PERCENTAGE CHANGES					YIELD %
	Initial	Subsequent	BEAR MARKET 8/14/81–8/13/82 %	BULL MARKET 8/13/82–8/12/83 %	5 Yr to 12/31/84 %	1 Yr to 2/28/85 %	3 Mo to 2/28/85 %	Annual Div to 2/28/85
Vanguard Specialized Portfolios								
Energy	1,500 *	250	n.a.	n.a.	n.a.	n.a.	-9.8	0.0
Gold & Precious Metals	1,500 *	250	n.a.	n.a.	n.a.	n.a.	-16.7	0.0
Health	1,500 *	250	n.a.	n.a.	n.a.	n.a.	-16.6	0.0
Service	1,500 *	250	n.a.	n.a.	n.a.	n.a.	17.0	0.0
Technology	1,500 *	250	n.a.	n.a.	n.a.	n.a.	15.4	0.0

GROWTH FUNDS

FUND NAME	Initial	Subsequent	BEAR MARKET 8/14/81–8/13/82 %	BULL MARKET 8/13/82–8/12/83 %	5 Yr to 12/31/84 %	1 Yr to 2/28/85 %	3 Mo to 2/28/85 %	Annual Div to 2/28/85
BMI Equity Fund	2,500	250	n.a.	n.a.	n.a.	20.3	14.1	0.4
Bowser Growth Fund	300 *	250	n.a.	n.a.	n.a.	n.a.	6.1	1.0
Calvert Fund Equity Portfolio	2,000 *	250	n.a.	n.a.	n.a.	11.5	11.8	2.5
Charter Fund, Inc.	2,000	250	-7.2	45.2	71.4	16.3	13.0	2.7
Columbia Growth Fund	1,000 *	500	-14.6	91.9	76.8	22.1	15.7	1.4
Dreyfus Fund Inc.	1,000 **	500	-27.2	45.0	67.9	11.5	9.4	3.8
Dreyfus Third Century Fund, Inc.	1,000	250	-24.1	51.4	47.6	14.0	11.4	2.7
Energy Fund, Inc.	500	500	-16.1	45.6	46.9	14.1	10.7	4.4
Fidelity Contrafund, Inc.	1,000 *	250	-12.3	57.1	58.2	14.9	13.0	2.7
Fidelity Discoverer Fund	1,000 *	250	-25.5	89.1	115.1	13.9	11.8	2.5
Fidelity Trend Fund Inc.	1,000 ***	250	-7.1	64.0	56.7	17.4	10.2	2.1
Financial Dynamics Fund	1,000 *	250	n.a.	69.5	56.9	11.1	21.5	1.6
Flex Fund	2,500 **	250	n.a.	n.a.	n.a.	14.7	14.3	4.7
Founders Growth Fund, Inc.	500	500	-12.4	68.0	93.6	10.1	11.7	2.6
Gintel Fund, Inc.	100,000	5,000	8.2	64.6	84.9	8.9	8.1	0.4
Hartwell Growth Fund	500	250	-31.9	129.7	19.1	8.5	19.9	0.0
Lexington Growth Fund, Inc.	1,000 *	250	-30.8	69.5	112.0	9.3	13.5	1.4
Manhattan Fund, Inc.	500	500	-12.6	71.5	63.6	28.6	13.6	1.5
Medical Technology Fund, Inc.	1,000 *	250	-14.0	86.8	n.a.	12.9	19.8	0.7
Newport Far East Fund	1,000	250	n.a.	n.a.	n.a.	n.a.	n.a.	n.a.
Newton Growth Fund	1,000 *	250	-12.1	94.2	108.0	14.4	8.4	1.9
Nicholson Growth Fund	1,000 **	250	n.a.	n.a.	n.a.	n.a.	n.a.	n.a.
Nova Fund, Inc.	2,000 **	250	-12.6	66.2	40.7	20.4	21.0	1.3
One Hundred Fund, Inc.	250	250	-21.9	89.4	81.5	11.3	20.0	2.1
Partners Fund, Inc.	500	500	4.2	38.9	71.1	20.8	11.7	4.4
Plitrend Fund, Inc.	250	500	-22.6	69.5	49.2	15.9	14.1	1.7
Pro Fund, Inc.	250	250	-19.2	53.1	42.2	22.7	13.1	3.3
T. Rowe Price Growth Stock Fund	1,000 **	250	-23.1	53.5	53.6	21.4	12.7	2.2
T. Rowe Price New Era Fund	1,000 *	250	-34.4	62.0	71.3	13.4	9.7	3.8
SAFECO Growth Fund. Inc.	1,000	250	-23.5	85.8	71.3	13.2	14.9	2.7

Fund	Min Initial	Min Subs.						
Selected Special Shares, Inc.	1,000 *	250	-23.1	76.4	60.8	11.3	11.1	2.6
Stein Roe & Farnham Stock Fund	2,500 *	250	-16.7	78.6	68.9	14.0	14.4	2.3
United Services Good & Bad Times	500	250	-7.2	37.8	n.a.	25.2	13.8	3.6
United Services Growth Fund	500	250	n.a.	111.8	n.a.	-1.6	12.8	0.9
Value Line Fund, Inc.	250	250	-0.2	31.6	53.2	12.3	20.5	1.6
Vanguard Ivest Fund	1,500 *	250	-23.5	78.8	91.8	12.3	10.3	2.5
Vanguard W.L. Morgan Growth Fund	1,500 *	250	-14.6	80.4	76.0	15.0	14.1	2.0

GROWTH & INCOME FUNDS

Fund	Min Initial	Min Subs.						
Analytic Optioned Equity Fund	25,000 *	1,000	-7.7	34.1	64.1	15.6	7.8	2.9
Bull & Bear Equity Income Fund	1,000 *	1,000	-6.5	31.1	60.5	16.5	7.1	6.1
Federated Stock Trust	25,000 **	250	n.a.	n.a.	n.a.	27.7	12.1	4.0
Fidelity Equity Income Fund #	1,000 *	250	-1.6	64.1	111.3	22.6	10.3	5.6
Fidelity Fund, Inc.	1,000 **	250	-7.1	60.0	78.6	19.3	14.1	3.6
Financial Industrial Fund	1,000 *	250	-1.6	51.7	52.6	17.8	14.3	3.5
Founders Mutual Fund	500	500	-16.5	60.4	n.a.	16.7	9.8	2.8
Guardian Mutual Fund, Inc.	500	500	-11.6	64.5	82.8	23.4	11.0	3.4
Ivy Growth Fund	1,000 *	250	-3.2	62.6	139.5	19.5	10.7	6.9
Ivy Institutional Investors Fund	1,000 *	250	n.a.	n.a.	n.a.	n.a.	7.4	4.1
Lehman Investors Fund, Inc.	1,500 *	250	-10.2	68.1	74.6	16.3	11.0	2.9
Lexington Research Fund, Inc.	1,000 *	250	-1.6	70.0	54.4	15.9	12.1	3.6
Mutual Qualified Income, Inc.	1,000 **	250	-4.5	46.3	94.4	16.9	8.1	6.2
Mutual Shares Corporation	1,000 **	250	-11.6	55.0	77.7	17.9	8.3	2.4
One Hundred & One Fund, Inc.	250	250	-17.7	81.7	n.a.	13.8	8.3	3.3
T.Rowe Price Growth & Income	1,000 *	250	n.a.	n.a.	n.a.	13.4	10.2	6.0
SAFECO Equity Fund, Inc.	1,000 **	250	-19.7	49.2	52.1	20.7	13.1	4.1
Scudder Growth & Income Fund	1,000 **	250	-23.7	47.9	32.5	17.2	14.2	3.2
Selected American Shares, Inc.	1,000 **	250	-3.9	40.1	87.7	28.1	11.9	4.0
Strong Investment Fund, Inc.	250	250	n.a.	61.2	n.a.	14.4	5.4	4.5
Strong Total Return Fund, Inc.	250	250	n.a.	57.0	n.a.	15.9	5.6	3.5
Vanguard Index Trust	1,500 *	250	-16.2	60.2	79.2	19.5	11.4	3.9
Vanguard Trustees' Commingled International Equity	25,000 *	1,000	n.a.	n.a.	n.a.	-6.6	-2.6	4.5
U.S. Equity	25,000 *	1,000	-15.1	59.6	n.a.	8.5	10.0	4.4
Vanguard Windsor Fund	1,500 *	250	-10.2	61.8	113.9	23.1	9.8	5.5

OPTION/INCOME FUNDS

Fund	Min Initial	Min Subs.						
Founders Income Fund	500	500	-5.9	31.6	73.8	13.2	4.4	6.2
Gateway Option Income Fund	500	250	-8.7	32.2	43.9	11.5	6.5	4.0

INCOME FUNDS

Fund	Min Initial	Min Subs.						
American Investors Income Fund	400 *	250	-13.4	51.5	35.4	-1.2	5.9	13.1
Bull & Bear High Yield Fund	1,000 *	250	n.a.	n.a.	n.a.	9.5	5.4	15.2
Capital Preservation Treas. Note	1,000 *	250	15.9	10.0	n.a.	10.8	1.8	9.4
Columbia Fixed Income Securities	1,000 *	250	n.a.	n.a.	n.a.	9.7	2.2	12.1
Federated GNMA Trust	25,000 *	250	n.a.	9.3	n.a.	12.0	1.3	12.0

| | PURCHASE MINIMUM REQUIREMENTS | | TOTAL RETURN PERCENTAGE CHANGES | | | | | YIELD % |
FUND NAME	Initial	Sub-sequent	BEAR MARKET 8/14/81-8/13/82	BULL MARKET 8/13/82-8/12/83	5 Yr to 12/31/84 %	1 Yr to 2/28/85 %	3 Mo to 2/28/85 %	Annual Div to 2/28/85
INCOME FUNDS *(cont'd)*								
Federated Income Trust	25,000 *	250	n.a.	10.2	n.a.	11.9	1.9	12.0
Federated Intermed. Gov. Trust	25,000 *	250	n.a.	n.a.	n.a.	12.7	2.0	11.5
Fidelity Mortgage Securities #	1,000 *	250	n.a.	n.a.	n.a.	n.a.	n.a.	12.9
Financial Industrial Income Fund	1,000 *	250	-2.6	47.5	69.1	18.3	10.7	5.5
Lexington GNMA Income Fund	1,000 *	250	19.9	5.5	37.0	8.6	0.3	11.1
Newton Income Fund	1,000 *	250	11.3	26.1	50.1	10.2	0.3	9.9
Northeast Investors Trust	500 *	250	14.2	29.4	55.2	12.5	5.6	12.7
Pro Income Fund, Inc.	300	250	14.7	24.3	43.3	8.8	2.2	10.5
SAFECO Income Fund, Inc.	1,000 *	250	-9.0	56.4	90.7	22.9	12.1	6.3
Scudder Income Fund, Inc.	1,000	250	10.8	25.6	48.5	12.5	2.4	11.0
Southwestern Investors Income	250	250	5.0	20.5	54.9	12.9	3.9	10.3
United Services Income	500	250	n.a.	n.a.	n.a.	11.5	7.8	5.6
Value Line Income Fund, Inc.	250	250	8.9	32.1	76.6	13.4	5.9	7.6
BALANCED FUNDS								
Dreyfus Special Income Fund	1,000 *	250	-6.4	40.1	59.0	9.2	5.1	7.9
Fidelity Puritan Fund, Inc.	1,000 *	250	0.4	44.3	94.0	19.1	8.5	7.5
Pax World Fund, Inc.	250 *	250	-10.4	54.0	65.3	17.9	7.9	4.5
SteinRoe Total Return Fund	2,500 *	250	-12.6	45.3	51.6	17.7	8.5	6.4
Vanguard Wellesley Income Fund	1,500	250	-4.5	34.7	78.6	16.6	4.4	10.1
Vanguard Wellington Fund	1,500	250	-3.0	47.5	87.0	16.8	7.0	6.9
SPECIAL PURPOSE FUNDS								
Bull & Bear Golconda Investors	1,000 *	250	-26.8	41.4	-3.8	-31.8	-11.1	2.3
Calvert Social Investment Fund	1,000	250	n.a.	n.a.	n.a.	15.6	7.5	2.2
Fidelity Overseas Fund #	2,500 *	250	n.a.	n.a.	n.a.	n.a.	n.a.	0.0
Gintel ERISA Fund, Inc.	10,000 *	1,000	n.a.	49.0	n.a.	11.9	6.6	3.1
Lexington GoldFund, Inc.	1,000	250	-27.9	77.0	-1.3	-33.4	-15.0	1.4
T. Rowe Price International Fund	1,000 *	250	-19.0	41.0	n.a.	-6.9	-0.8	2.3
Scudder International Fund, Inc.	1,000 *	250	-17.3	47.0	53.5	-3.3	0.8	0.5
United Services Gold Shares	500	250	-21.4	127.5	56.4	-43.5	-20.6	6.0
United Services Prospector Fund	500	250	n.a.	n.a.	n.a.	-41.2	-10.0	0.0
Vanguard Qualified Dividend								
Portfolio I	3,000 *	250	6.3	59.5	136.6	27.0	8.2	7.9
Portfolio II	3,000 *	250	14.7	26.1	49.6	12.5	5.7	12.5
Portfolio III	25,000 *	1,000	n.a.	n.a.	n.a.	15.1	5.0	10.5

TAX-EXEMPT FUNDS

Benham California Tax-Free Trust								
Intermediate Term	7.4	3.4	6.8	n.a.	n.a.	n.a.	1,000	250
Long Term	9.1	6.5	8.3	n.a.	n.a.	n.a.	1,000	250
Benham National Tax-Free Trust								
Intermediate Term	8.8	1.6	n.a.	n.a.	n.a.	n.a.	1,000	250
Long Term	9.4	4.0	n.a.	n.a.	n.a.	n.a.	1,000	250
Short Term	7.0	1.9	n.a.	n.a.	n.a.	n.a.	1,000	250
Dreyfus Calif. Tax-Exempt Bond	8.8	4.9	5.9	n.a.	n.a.	n.a.	1,000	250
Dreyfus Intermd. Tax-Exempt Bond	8.2	3.5	7.7	n.a.	n.a.	n.a.	1,000	250
Dreyfus NY Tax-Exempt Bond	8.6	4.4	8.4	n.a.	n.a.	n.a.	1,000	250
Dreyfus Tax-Exempt Bond Fund	9.2	4.6	8.8	18.9	24.0	11.1	1,000	250
Federated Shrt-Intrmd. Muni.	6.3	1.9	6.9	n.a.	7.3	n.a.	25,000	250
Fidelity California Tax-Free								
Municipal Bond	9.4	4.8	n.a.	n.a.	n.a.	n.a.	2,500	250
Short Term	5.6	1.5	n.a.	n.a.	n.a.	n.a.	2,500	250
Fidelity Gov. Securities Fund	11.3	1.5	9.3	53.4	10.5	20.8	1,000	250
Fidelity High Yield Muni. Bond	9.4	6.0	10.7	24.2	n.a.	13.3	2,500	250
Fidelity Limited Term Muni. Bond	7.8	3.9	8.6	28.4	15.7	11.9	2,500	250
Fidelity Municipal Bond Fund	8.6	6.0	10.2	12.8	20.2	11.9	2,500	250
Fidelity New York Tax-Free								
Municipal Bond	8.9	5.6	n.a.	n.a.	n.a.	n.a.	2,500	250
Short Term	5.5	1.5	9.3	n.a.	n.a.	n.a.	2,500	250
Financial Tax-Free Income Fund	8.9	5.2	9.1	n.a.	n.a.	n.a.	1,000	250
Nuveen Municipal Bond Fund	7.2	4.2	6.9	19.7	23.3	7.9	1,000	250
T.Rowe Price Tax-Free Income	7.8	3.0	9.3	30.4	23.9	10.1	1,000	250
SAFECO Calif. Tax-Free Income	8.5	7.5	11.6	n.a.	n.a.	n.a.	2,500	250
SAFECO Municipal Bond Fund	9.2	5.6	11.0	22.7	22.9	12.9	2,500	250
Scudder California Tax-Free Fund	9.0	6.4	8.2	n.a.	n.a.	n.a.	1,000	250
Scudder Managed Municipal Bonds	8.4	4.9	9.5	n.a.	n.a.	n.a.	1,000	250
Scudder New York Tax-Free Fund	8.3	n.a.	n.a.	n.a.	n.a.	n.a.	1,000	250
Scudder Tax-Free Target Fund								
1987 Portfolio	6.4	5.0	7.6	n.a.	n.a.	n.a.	1,000	250
1990 Portfolio	7.6	5.4	7.8	n.a.	n.a.	n.a.	1,000	250
1993 Portfolio	8.0	6.0	8.6	n.a.	n.a.	n.a.	1,000	250
Selected Tax-Exempt Bond Fund	8.3	4.6	8.3	9.1	20.7	5.6	1,500	250
SteinRoe Tax-Exempt Bond Fund	8.4	5.1	12.1	29.2	25.9	13.8	2,500	250
Value Line Tax-Exempt Fund,Inc.	10.0	5.3	n.a.	n.a.	n.a.	n.a.	1,000	250
Vanguard Municipal Bond Fund								
High Yield	9.5	5.5	10.1	20.4	21.7	8.9	3,000	250
Intermediate Term	8.6	4.1	8.9	18.1	17.0	9.1	3,000	250
Long Term	9.2	6.1	9.8	12.4	21.5	9.3	3,000	250
Short Term	6.5	2.2	6.9	35.0	6.8	9.3	3,000	250

BOND FUNDS

FUND NAME	PURCHASE MINIMUM REQUIREMENTS		TOTAL RETURN PERCENTAGE CHANGES					YIELD %
	Initial	Sub-sequent	BEAR MARKET 8/14/81- 8/13/82 %	BULL MARKET 8/13/82- 8/12/83 %	5 Yr to 12/31/84 %	1 Yr to 2/28/85 %	3 Mo to 2/28/85 %	Annual Div to 2/28/85
Dreyfus A Bonds Plus, Inc.	1,000 *	250	18.2	16.2	51.7	11.8	1.2	12.4
Fidelity Corporate Bond Fund	2,500 **	250	19.5	16.2	43.5	9.9	1.5	12.2
Fidelity High Income Fund, Inc.	2,500 **	250	15.6	32.7	63.8	11.8	4.4	13.3
Fidelity Thrift Trust	1,000 *	250	20.6	15.1	64.7	11.7	1.8	11.5
Financial Bond Shares								
Bond Shares	1,000 *	250	18.7	14.3	39.5	4.1	0.8	11.8
High Yield Bond	1,000 **	250	n.a.	n.a.	n.a.	n.a.	3.9	10.4
Liberty Fund, Inc.	500	500	6.0	27.8	36.7	7.5	4.4	10.2
T. Rowe Price New Income Fund	1,000 *	250	17.2	17.1	45.8	10.7	2.1	11.5
Scudder Target Fund								
General 1985 Portfolio	1,000 *	250	n.a.	n.a.	n.a.	9.7	2.1	7.0
General 1986 Portfolio	1,000 **	250	n.a.	n.a.	n.a.	10.0	2.8	6.8
General 1987 Portfolio	1,000 **	250	n.a.	n.a.	n.a.	11.1	3.4	7.3
General 1990 Portfolio	1,000 *	250	n.a.	n.a.	n.a.	12.0	3.4	8.6
U.S. Gov't 1985 Portfolio	1,000 *	250	n.a.	n.a.	n.a.	9.7	1.6	7.2
U.S. Gov't 1986 Portfolio	1,000 *	250	n.a.	n.a.	n.a.	9.7	1.5	7.0
U.S. Gov't 1987 Portfolio	1,000 *	250	n.a.	n.a.	n.a.	10.6	2.1	7.6
U.S. Gov't 1990 Portfolio	1,000 **	250	n.a.	n.a.	n.a.	11.7	2.7	8.5
SteinRoe Bond Fund, Inc.	2,500 **	250	19.0	15.1	35.3	9.9	0.8	11.1
Value Line Bond Fund, Inc.	1,000	250	n.a.	17.6	n.a.	11.0	1.2	11.0
Vanguard Fixed Income Securities								
GNMA Portfolio	3,000 *	250	24.4	14.9	n.a.	10.5	3.4	12.0
High Yield Portfolio	3,000 **	250	16.8	23.7	52.0	9.2	2.5	14.1
Investment Grade Portfolio	3,000 *	250	20.9	16.2	54.5	10.8	0.8	12.6
Short Term Portfolio	3,000	250	n.a.	n.a.	n.a.	12.4	2.3	10.6
S & P 500			-16.6	62.9	86.7	20.2	11.9	4.2
DOW JONES INDUSTRIAL AVERAGE			-10.5	57.2	78.0	16.4	9.3	4.7

#Low load funds.   *Lower minimum available for Keogh and/or IRA plans.

APPENDIX D

The Paul A. Merriman Timing Models

Paul A. Merriman, one of the authors of this book, is the president and founder of Paul A. Merriman & Associates, Inc. (PM&A). Many of the concepts and much of the data included in earlier chapters are the result of his research and experience.

Paul A. Merriman & Associates, Inc., is an investment advisory firm registered with the United States Securities and Exchange Commission (SEC). The primary business of PM&A is to develop and distribute mutual fund timing information. The investment management programs offered by PM&A and used by thousands of investors can be used by any investor—with or without experience.

Three market timing models offer investors a reasonable range of alternatives depending on their risk tolerance, age, investment objectives, and income. The three models include the Merriman Equity Switch Model, the Merriman Bond Switch Model, and the Merriman Gold Switch Model. One or all of these investment opportunities will likely fulfill the objectives of most investors.

The Merriman Equity Switch Model calls for investors to be in mutual funds with portfolios of equity issues during general stock market advances and in money market funds during periods when the market is declining. The Merriman Equity Switch Model is developed around a switching discipline that can be used with aggressive growth stock funds, quality or conservative growth stock funds, and the most conservative dividend-oriented stock funds.

The Merriman Bond Switch Model provides a switching discipline that can be used to invest in corporate, government, and tax-exempt bond funds. As interest rates fall, bond prices tend to rise. During these rising markets, the goal of the Merriman Bond Switch Model is to be in those mutual funds holding portfolios of long-term bonds. As interest rates rise, bond prices tend to fall. As interest rates begin to rise, therefore, the goal is to protect the values built up in the bond funds by switching into money market funds.

The Merriman Gold Switch Model is specifically devised to be used with most gold or precious metal funds. As gold prices rise and fall, gold funds tend to follow—but not always in tandem. Further, gold funds seldom follow the price trend of the general equity market. Therefore, a switching model adaptable to gold mutual funds must analyze those specific trends rather than gold itself. When gold funds are in an upward trend, the goal is to keep investments in gold funds. When the trend reverses, assets invested in gold funds are switched into a money market fund.

Investors can avail themselves of PM&A management services in one or more of three ways:

1. *The Fund Exchange*. This is a newsletter published by PM&A to advise subscribers outside the state of Washington of the signals needed for timely switching; it also offers other information of interest to investors in no-load mutual funds. Regular reporting of results of the three Merriman switching models keeps subscribers up to date on relative performance. Supplying timing signals to individual investors via a newsletter mailed to subscribers is routine for many market timing organizations. Some form of "call in" service on a hotline may also be offered by market timers to supplement mailed information. As far as is known, however, PM&A is the only service for equity, bond, and gold fund switching to take the guesswork out of the timing signal delivery process.

Delivering the switching signals is probably the most important link in market timing investment management. If you don't receive the switching signal immediately, you are unlikely to gain optimum results. Subscribers of *The Fund Exchange* who elect the personal call option are called personally when any of the three switching models generates a switching signal. To confirm this telephone message, subscribers are immediately sent a switch signal by first-class mail.

Subscribers who fail to act promptly following receipt of a switching signal will not gain the full benefits built into the switching models. Each investor is responsible for acting on the signals, but sometimes prompt action is not possible—being away on vacation, for example. PM&A therefore offers the private management of accounts.

2. *Private Management*. PM&A will recommend investment in one

or more mutual funds and switch assets between the equity, gold, or bond funds and a money market fund in accordance with signals generated by one of the three specific switching models. This service is particularly useful for those investors who have neither the time nor the inclination to manage their mutual fund investments on a timely basis. As a first step, PM&A will help clients determine their investment objectives. Next, they assist the client in selecting and opening accounts in the appropriate equity or bond mutual fund and an associated money market fund. Once these accounts are established in the name of the client, a limited power of attorney is prepared and signed; this authorizes PM&A to switch money in the accounts between the funds on the basis of the switching signals. This authority is communicated to each of the funds, and the stage is set for the next switch. When one of the Merriman Equity, Bond, or Gold Switch Models generates a signal, PM&A immediately notifies each of the affected funds and the funds are switched immediately.

3. *Diversification.* As long-time stockbrokers, both authors recognize the value and importance of diversification. As a client's account continues to grow, PM&A may suggest that some of the funds be split off for diversification. Different market timers may use other techniques for generating switching signals, and PM&A has carefully qualified three other nationally known market timers. These three other organizations use technical analyses different from PM&A's, but they all maintain a strict buy-and-sell discipline.

Diversification starts to make sense when an account reaches $50,000 to $100,000. Most market timers are fully confident of their own timing techniques and the effectiveness of their timing models. The Merriman Equity, Bond, and Gold Switching Models are no exception. PM&A is the only market timing service that offers this diversified approach to timing mutual funds. The service is available without extra cost.

Rather than attempt to describe all of the specifics in the PM&A program, we are including here the questions most often asked by clients. The answers are by Paul Merriman.

Q. How does PM&A choose the mutual fund family within which I will switch?

A. The first thing we consider is the fund family's position on timing. The mutual fund family must permit liberal switching on a nominal or no cost basis. We also consider the fund's "track record," that is, its results over a meaningful period of years. Typically, we look at its performance over the last five to ten years rather than the last one or two. The fund's bottom-line performance offers a good indication of the fund manager's ability to pick stocks that outperform the market. The fund family must also include at least one money market fund.

Q. Should I diversify my mutual fund holdings among several different funds?

A. Yes. You may wish to choose funds with different investment objectives. The basic choices are aggressive growth, growth, conservative growth, growth-income, bonds, and gold.

Q. What level of return may I expect from my mutual fund investments managed by PM&A?

A. We cannot, of course, guarantee any return. We believe, however, that our goals are attainable. We aim to achieve a compound rate of growth of 18 percent to 22 percent for aggressive growth funds. Our goals for other fund categories are as follows: conservative growth, 16 percent to 18 percent compounded yearly; growth-income, 12 percent to 15 percent compounded yearly; gold, 20 percent or more compounded yearly. For bond funds our objective is to earn between 3 percent and 5 percent more each year than a buy-and-hold strategy would have earned. You should recognize that our switching models are designed to produce these results over several years and that results for individual years may be higher or lower than these stated goals. Market timing is a long-term investment strategy.

Q. Is the Merriman program suitable for qualified retirement programs, such as IRAs, Keoghs, or 401(k)s?

A. Absolutely. In fact, PM&A's basic philosophy is to provide quality, inexpensive service for investors with these types of plans. Qualified retirement plan holders make up the largest single group among our clients.

Q. Will PM&A analyze a portfolio of individual stocks and/or bonds?

A. No. Our switching models are not designed for individual issues of stocks or bonds. Our models follow market trends for the broad categories of equity, bond, and gold issues, and therefore apply to mutual funds only.

Q. What are the risks of market timing?

A. Our program involves two types of risk in addition to the normal market risks of any investment. First is the risk inherent in the switching techniques used by market timers. Timing systems based on trend analysis may be subject to "whipsawing"; that is, you may get a series of premature signals that produce losses before you get onto a prolonged profitable trend. Second is the risk associated with the point at which you enter the market. If you enter the market at its peak, you may initially suffer a small loss before a switching signal moves your investment into a money market fund.

Q. Over what period may I expect to see the impact of market timing?

A. In a generally declining market, we think you will see definite benefits from our market timing management within one year. Otherwise, our market timing program should be judged over a complete market cycle that generally spans four to five years.

Q. Should I market-time my investments even though most of the transactions may be short-term (less than six months), and thus incur taxation at ordinary income rates?

A. Yes. If your account is protected from current tax impacts in a qualified plan, short-term profits will have no effect on your investments. But if you plan to open a regular or non-tax-sheltered investment account, consider this: At PM&A we feel that you are far better off earning a short-term profit, even if it is fully taxed, than to watch profits turn into losses while waiting for long-term capital gains. Unfortunately, many investors become locked into losing investments that end up being very long-term holdings.

Q. Do mutual funds like timers and market timing?

A. Yes, the smart ones do. Since our timing models are designed to increase the value of our clients' accounts, the mutual funds benefit by having larger and larger investments under management. Switching sometimes causes problems for a fund if too many investors move at exactly the same time; however, people who consistently time their accounts represent a small percentage of a fund's shareholders. Further, there are many market timers advising investors, and each timer uses his own models that generate a variety of switching signals, usually at different times. At PM&A we recognize the potential problems facing mutual fund managers and have designed our models to work with them rather than against them.

Q. Out of the hundreds of timing indicators available, why has PM&A picked price reversal analysis?

A. Basically, the success or failure of an investment reflects the prices at which it is bought and sold. We believe, and our analyses confirm our belief, that the price reversal analysis technique is the analytical method most closely related to the actual direction of the market. It is thus very likely to produce positive investment results.

Q. Do you tell your clients how your models work?

A. Only in general terms. We view our models as proprietary and use them exclusively in the management of our clients' accounts.

Q. Do you ever resort to using your intuitive judgment in determining a switch signal?

A. No. We rely entirely on our models.

Q. When your models generate a switch signal, are you anticipating a certain market move?

A. No. We're not fortune tellers— although we would like to be fortune makers! When one of our models generates a switch signal, it indicates a change in trend, not a prediction of what might happen in the future. A new trend could last a week, or it could last a year.

Q. You have been in business only since 1983. How do you know your PM&A models will continue to be successful?

A. We don't know for certain. We believe that our approach to the management of investments in mutual funds exhibits the qualities that produce successful results—common sense and strict discipline. Market timing is not a new science, nor is it difficult to understand, but few investors have the time and patience needed to manage their own accounts with consistent success. The actual models that most timers use, including ours, are refinements of proved investment strategies found in many books on market timing and technical analysis. We believe that market timing strategies do work and that the most important factor in making them work is the discipline to apply the strategies consistently over a long period. That is our purpose, and that is what we are paid to do.

Q. What percentage of the time do you expect to be in equities or bonds, and what percentage of the time do you expect to be in money market funds?

A. We expect to be in the market (equity, bond, or gold funds) about 50 percent of the time and in a money market fund earning interest for the rest of the time.

Q. Is market timing more risky than simply buying and holding shares in a mutual fund?

A. Actually, market timing your holdings in a mutual fund reduces your risks. When you buy and hold mutual fund shares, you are exposed 100 percent of the time. While your account is invested in a money market fund, you incur no risk of a capital loss; therefore, our clients experience about half as much risk as those investors who buy and hold shares in mutual funds.

Q. Do the Merriman models pick market bottoms and market tops?

A. No. Our switching models are trend followers. A change of trend direction is always identified after a bottom or top has been reached. When our models signal a time to switch, they are telling us that a change in trend has *already* occurred. Trend following signals differ significantly from forecasting signals for one very important reason: While forecasting signals may depend on a variety of patterns observed in the past, there is no clear case for those patterns to predict future market directions. With trend following signals, the reasons for changes in trend direction may vary from time to time, but the signals recognize the trend changes regardless of the reasons. Trend following signals recognize the facts of a price reversal rather than attempt to predict directions.

Q. Is it possible for my mutual fund to decline when the market is going up or vice versa?

A. Yes. If your mutual fund holdings include a large percentage of stocks that are not following the general trend of the market, then the mutual fund will be "out of sync." Such contrary moves are not at all unusual. If you noticed a typical day's stock activity, you would see that as many as half of the stocks traded decline while the other half rise or remain unchanged. On any given day numerous stocks record a new high price for the year while others reach new lows. The makeup of a mutual fund's portfolio, particularly if it specializes in a particular industry such as oil, determines whether the fund follows the general market.

Q. How often will the Merriman Switching Models signal for a switch in my portfolio between equity and money funds?

A. We expect our equity model to average two switches or complete cycles (equity to money fund to equity, or vice versa) each year. However, these cycles are entirely unpredictable. During one recent period investors in our equity switching program remained in money funds for more than eight months before switching into an equity fund.

Q. How often will my investment in a bond switching program be switched?

A. We expect our bond model to call for an average of three to four complete cycles per year.

Q. How often will my investment in a gold switching program be switched?

A. We expect our gold model to call for an average of one to two complete cycles per year.

Q. What kinds of investors choose the Merriman Equity Switch Model?

A. Any investor who currently owns shares in one or more mutual funds holding a portfolio of common stocks can use the Merriman Equity Switch Model effectively. This model is applicable to the most aggressive or the most conservative equity-oriented mutual funds. Generally, investors who have many years for investing before retirement can apply the switching signals profitably to aggressive funds. Investors with only a few years until retirement or those in retirement may apply switching to the more conservative equity funds or the equity-income funds. All funds, aggressive or conservative, can tumble in major bear markets.

Q. What kind of investor chooses the Merriman Bond Switch Model?

A. Before answering this important question, allow me to comment on the risks of owning bonds. Most investors do not realize that proper diversification within a bond portfolio is just as important as diversification within a stock portfolio. The portfolio manager of one of the nation's largest bond funds believes that an investor must have more than $500,000 invested in bonds to achieve proper diversification, so most bond investors are better off if they buy into a diversified bond fund. Any investor who was caught in the tax-exempt bond market during the declines, ranging from 30 percent to 40 percent, between 1978 and 1981 is painfully aware of the potential risks of bond funds on a buy-and-hold basis. Therefore, any investor with part of his holdings in mutual funds that invest in either tax-exempt municipal, U.S. government, or corporate bonds could use the Merriman Bond Switch Model. Those investors paying marginal tax rates of 35 percent or higher will probably prefer to market-time a tax-exempt bond fund. We have clients who keep their emergency funds in a bond switching program that alternates holdings between a tax-exempt money fund and one or more tax-exempt bond funds. A checking account can be opened with the tax-exempt money market fund to permit the investor to write checks for rapid liquidity.

Q. What kind of investor chooses the Merriman Gold Switch Model?

A. Many financial planners are known to recommend that 10 percent to 15 percent of a client's investable funds be channeled into gold-related securities. But mutual funds holding a portfolio of gold mining stocks can be great winners—or horrible losers. All of our backtested studies indicate that anyone who is buying shares in one or more of the gold funds should apply some form of market timing discipline to avoid or minimize the substantial declines that have occurred over the past decade.

Q. Can I margin my mutual fund account?

A. Yes. Charles Schwab and Co., Inc., offers a program that allows the purchase of mutual fund shares on margin. Fidelity also permits the purchase of their own shares on margin. The Jack White Company also permits buying mutual fund shares on margin.

Q. How does a margin account work?

A. Buying securities of any kind on margin simply means that a brokerage company will lend you part of the purchase price of the securities you are buying while they hold the securities as collateral for the loan. As an example, if the margin rate is 50 percent—that is, you can borrow funds to buy as much as 50 percent of the total share purchase—and you wish to purchase $20,000 worth of securities, you would be required to deposit only $10,000 in cash. Margining the purchase of mutual fund shares is actually easier than buying shares of stock on margin because the additional shares do not have to be borrowed from another owner. The margined shares simply represent additional purchases from the mutual fund.

Q. Can I margin my IRA or Keogh account?

A. No.

Q. Are PM&A's fees tax deductible?

A. Generally, our fees are deductible under the Internal Revenue Code, Section 212 (1). We recommend, however, that you check with your tax advisor.

Q. How do I follow the performance results of your switching models?

A. We provide three sources of information by which you can follow our performance and check results. First, you will receive a statement from us at the end of each quarter detailing the current status of your account. Second, you will receive a quarterly newsletter that reports on our performance for the funds we manage. Third, you will receive confirmations from the fund(s) whenever a transaction occurs in your account. Remember, the mutual fund accounts are registered in your name.

Q. How can I evaluate my portfolio daily?

A. It's easy. Changes in the NAV (net asset value) of the mutual fund where you own shares are reported in the financial section of your newspaper. You can follow the changes as you would for a stock. You should recognize, however, that the value of mutual fund shares is also affected by dividends declared and capital gains realized and distributed periodically.

Q. Where are my mutual fund shares held?

A. Your mutual fund shares are held in trust for you by the custodial bank for your mutual fund. They are held in your name only, and the custodial bank regularly reports via computer printout on the status of your holdings. Attempting to collect and hold certificates representing your ownership of shares in your mutual fund is impracticable in a switching program.

Q. Does PM&A have the right to switch my shares to a different fund without my approval?

A. Absolutely not! Our contract specifically restricts PM&A to switching between the two funds you select within a specified mutual fund family. As further protection for you, the mutual funds holding your shares permit PM&A to initiate switch transactions only in accordance with our limited power of attorney.

Q. How liquid is my investment?

A. Mutual funds offer one of the most liquid investments available. In most cases, your cash is available immediately. All you need do is write a check on your money market fund, assuming you have elected this option at the time you open the account. Of course, you should first contact us to be certain that your money is currently invested in the money market fund. If not, we will assist you in making the necessary arrangements. The only exception is for qualified plans. Check writing is not available, and withdrawals from qualified plans, such as IRAs or Keoghs, may be subject to penalties in addition to taxes.

Q. Are there penalties if I choose to cancel your service?

A. No. We offer an unconditional money-back guarantee that entitles a client to a prorated refund of fees at any time without question. All you need do to cancel your contract is drop us a note. Of course, if you were to liquidate a qualified plan, such as an IRA or a Keogh, there could be substantial penalties and taxes unless the account is reinvested within the penalty-free period.

Q. Do large accounts receive any special services?

A. No. We provide the same service to every account without regard to size.

Q. Will PM&A notify me in advance of each trade?

A. No. We have two reasons for not contacting each client in advance of each trade or switch. First, if we accepted that responsibility, the time involved in contacting each client would delay the actual trade, thus defeating the timeliness of our switching signals. Second, your mutual fund will automatically confirm every transaction in your account; in this way you keep abreast of any changes on a timely basis.

If you have a question that was not answered or if you require additional information, please do not hesitate to contact Paul A. Merriman & Associates, Inc., at their Seattle office: 1200 Westlake Avenue North, Seattle, WA 98109. The telephone number is (206) 285-8877.

Selected Bibliography

American Association of Individual Investors. *The Individual Investor's Guide to No-Load Mutual Funds* (paperback).
Presents detailed data analyses on no-load mutual funds. Updated annually in August and mailed free to members of the association. Non-members can receive a copy by sending a mail inquiry to American Association of Individual Investors, 612 N. Michigan Ave., Chicago, IL 60611.

Appel, Gerald and Fred Hitschler. *Stock Market Trading Systems: A Guide to Investment Strategy for the 80's.* Dow Jones-Irwin, 1818 Ridge Road, Homewood, IL 60430.

Bernstein, Jacob. *The Investor's Quotient.* John Wiley & Sons, Inc., 605 Third Avenue, New York, NY 10158.

Julian Block's Guide To Year-Round Tax Savings (annual editions). Dow Jones-Irwin, 1818 Ridge Road, Homewood, IL 60430.

The Donoghue Organization, Inc. *Donoghue's Mutual Funds Almanac,* 1986 (paperback).
Provides a complete directory for over 650 funds. Gives statistical information, including 10-year performance figures. Also contains some basic information on mutual fund investing.

Droms, William G. *Mutual Fund Yearbook.* Dow Jones-Irwin, 1818 Ridge Road, Homewood, IL 60430.

Editors of The No-Load Fund Investor. *The Handbook for No-Load Fund Investors: 1986 Edition.* P.O. Box 283, Hastings-on-Hudson, NY 10706 (paperback).

Includes basic information for the investor who wants to understand the workings of a no-load fund, how to invest, and how to choose a fund.

The Investment Company Institute. *1986 Mutual Fund Fact Book* (paperback).
Provides statistical data on specific funds, basic historical background, plus some mutual fund terminology and definitions. Published annually by a major mutual fund industry association. Send mail inquiry to Investment Company Institute, 1775 K Street, N.W., Washington, DC 20006.

Directory—Your Guide to Mutual Funds (updated annually). No-Load Mutual Fund Association, Inc.; 1983 (paperback).
Lists and describes over 240 no-load funds by objective category. Includes a glossary of mutual fund terms. Send $2 to The No-Load Mutual Fund Association, 11 Penn Plaza, New York, NY 10001.

Pope, Alan. *Successful Investing in No-Load Funds.* John Wiley & Sons, Inc., 605 Third Avenue, New York, NY 10158; 1983 (hardcover).
Covers everything from getting started in no-loads to selecting, buying, managing, and selling them. Also suggests different investment strategies.

Pring, Martin. *Technical Analysis Explained,* second edition. McGraw-Hill Book Co., 1221 Avenue of the Americas, New York, NY 10020.
Explains how to track and chart investments in order to predict their future behavior. Provides detailed information needed by investors to understand, interpret, and forecast major market moves.

Rugg, Donald D,. and Norman B. Hale. *Dow Jones-Irwin Guide to Mutual Funds.* Dow Jones-Irwin, 1818 Ridge Road, Homewood, IL 60430.

Index

I wish to compute and keep current my own "3-A Signal System" averages for instant action in case of a switch. Please send me updated "3-A Signal System" averages. These are FREE, but I am enclosing a stamped, self-addressed business envelope.

Name _____

Address _____

City _____ State _____ Zip Code _____

Mail this coupon to:
    Paul A. Merriman & Associates
    1200 Westlake Avenue N., Suite 507
    Seattle, WA 98109-3530
Or, call 1-206-285-8877.